Confronting
Homelessness

Social Problems, Social Constructions

Joel Best and Scott R. Harris, series editors

What Is Constructionism?
Navigating Its Use in Sociology
Scott R. Harris

Judging Victims: Why We Stigmatize Survivors,
and How They Reclaim Respect
Jennifer L. Dunn

The Paradox of Youth Violence
J. William Spencer

Confronting Homelessness:
Poverty, Politics, and the Failure of Social Policy
David Wagner, with Jennifer Barton Gilman

Making Sense of Social Problems: New Images, New Issues
edited by Joel Best and Scott R. Harris

Confronting Homelessness

Poverty, Politics, and the Failure of Social Policy

David Wagner,
with Jennifer Barton Gilman

LYNNE
RIENNER
PUBLISHERS

BOULDER
LONDON

Published in the United States of America by
Lynne Rienner Publishers, Inc.
1800 30th Street, Boulder, Colorado 80301
www.rienner.com

and in the United Kingdom by
Lynne Rienner Publishers, Inc.
3 Henrietta Street, Covent Garden, London WC2E 8LU

Library of Congress Cataloging-in-Publication Data
Wagner, David.
  Confronting homelessness : poverty, politics, and the failure of social policy /
David Wagner with Jennifer Barton Gilman.
      p.   cm. — (Social problems, social constructions)
  Includes bibliographical references and index.
  ISBN 978-1-58826-823-5 (hc : alk. paper)
  ISBN 978-1-58826-931-7 (pb : alk. paper)
  1. Homelessness—United States. 2. United States—Social policy. I. Gilman,
Jennifer Barton. II. Title.
  HV4505.W233 2012
  362.5'925610973—dc23

                                                    2012009733

British Cataloguing in Publication Data
A Cataloguing in Publication record for this book
is available from the British Library.

Printed and bound in the United States of America

The paper used in this publication meets the requirements
of the American National Standard for Permanence of
Paper for Printed Library Materials Z39.48-1992.

10 9 8 7 6 5 4 3

Contents

Figures and Tables

Figures

Tables

Preface

I am lucky to come from a family that had strong social values, which early on sensitized me to issues such as poverty and civil rights. My parents' values and the events of the 1960s as I was growing up provided the roots of my own ideas and the perspective that one has an obligation to work for people's rights and against the humiliation and pain of being poor.

There were no (or few) homeless people where I grew up, and I can still remember seeing a homeless person for the first time in New York City in 1979; I was shocked. Later, in the mid-1980s, when my wife, Marcia B. Cohen, was Columbia University Community Service's on-site faculty field instructor at the Travelers Hotel in midtown Manhattan, I ran an art group at the hotel and got to know some of the women there who had been homeless. I experienced firsthand these women's resilience and vibrancy, despite the awful stigmas of the labels "homeless" and "mental illness." Also at that time, I taught a class at Columbia University whose students tried to assist an (ultimately failed) effort by the National Union of the Homeless to organize the homeless.

In the more than twenty years since, I have continued to be active in organizing efforts with homeless and poor people in Maine and, more recently, California. Through one of my students at the University of Southern Maine (USM) in Portland, who was a leader of a "tent city" protest, I became very active with some of the groups in the area and went on to do participant observation research, which led to my book *Checkerboard Square: Culture and Resistance in a Homeless Community* (1993). That project, though I did not realize it then, gave me a unique view of some formerly homeless people. Because of Portland's relatively small size, I continue to meet and have become friends with some of the book's subjects.

Over the years, I have continued to focus on poverty and homelessness in Portland. In the early 2000s, having become familiar with the Poor People's Economic and Human Rights Campaign, I was able to use a conference on poverty in Portland to help poor people form a new group, the Portland Organization to Win Economic Rights (POWER), which achieved modest success and a strong membership for a time. Jennifer Barton Gilman, the coauthor of this book and a student of mine at USM, decided to do her field placement with POWER. Our partnership and friendship gave me my first experience as a social work supervisor by allowing me to help her with community organizing. As she went on to complete her master's degree, I became increasingly impressed by her abilities and found that she held views similar to mine.

In recent years, I have had the great pleasure of meeting the wonderful people of Los Angeles Community Action (LACAN) and assisting them in their strong organizing efforts on Skid Row in Los Angeles. I am thoroughly impressed by the day-to-day work of LACAN, especially the organizers and their codirectors, Becky Dennison and Pete White.

My coauthor and I want not only to achieve major reforms, but to end homelessness. We hope that this book furthers these goals.

Acknowledgments

This is the first book I have written that includes an official coauthor. Jennifer Barton Gilman has been such a pleasure to work with. She is a fine researcher and a wonderful person with whom to discuss these issues. Thanks, Jenn!

My wife, Marcia B. Cohen, remains an unofficial partner in most of my work. She constantly reads and otherwise attends to my writing, even when she herself is inundated with work. Marcia also was responsible for some of my first organized contacts with homeless people in New York City back in the 1980s, when she managed an on-site team at the Travelers Hotel through Columbia University Community Service (now renamed and under different auspices).

My activities with homeless people have spanned New York, Maine, and California. I am particularly grateful to those in the homeless and low-income community in Maine whom I have studied, spent time with, and organized through the Portland Organization to Win Economic Rights. I was lucky to be able to spend a semester in the Los Angeles area when I was chosen as a distinguished visiting professor at California State University–Dominguez Hills (CSUDH). In addition to having time there to work on my writing and present it to faculty, I learned a great deal through contact with the Los Angeles Community Action Network and its accomplished work with low-income and homeless people. The insights of the network's codirectors, Pete White and Becky Dennison, were invaluable to my thinking. I would also like to thank Clare Weber, chair of CSUDH's Sociology Department, and longtime policy activist Gary Blasi, who helped me get the "lay of the land" in the Los Angeles area. I also thank Michael Stoops, a longtime activist in the Coalition for the Homeless, who quickly made available to me many documents from the coalition's collection.

—D. W.

Confronting
Homelessness

1

Homelessness:
From Crisis to Routine

In the late 1970s and early 1980s, many residents of the major urban areas of the United States found themselves suddenly awakening to the fact that people were living out of cardboard boxes, sleeping over heating grates, or living in their vehicles. For the first time since the Great Depression, homelessness reemerged in the United States as a social problem. Despite broad disagreement about the "deservedness" of such people and what caused them to become homeless, there was little question that something apparently new and stunning was happening. Seeing sleeping and prostrate people in bus and train stations was shocking, and being asked for change by groups of people who looked like beggars and vagabonds from a Charles Dickens novel aroused people: some to anger, some to shock, some to anxiety, some to concern. Advocates testified that there were millions of such people and that their presence signaled an "impending catastrophe" (Montgomery, 1981). In September 1980, the Community for Creative Non-Violence (CCNV), an activist group, testified before Congress:

> Envision, if you will, an infinitely long line of people, stretching—five, ten, twenty abreast—as far as the eye can see. There are literally millions of them—men, women, and children. Slowly, painfully, some walking, others shuffling, limping, crawling, they pass before you. These are the nation's untouchables. America's pariah: invisible, disposable, surplus. They are the destitute homeless. . . . This, the vast army of America's homeless: the progeny of our ignorance, our indif-

ference, our insulation, and our pathological demand for conformity and productivity. They are a reflection of our unwillingness to confront difficult problems. (Hombs and Snyder, 1983, p. 129)

While some observers urged compassion, assistance, and even radical change, others assigned blame, declaring personal problems and dysfunctions as causes of homelessness. Regardless, the reality of this apparently new and challenging situation was clear:

> They can be seen any night now, sleeping on the floor of North Station—or any of scores of other sites around Boston—sitting unsteadily on benches or in doorways, mumbling nonsense. Some are alcoholics. Some are deinstitutionalized mental patients. As winter closes in, they are all even more homeless. The shelters for alcoholics are filled. The mental hospitals can't take patients in unless they are considered dangerous. (Dietz, 1980c, p. 1)

Homelessness would become a major social issue in the United States by the 1980s, a newly emerged social problem, seemingly forgotten since the Great Depression. Nearly every city (and some towns and counties) organized homeless shelters, soup kitchens, and food or clothes pantries. Volunteer efforts took hold, including those that would become famous: "Second Harvest," which collected food thrown out by restaurants and others for presumed use among the poor; "Hands Across America," which challenged people to respond to homelessness with goodwill; and "Comic Relief," a comedy-led marathon organized by Billy Crystal, Whoopi Goldberg, and Robin Williams, which raised funds for the homeless. New classes on homelessness were established at universities, new departments devoted to homelessness and housing were created in some cities, and new movements of the very poor emerged. But there was opposition to the homeless as well, with some citizen groups opposing shelters and other "handouts," and "not in my backyard" (NIMBY) movements flourished. Some young people would harass or even physically attack homeless people. Conservative commentators countered liberal and radical advocates by minimizing homelessness and blaming the homeless themselves for their own problems (see, for example, Awalt, 1991; Limbaugh, 1991).

What is of interest here is how time-limited the new social problem of the homeless was. The term "homelessness" was not used by the major media outlets (the *New York Times* was still using the term "vagrant") in the early 1980s. The *New York Times* published only 12 stories citing "homelessness" in 1981, compared to 352 stories in 1990. But by 1995 the number had halved, to 156 citations, and by 2005 only 92 references were found. On the opposite coast, in the *Los Angeles Times,* the number of references to "homelessness" soared from 5 in 1981 to 444 in 1990, but then dropped to 234 in 1995 and to only 97 in 2005.[1] In the 1980s, political figures spoke of homelessness as an emergency or, like President Ronald Reagan, dismissed it as exaggerated, but by the 1990s and 2000s, political candidates of both major parties would hardly utter a word about homelessness. The 1988 election was the last time that "homelessness" or "extreme poverty" was even mentioned in a presidential campaign. It was not an issue in the two Bill Clinton elections in the 1990s, the George W. Bush elections of 2000 and 2004, or the Barack Obama election of 2008. The Vanderbilt Television News Archive, which archives the broadcasts of the major media networks, confirms this pattern. A tiny number of stories on the homeless typified the early 1980s, but by 1986 (the year of "Hands Across America") the number of stories grew to forty-six, and reached an all-time high of fifty-three stories in 1990. By the early 1990s there were about thirty-five stories a year on average, but this number trailed off to eighteen stories a year by the late 1990s and early 2000s (see Figures 1.1–1.3).[2] These figures may exaggerate the issue, as it is not al-

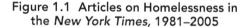

**Figure 1.1 Articles on Homelessness in
the *New York Times,* 1981–2005**

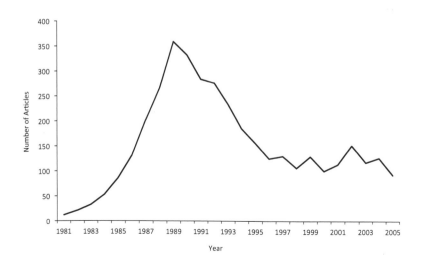

4

Figure 1.2 Articles on Homelessness in
the *Los Angeles Times*, 1981–2005

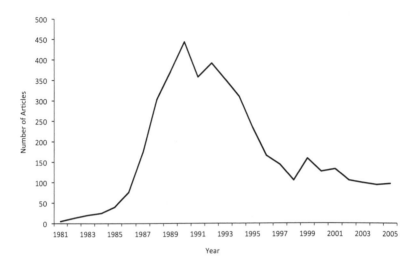

Figure 1.3 Network News Pieces on the Homeless, 1980–2007
(coverage from ABC, CBS, CNBC, CNN, FOX, and NBC)

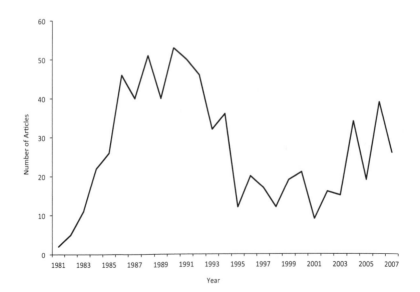

ways possible to separate out stories about people who become homeless due to fires and tsunamis in other nations from stories about the homeless in the United States.

Of course, no one would be sorry if this decline in mass media coverage and political attention had happened because the problem of homelessness has been solved. But no one, from either left or right, from government or advocacy groups, or from any major media outlet, has argued this; the current debate is only about how many hundreds of thousands of citizens are homeless each night, and how many millions are homeless each year. Two advocates put this dilemma of the issue of "falling from the scene" into perspective:

> Something remarkable has happened to the spectacle of the street-dwelling poor in the two decades since it reappeared on the public stage: Homelessness became domesticated routine; an all-but-expected feature of the urban landscape. No longer cause for vocal concern, let alone outrage, it has been integrated into that cheerless diorama of unabashed wealth and relentless poverty that now passes for "normalcy" in American cities. (Hopper, 2003, p. 193)

> Decades and decades have passed without the resolve to end such an epidemic. . . . [H]omelessness doesn't end. Year after year, shelters provide refuge, churches and temples provide meals, downtown missions offer care, social service agencies provide employment training and transitional housing. . . . Every Thanksgiving season, plastered on the pages of the local newspaper, you see a picture of a tattered homeless child or a hungry toothless homeless man smiling in front of a hot, piping meal. (Roberts, 2004, p. 17)

How is it that interest in social problems such as homelessness can rise and fall so rapidly, and often with no relation to the extent of the problem? Why did the mass media, politicians, advocates, and others react to the issue of homelessness in the 1980s, but relatively ignore it by the 1990s and 2000s? Why was homelessness expected to be a time-limited problem by both advocates and critics?

The Social Construction of Problems

Although many intelligent people assume that social problems receive attention when they first arise or when their scope reaches a certain level, this view has been widely criticized in the social sciences. In sociology and related disciplines, social constructionist thinkers have compellingly argued that issues are constructed by certain forces—political leaders, the media, social movements, and others—and not necessarily at the time when these issues arise or when they become more problematic in any empirical way. This perspective begins with the idea that social problems do not exist "out there" in the world; they have to be defined, made known to much of the public, and accepted by experts and others in order to be legitimated (Blumer, 1971).

To take one example, Joel Best's (1989) seminal work on the "missing children" crisis of the 1980s conclusively illustrates that there was no increase in missing children in this period; nor is there any support for the idea that abduction by strangers was a serious issue at this time. Explaining how the issue of missing children became a national issue—with pictures of kids even appearing on milk cartons—is quite different from looking at the raw numbers of missing children. It was breathless mass media coverage, and increased police and criminal justice budgets devoted to this issue, that made us think more about missing children. To take another example, Craig Reinarman and Harry Levine (1997), among others, have illustrated how the problem of illegal drugs was far more widespread in the 1970s, well before the declaration of the "war on drugs" by the Reagan administration, than it was in the 1980s and 1990s. It was politics that dictated attention to illegal drugs, not anything "out there" in the empirical world.

Political scientists have also weighed in on the rise and fall of social problems. Going back to the work of Anthony Downs (1972), they have noted that Americans have an "issue attention cycle" that corresponds with political factors, not any objective reality. Barbara Nelson's important book *Making an Issue of Child Abuse* (1984) illustrates how forces in the 1960s helped make child abuse a public issue, although such behavior has long existed in the family and was already, by the 1980s as Nelson wrote, becoming less compelling to media and lawmakers, and hence to the public.

One can further note the many problems and issues that are always "out there" in the world, but about which we are silent. Poverty, for example, has long existed in the United States, yet it goes through cycles of discovery and rediscovery by experts and the mass media (see Ehrenreich, 1989). Environmental hazards have long been present, but were often not remarked upon prior to the rise of the modern environmental movement beginning in the late 1960s. It is not the problem that makes an issue, but its compelling discovery.

Interestingly, most of the social problems taken up by sociologists and political scientists can be considered as postmodern or cultural issues, but not economic problems. For example, social problems that have arisen since the 1960s and 1970s, including street crime, rape, domestic violence, drugs, missing children, hate crimes, and sexual abuse, have been subjects of articles and books describing their "social construction." Rarely, however, has a critique of economic issues—unemployment, poverty, wealth, the growing gap in incomes—been the subject of social constructionist critique. One reason may be that even social constructionists assume more of a "social fact" orientation (in other words, they somehow do not believe their own perspective that problems require discovery and claims and contestation) to economic conditions than to cultural ones. For example, despite disputes about the unemployment rate, there may be more widespread trust in the veracity of these statistics, at least relatively, than in what has been labeled "claims-making" by movements and media around certain cultural issues. Indeed, while we can criticize the way the unemployed are counted, the figures prove relative validity: for example, if the unemployment rate increases from 5 to 6 percent, we can all agree that things are getting worse. Another factor is that with "new" social problems, such as sexual abuse, the amount of previous abuse or its existence as a social problem is more speculative before its definition and naming, so perhaps these problems are more interesting to probe than better-known issues such as poverty and unemployment. A third possibility is that sociologists and other social scientists may assume, like advocates and other issue-oriented academics, that economic problems are *always* important. Therefore, that poverty or wealth has an attention cycle may be difficult to admit. In Chapter 2, I discuss the utility of theory to the social problem of homelessness generally. I also argue for the compatibility of social conflict theories and a social constructionist perspective. I do not, by any stretch of the imagination, argue that homelessness and extreme poverty are not facts for many in the United States, or that homelessness did not increase beginning in the late 1970s. However, I do suggest that, absent the strong influence of politicians and politics, mass media, activists, and movements in constructing the issue of homelessness, it may well have been ignored or been back-page news. There are those, ranging from family members to social workers to activists, who will always be concerned about homeless people. But in order to understand the career of homelessness as an issue, one needs to understand how the issue was presented to the public and why audiences respond (and sometimes do not respond) to issues.

Organization of the Book

After a discussion of theory and the proposed use of a stage theory of the development of social problems in Chapter 2, I introduce a historical approach in Chapter 3, as this is sometimes insufficiently developed in social constructionist interpretations. Again, perhaps the tendency of many theorists to discuss recently documented or defined social problems has been a cause of this insufficiency. With homelessness, there is a long history of such insufficiency, and generally it is fair to say that the treatment of the homeless and very poor has never been good in the United States. It is true that at some points in US history there were subcultures that saw the "hobo" and "tramp" as potential revolutionaries and romanticized them. But even when this was so, most famously in the organizing days of the Wobblies (the Industrial Workers of the World, who organized unskilled workers in the first two decades of the twentieth century), the vast majority of people did not subscribe to this view; nor did those who had power over the poor (police, railroad officials, and town, city, and county officials) treat them with respect. US history in many senses predicts that despite the very different construction of homelessness in the early 1980s (advocates christened them the "new homeless" in a clear attempt to distinguish them from the old "tramp"), the results would be similar to those of past epochs.

The remaining chapters move chronologically through the past three decades in the definition of and contestation over homelessness. In the very late 1970s, people became, for the first time in a generation, very visibly homeless, and this was a shocking sight. It also was a blow to the concept of self in the United States, which was then steeped in the idea of US prosperity. Almost immediately, however, homelessness became identified in a symbolic way. For activists, advocates, and those on the left and liberal wing of the Democratic Party, homelessness was a key issue of the 1980s, illustrating primarily the greed and heartless policies of the Ronald Reagan administration. Interestingly, this rhetoric was employed even by those groups, such as the Community for Creative Non-Violence (CCNV) in Washington, D.C., and the Coalition for the Homeless in New York City, that were active in advocating for the homeless under the Jimmy Carter administration, and hence were aware that the issue preceded Reagan taking office. It is perhaps telling that advocates often expected homelessness to end with Reagan and his policies. But, in retrospect, what the United States was witnessing was far broader: a major long-term downturn in the US economy and, in many areas of consumption, particularly housing, a long-term decline in people's ability to sustain life's basic necessities.

Whereas the most stubborn denial of homeless people's suffering and the size of the problem came from the Reagan administration and its conservative allies, this is not to say that there was a direct correlation between political position and views about homelessness. Within academia and the professions, for example, many argued that issues like unemployment, deindustrialization, lack of affordable housing, and social service cutbacks were responsible for the rise in homelessness; others, however, including at least some liberals, stressed deinstitutionalization of mental hospitals and alcohol and drug issues as causing the rise in homelessness (for one example of an academic attack on the common wisdom about homelessness, see Baum and Burnes, 1993). Interesting changes would occur with time, as early advocates declared large numbers of homeless people to be mentally ill, a perspective they moved away from, in part, because this explanation was more of a characteristic stand of conservatives and some government officials. Also standing in the middle, where most Americans were as well, was the charity establishment, which recognized a new issue and source of funding and volunteering. Despite some local differences, a fair degree of symmetry occurred in such charitable appeals and programs, with temporary shelter and other palliative, nonthreatening services being offered. People jumped into the voluntary task with enthusiasm, optimistic about serving the most needy.

The liberal social construction of homelessness had its downside even in the halcyon days of the issue in the 1980s. Advocates and opponents alike tended to equate beliefs about the causes of homelessness with solutions, and with convincing the public and social service providers of one belief or another. However, the very definition of homelessness as a new emergency in some ways naturally supported the charitable approach to homelessness, which stressed homeless shelters and soup kitchens (see, for example, Lipsky and Smith, 1989; Hoch and Slayton, 1989). Moderates and even conservatives ultimately found the mild solutions to homelessness hard to be against (who can be against a soup kitchen?), and, as with other issues, it is not surprising that Reagan's successor, George H. W. Bush, who had called for "a kinder, gentler" nation, did not bother to fight the claims made about homelessness. The gap between critique and actual political changes or solutions to homelessness was huge, yet it seemed for a while that no one but a few radicals noticed this. In other words, shelters and soup kitchens and case managers would not end homelessness, yet few admitted or were willing to say this.

Equally paradoxical was the gap between liberal and charitable elements of the loose coalition to do something about homelessness, and their charges, the homeless themselves. Initially the clientele themselves seemed left out of the discussion. As time went on, however, more grassroots efforts occurred, with tent cities or encampments separate from official shelters being set up. In some cities, pitched battles would rage, most notably in New York City around Tompkins Square Park in the late 1980s and into the 1990s. Homeless activism, although supported to an extent by advocates, often contradicted the right of others to speak for them, and complicated the solution to homelessness as being one of shelters and social services. Many efforts by homeless and poor people themselves (sometimes joined by other radical elements in local communities) rejected these palliatives as forms of repression and social control, and demanded housing, jobs, and income.

It may well be that the intractability of homelessness to solution would have caused a decline in public attention to this issue in any case. By the late 1980s, the term "compassion fatigue" was being widely used to describe the middle-class and charitable weariness about the issue (Uzelec, 1990). The achievement of one legislative victory, the Stewart B. McKinney Homeless Assistance Act of 1987, which for the first time provided federal monies to localities to benefit the homeless, and the expanding rift between a more radical solution to homelessness and charitable efforts, both probably in turn eased pressure on the issue, while also complicating it by splitting the ranks of people concerned about the homeless. Also important to this analysis is the election of Bill Clinton in 1992, and the end of Reagonomics as a target of advocacy groups. This election led to a decline in any mobilization for the homeless. As with many other issues of the 1980s, from AIDS to nuclear disarmament, the election of a Democrat caused a drop in activism. Some leaders of major advocacy and charitable groups, hoping for intervention from above as well as jobs themselves in the administration, certainly consciously moderated their demands and goals. But for most activists, service providers, and community leaders, it was not so much a conscious change, but a disorientation, that would prevail. While the Clinton administration, unlike the Reagan administration, was ready to frankly acknowledge this problem (as George W. Bush would do as well), neither administration took any major action to diminish homelessness. In fact, both arguably took policy actions that increased homelessness (for example, under Clinton, the passage of the North American Free Trade Agreement in 1993 and of the Personal Responsibility and Work Opportunity Reconciliation Act in

1996). The fact that these administrations would have little positive impact on homelessness and other problems of the poor was profoundly disorienting, because the issue had been defined in such a politically partisan way since 1981. It is true that, for now, more service providers and advocates (though they are small in number compared to the public) do advocate a "housing first" approach to homelessness, in which after nearly thirty years, palliative aids such as homeless shelters and social services are seen as less of a solution than is housing. Providers themselves have found it much easier to help people "get their life together" once those people have a roof over their head. Generally, though, for most Americans, homelessness entered the realm of a retinue of "back burner" problems, from child abuse to AIDS to illicit drugs, that are acknowledged but not considered very critical or immediate issues.

In concluding the book, Chapter 8 briefly explores how to assess the social construction of homelessness in the 1980s. It is difficult to know whether different outcomes could have occurred if the issue had been presented differently. In some ways, given the absence of broader social movements in the last decades of the twentieth century that would unite larger groups of people behind an economic justice campaign, it was perhaps inevitable that, like child abuse or other recent issues, homelessness would become primarily an issue of social service. Chapter 8 also briefly explores what this study can contribute to social constructionist perspectives, which so rarely tackle economic issues.

Homelessness, Poverty, and Definitional Issues

Homelessness presents problems of definition, first because it is a moving subset of poverty that is constantly changing despite stereotypes (people move onto and off the streets daily), and second because, both today and in other historical periods, people do not always mean the same thing by the term "homelessness." In some cultures and even in Western culture before the rise of capitalism and Protestantism, living on the street and begging was not stigmatized, and students, minstrels, and religious pilgrims shared the road with the poor. But even when the poor became highly stigmatized, it was not necessarily possible for the observer to always differentiate who was "sleeping rough," as the British say, from those who were merely on the move to a different abode or who looked "down and out." In the United States, there has been so much migration in our history that huge minorities could be considered technically homeless at any given time (see Jasper, 2000). Social welfare and police officials were concerned only about those people who asked for aid. These officials enforced the Laws of Settlement, first passed in England, which required one to be the resident of a town or city for a certain period of time to be eligible for aid (usually also based on taxes paid; for women, settlement was based on the settlement status of the father or husband). Towns and cities set up extremely harsh penalties for the nonsettled, from warning them out of town to sending them to workhouses or houses of correction. But the ambiguity was strong, because if the person did not ask for aid or left the workhouse to go elsewhere, then, as Henry Miller notes, "the vagrant was a vagrant only so long as he or she stayed in town; if vagrant people took off for Kentucky or Ohio, they became something else: pioneers, perhaps settlers" (1991, p. xviii). During the era between the Civil War and the Great Depression, things became even more complicated, as the tremendous surge in railroads and industrial growth required a highly mobile transient labor force. Despite the fact that millions of men (and to a lesser degree families) moved across the country for work, they were harshly stigmatized as "tramps" by the newspapers and magazines. Others differentiated "tramps," "hobos," and "bums," with the usual sense that tramps were transient workers, hobos were local settled wage workers, and bums were those who did not want to work. In practice, of course, these all became highly stigmatized terms, and many people, workers or not, homeless or not, ended up caught in the harsh vagrancy laws of the time and sent to jail. The needs of mobile capitalism clashed, as we shall see in Chapter 3, with the social control needs of the state and, perhaps in some cases, of local businesses, to have a settled citizenry, just as today's debates on immigration split employers and others.

Homelessness was even more ambiguous in the Great Depression. Were those who lived in "Hoovervilles," the large shantytowns set up usually on the edges of US cities, always homeless? Not necessarily. Millions traveled the rails, and some had no home, but others were young men who left their parents' homes or even their own homes with their wives and children to find a job. Some authors refer to the famous Bonus Marchers of 1932 (see Kusmer, 2002, pp. 202–203) as being homeless, but again many of the veterans who lived in the mass camps surrounding Congress had homes elsewhere. So many people were poor and unsettled in the Great Depression that the line between poverty and homelessness broke down. Only the short-lived Federal Transient Bureau (as well as all the local public welfare officials) checked on the actual settlement of applicants.

Although there is strong evidence that homelessness arose anew beginning only in the late 1970s, it is also true that naming a problem changes it, and that the added attention to the new homelessness may have led to an understatement of the older problem. There were many young people living on the street in the 1960s and 1970s, but they were not usually considered a social problem. Christopher Jencks makes a good point when he contrasts the 1970s with the 1980s: "in the late 1980s most Americans assumed that everyone on the streets who looked unkempt or confused was homeless. In the late 1970s, we assumed such people had a home unless we saw clear evidence to the contrary, such as a grocery cart full of personal belongings" (1994, pp. 14–15). Usually in the 1970s, the "unkempt" poor went back to a lodging house or single-room occupancy in the central city. By the 1980s, many lacked a room at all. But this is only generally true, not always.

In any case, since the reappearance of homelessness, a rousing debate about the numbers of homeless people has occurred, with methodology, interpretation, and definition all contested. Generally, government has favored a restrictive definition that accepts as homeless only those who are literally homeless—meaning those who have absolutely no place to sleep—and often relies on shelter counts as a major part of its censuses. Advocates have consistently called for a broader definition that would include people living out of vehicles and in abandoned housing, people "doubled up" on floors and elsewhere in others' apartments, and even people who lack a regular home because they are in prison or other institutional quarters. When the US government sought to undertake a census of homeless people in 1980, 1990, and 2000, each time considerable opposition emerged among advocates, because clearly many homeless people do not readily make themselves available to government officials, and advocates believed that low counts would only hurt their cause (see Rossi, 1989; Wagner, 1993; Hopper, 2003). It is not the intent of this book to minimize the importance of numbers, which can vary from several hundred thousand a night on the street to several million, but rather to suggest that the debate is unsolvable, because it is not primarily methodological but rather political. Government and social service sources seek to define a clientele for shelters and case management, and hence are defining homelessness as an immediate, emergency service issue. Advocates are correct that the problem of homelessness is far more widespread, and if one includes those at risk of homelessness at some time in the year, we have huge numbers. But these numbers are supportive of political arguments for housing, income, jobs, and other broader aid.

We are to a certain extent at the mercy of historians and mass media when exploring the story of homelessness. Many homeless people do not look homeless, for the very reason of seeking work, going to school, and blending in with society. Some people may look homeless, but only be poor. The English term *roofless* would also help us differentiate those without any place to stay from those the advocates call homeless but who do have a roof—a motel, a friend or relative's couch, or a jail cell. We must keep in mind throughout the account of homelessness the fact that, for the most part, those who go through the experience are not usually writers, and that we do not have precise empirical details on homelessness.

Sources of Data and Methods of Inquiry

Following the theoretical and historical discussions in Chapters 2 and 3, I analyze the developments in homelessness over the past three decades with the aid of several sources of data. The Coalition for the Homeless, the largest advocacy group for the homeless in the United States, kindly allowed access to all of its newsletters, which began in early 1983. In addition, four major newspapers—the *New York Times,* the *Chicago Tribune,* the *Los Angeles Times,* and the *Boston Globe*—have been analyzed between 1979 and 2008, with a complete sampling every other year of the period (but varying the skipped years among the papers in order not to miss event coverage). Although there is little precision when studying newspapers, the few studies done on reports of homelessness in newspapers have perhaps overemphasized developments in New York City and Washington, D.C. (see Bogard, 2003). While developments in New York City in particular are reported elsewhere, the *New York Times* still lays claim to being the "paper of record," so it was included in the analysis. But in order to gain a more regionally and politically balanced look at the issue of homelessness, Los Angeles and Chicago as well as Boston were included (politically, the *Chicago Tribune* is the most center-right and the *Boston Globe* is the most liberal). One idea in particular, that the advocacy of Mitch Snyder's D.C.-based CCNV and Robert Hayes's New York City–based Coalition for the Homeless was critical in the social construction of homelessness, was not borne out by this research; the press made very few references to Mitch Snyder or Robert Hayes or their groups in the first few years of the homeless crisis.

In most ways, the articles in the papers, including news stories and editorials, were far more similar than different. Only in the early years of the "new" homeless problem was there a contrast: the *New York Times* gave rather consistent attention to the idea that homelessness was caused by deinstitutionalization of the mentally ill, in part, no doubt, because of Mayor Edward Koch's campaign in the 1980s to secure state funding for the homeless by blaming the state of New York's policies. The *Los Angeles Times* and *Chicago Tribune* emphasized the deep recession of the period as causing homelessness, while the *Boston Globe* covered a variety of causal issues. Still, overall, not only is there evidence that the media handled homelessness similarly, but also there is no evidence that coverage of different issues as causal actually led to any different social policies. Generally, US cities followed the discovery of homelessness by building shelters, opening soup kitchens, and providing social services, but none came close to reducing the number of homeless people in their cities. Additionally, I analyzed the Vanderbilt Television News Archive to gather information on broadcast media coverage (networks only) of the homeless in abstract form. I also analyzed the approximately three dozen major books on homelessness in this period as well as major academic articles on the topic.

All materials about homelessness in the four newspapers, the Vanderbilt Television News Archive, the National Coalition for the Homeless newspaper, and other sources were coded so that counts could be made of positive and negative stories about the homeless, of discovery and naming of the issue, of quests for charity and shelter provision, and later of compassion fatigue and anger about the issue, for example. This qualitative examination was done in conjunction with the quantitative examination of the decline in homeless stories. Throughout the years of the study (1979–2009), there were stories of three types in each period— "enthusiastic excitement," "sober realization," and institutionalization— however, the balance among these types of story would differ considerably. Even advocates limited their focus as time went on, moving from rousing calls to action to reports on annual budgets, job postings, and the ins and outs of legislative work.

Perhaps most interesting, in talking with advocates and experts on the homeless issue, we found no dissension that the issue of homelessness, once a subject of front-page news, had fallen from public attention. In fact, many people expressed retrospective surprise that the issue of homelessness was still with us in the twenty-first century. The only question was whether the current lack of interest in homelessness was inevitable given the short attention span of Americans, or whether the decline represented something more fundamental about the way the issue had been framed. Of course, for this type of social science hypothesis, it is impossible to prove. Nevertheless, there is evidence to suggest that, in many ways, and regardless of the short attention span of the US population, the very manner in which advocates, experts, and the mass media constructed the issue laid the seeds of its decline over time. While the focus was on public sympathy, charity, and palliative aid such as shelters, these were never sufficient to solve homelessness or even to have a major ameliorative effect. Moreover, while the tendency early on to blame the Reagan administration and construct a "new" homeless population is understandable, such constructions are not sustainable in the long term. This view is not meant as a critique of the merits of homeless advocacy per se, but as a reflection of the limits of social reform in the United States, particularly with regard to deeply entrenched social and economic issues.

Notes

1. With the newspapers, given the large number of citations, it was not possible to separate stories about the "homeless" that were not exactly about the new period of homelessness in the United States; for example, some stories about people made homeless due to floods, wars, disasters, and other causes in foreign nations could not be excluded, nor could even stories about "homeless pets." Instead, we decided to search for the word "homelessness," although this reduced the count, it ensured that the articles were consistently related to the desired topic. With the Vanderbilt Television News Archive, because the number of stories was far more limited, stories that contained the word "homeless" in them but that were not about homeless people in the United States were more easily excluded.

2. Of course, any definition of homelessness is arbitrary. Although we do not usually include flood victims who are homeless as part of the broader problem of homelessness, many advocates at the time of Hurricane Katrina used the tragedy, as exemplified in the footage of New Orleans, to remind Americans of the large numbers of poor and homeless people in the nation.

2

The Rise and Fall
of a Social Problem

Homelessness has not always been looked upon as a social problem, although today most people, including social scientists, view it as one. Prior to the beginnings of modern capitalist society, homelessness was not particularly stigmatized or vilified, but was a condition shared by pilgrims and religious wanderers, students and teachers seeking money for their studies, craftsmen and tinkerers, as well as the abject poor (see, for example, Geremek, 1994; Miller, 1991). Those who wandered carried on the religious example of Saint Francis of Assisi, while others were those lucky enough in a medieval society to be free of restraint (escaped slaves and serfs, for example). Nevertheless, it is true that in modern society, most people's "common sense" about the homeless and very poor, perhaps even their "local knowledge," to use anthropologist Clifford Geertz's term (1973, 1983), is quite negative. Many observers are quick to label homeless people as failures or as "drunks," "mentally ill," or "lazy," among other such pejorative terms.

There has been little study of why this is so. Modern humans seem to rely on visual perception or oral and other sense cues, as well as common stories and traditions, to explain conditions they see or hear about. Historically, for example, while visible physical disability has been easily recognized and generally accepted as not the person's "fault" (there are some notable exceptions to this), even today the existence of severe mental disabilities in people who have no obvious visible problem has been a difficult issue in Western societies. What people cannot see per-

17

plexes them more. The depressed or schizophrenic person was often in our history not believed to have a problem, and to be "malingering" if he did not work or "act normal." Race provides another obvious example of sense perceptions making for generalizations. Large groups of people make judgments about others based on characteristics such as skin color and other emblems of what we erroneously refer to as "race." Although we are all 99.9 percent the same in our DNA, not only does racial stereotyping continue, but even anti-racists often continue to make broad statements about "whites," "blacks, "browns," and so forth, often without much data to support their generalizations. Added to humans' reliance on simple perception to generalize about people and events are the tales and oral histories of neighbors and families. The beliefs of those who saw people of a certain "race" do a certain thing or those who traditionally think that a certain group dislikes them or is lazy or dangerous often influence the next generation.

In a similar way, one can say that, at least for the majority of nonpoor citizens in majority cultures (based on race and ethnicity, for example) in the United States, people rely on anecdotal observation and local tales to explain homelessness, with particular reliance on beliefs about alcohol and drug use, "craziness," "laziness," and other negative attributes or personal deficiencies. Although, as many argue, there may be personal comfort in these explanations (it happens to them, not to us), still we cannot discount a type of localized common sense (someone visits a particular street and sees a particular homeless person who always seems to be drunk, and concludes that all homeless people tend to be drunks). These depictions, of course, are much less the case when major economic depressions or downturns occur. So, as we shall see in Chapter 3, economic depressions change consciousness of homelessness. Like floods or fires, which are easily visible to people, suddenly the specter of deep poverty comes to be connected for most people to economic downturn at certain exceptional times.[1] Of course, some communities, including those that are very poor and those with minority groups who have suffered extraordinary poverty, may have enough firsthand experience and perceptual differences from majority society not to completely share the stigmatized view of extreme poverty (someone who knew a homeless person before she began drinking in order to cope with unemployment and then eviction).

Although advocates and scholars have much criticized the mass stigmatization of poverty and homelessness, we must recognize that these elements are part of many people's "common sense." Particularly since the most visible homeless persons are often panhandlers or quite often have "discreditable" signs (smell of drink, for example), observers draw negative conclusions. It is part and parcel of the major split in perception between lay observers, on the one hand, and scholars and experts on the other, not to see the hidden nature or long-term effects of many social phenomena. In fact, we might say that it was the great discovery of many modern social thinkers—Marx, Darwin, Freud—that causation of human action and motivation is often hidden from individuals themselves. Corporations do not announce that some of the people laid off may become homeless (and this process may take six or seven years), nor do landlords usually publicize evictions or what happens to the evictees. It becomes a vicious cycle as well, as the individuals or families involved often feel so ashamed that they do not share these events with friends or neighbors and may simply disappear from their communities. Hence we can see some reality in why people easily identify fire and other disaster victims with their cause, but do not associate the very poor and homeless with hidden and long-term economic, political, and social phenomena. They do not know that the people whom they now see only as homeless may have once been "regular" working people with homes.

The reliance of many citizens on perceptual information and "common sense" does tend to fit with more conservative (and ahistorical) interpretations of homelessness. In the 1980s, when homelessness became a political issue in the United States for the first time in many decades, the comments of President Ronald Reagan questioning the deservedness of the homeless no doubt spoke for a large segment of people in the United States who believed character flaws were at work in homelessness. As early as 1984, Reagan stated: "What we have found in this country, and maybe we're more aware of it now, is one problem that we've had, even in the best of times, and that is the people who are sleeping on the grates, the homeless who are homeless, you might say, by choice" (Taylor, 1984, p. 1). Conservative writers, mostly in retort to liberal and leftist advocacy, arose to further support character flaws as the main cause of poverty and homelessness (Awalt, 1991; Derbyshire, 2003; Limbaugh, 1991; Magnet, 1987; Mead, 1986; Murray, 1984; Rosen, 2003). But arguments about drug use and mental illness, not deep structural social conditions, were common as well among many nonconservative social scientists. A body of literature sought to connect deinstitutionalization of the mentally ill to homelessness (Arce et al., 1983; Belcher and Toomey, 1988; Lipton, Sabatini, and Katz, 1983; Torrey, 1988, 2008) and, in some cases, to connect the baby boom generation's attitude toward drugs and mental illness with homelessness (Baum and Burnes, 1993).

The appeal of these ideas is strong and fits with "common sense" views of some citizens. Yet when confronted with larger views of both history and social science, "common sense" views become weak explanatory systems. We can document no increase in alcohol or drug consumption in the United States at the time homelessness rose in numbers (beginning in the late 1970s and early 1980s), nor can we document any rise in mental illness at this time, nor does the pattern of deinstitutionalization fit the timing of the rise of homelessness very well.

Deinstitutionalization started in the 1950s and most of the reduction in psychiatric hospital beds had occurred before the rise of homelessness. This is not to suggest that deinstitutionalization did not have a negative effect on people, and that it did not have some effect on the numbers of homeless people. Yet prior to the very late 1970s, most former patients were housed in the community. Much less does the idea of "laziness" (a very difficult thing to measure) make sense to have grown at this particular time. In the longer haul, the socioeconomic arguments for homelessness fit the time period of the late 1970s onward as one of deindustrialization and wage decline, with the added issues of gentrification of housing and a decline in social benefits. However, when compared with previous periods of highly visible poverty and homelessness (the depressions of the nineteenth and twentieth centuries), the highly differentiated social and economic scene in the United States does make such connections more difficult for some people to make. After all, neighborhoods and communities today are more separate from each other than they were in the 1930s, and the impact of economic decline is so different now among the rich, middle class, working class, and poor. The period of the past three decades stands in strong contrast to the Great Depression period. In those days, few who looked outside could not see visible strains of economic change. Even in the midst of the current, severe economic recession, it is still very possible, dependent on one's neighborhood and social networks, not to see distress, particularly severe poverty, from one's front door.

Discussion of theory and even policy does not determine political or social action as much as many people believe. To the extent people feel sympathy for the homeless, compassion crosses a variety of political and causal views of poverty and homelessness. Some people assert the mental incapacity or substance abuse problems of the homeless, but still assist them in soup kitchens or through donations. Others take an approach more akin to conflict theory, but without taking any social action to express these beliefs. We might say that compassion or sympathy is a different vector in the American consciousness that can still fit with "common sense" interpretations. Following the Christian tradition of charity (as well as Jewish and Muslim), many people hold contradictory views: they may see the homeless as failures, but still believe they need help. Others may believe structural causes are to blame, but see no other method but charity as a way to aid people.

The following analysis of social conflict and social constructionist theories and their approaches to homelessness is not meant to imply that no work has been undertaken through other lenses on poverty and homelessness. However, despite the occasional postmodern or symbolic interactionist article (which can be subsumed to some extent under social constructionism), and the presence of some authors who go back to the days of structural functionalism (see Gans, 1994, for example), these two theories are generally most relevant to this discussion.

Social Conflict Theory and Homelessness

Conflict theory is perhaps most associated with Karl Marx and Marxism, which saw the primary social engine of human history as being a conflict of social classes (classically, under capitalism, being the bourgeoisie and the proletariat). However, conflict theory, as a general set of theories that see parts of society being at odds with other parts, is also built into most feminist theory, Afrocentrism, and, to various degrees, the theories of social scientists who adopt liberal, "progressive," or social democratic views. Because Marxists, radicals, and other conflict theorists were most attuned to conflict, the rise of homelessness as the most extreme form of poverty was generally noted and written about in the 1980s–1990s mostly by scholars and activists holding conflict theories, either explicitly or implicitly (for example, Baxter and Hopper, 1981; Blau, 1992; Golden, 1992; Hombs and Snyder, 1983; Kozol, 1988; Marcuse, 1988; Snow and Anderson, 1993; Timmer, Eitzen, and Talley 1994; Wagner, 1993; Wright, 1997).

Marx asserted in his most famous works, *The Communist Manifesto* (1848) and *Capital* (1872), that class conflict began with the private ownership of the "means of production"—which began under slavery and then advanced to feudalism and later to capitalist societies. It is in the interest of the capitalist or bourgeois class in capitalist society to increase its wealth at the expense of the proletariat, which it does constantly by seeking out more surplus value (in profit, rent, and dividend). It may increase its surplus value by making workers work harder (more productivity) or it may do so by making them work more cheaply by driving down labor costs. It has been axiomatic since the beginning of Marxism that the creation of a large body of poor people was natural to capitalism, both because Marx and Friedrich Engels predicted increased immiseration of the proletariat and because it is in the interest of the wealthy bourgeoisie to have a large pool of available cheap labor. Perhaps this basic principle is best put by social welfare historians Frances Fox Piven and Richard Cloward in their well-known work *Regulating the Poor,* in which they argued that terrible conditions for the poor were intentional and designed "to spur men . . . to contrive ways of supporting themselves by their own industry, to offer themselves to any employer on any terms" (1993 [1971], p. 33). Many feminist and critical race theorists would agree, while seeing women and members of disenfranchised races as having always been the worst hit by capitalist exploitation. Women have subsidized production in the domestic sphere, and when they do enter the formal labor market, they have been paid less than men. African Americans, since the days of slavery, have helped Western society secure tremendous surplus value at little or no cost through vicious exploitation of their labor. The cheaper the labor (including free labor, in the case of slavery), the more profit for those in power.

For most conflict theorists—whether or not they are specifically Marxist—the process of deindustrialization, which began in the 1970s (together with the broader process of globalization, which coincided with deindustrialization), was key in reducing labor costs, and increasing poverty, in the United States. Peter Marcuse, the most explicitly Marxist of many scholars of homelessness, cited deindustrialization as a major contributing factor in the increase in homelessness during this time period; the decline in jobs specifically in manufacturing spurred an increase in low-paying, low-benefit service economy jobs. "It is this last pattern of homelessness which characterizes the current phase of homelessness in the United States and differentiates it from other historical patterns of homelessness. . . . [T]oday's homelessness differs quantitatively from that of all earlier periods. . . . [I]t is not the result of general poverty, rather it is occurring in one of the most advanced industrial economies of the world" (1988, p. 72). Among the Catholic activists who formed the Community for Creative Non-Violence in the late 1970s, the sense of productivity, surplus, and a capitalism gone awry was deeply present. Mary Ellen Hombs and Mitch Snyder asserted that "the homeless are our human refuge, remnants of a culture that assigns a pathologically high value to independence and productivity. America is a land where you are what you consume and produce. The homeless are simply surplus souls in a system firmly rooted in competition and self-interest" (1983, p. 9).

Put in more specific terms, conflict theorists would argue that when the US economy began to decline after the recession of 1973, it succumbed to increasingly successful foreign competition. In addition to the decline of manufacturing jobs in the United States as jobs moved overseas, corporations began a concerted campaign against unions, wage increases, benefit packages (for example, either shedding altogether or cutting healthcare benefits), and public provision (hence the cuts in social benefits that followed particularly during the Reagan administration, but essentially from the late 1970s onward). Many conflict theorists, of course, would differ on how planned the anti-labor campaign was, and how connected corporate strategies were to political strategies that sought cuts or privatization of the public sector. Throughout the world, the move toward privatization and cutting labor costs spread, with workers from Sweden to Australia to Japan to Bulgaria feeling the economic decline and poverty rising in many of these nations, if not always homelessness per se. Some nations, such as the European community, have experienced high unemployment rates and decreased labor costs, but because of strong social welfare systems have had far fewer people falling into abject poverty than in the United States.

The figures on economic change since the early 1970s are dramatic. The 2011 *Economic Report of the President* shows not only a dramatic decline in the number of manufacturing jobs (sliding from well over a quarter of the nation's jobs to less than 9 percent in 2010), but also a decline in real wages over the past four decades that has left hourly wages in 1972–1973 (adjusted for inflation) higher than wages now. It is astounding to many conflict theorists that many discussions of homelessness and other dramatic signs of poverty do not include the basic economic context in the United States.

Few social scientists, however, think that the desire to reduce labor costs is the sole reason for the huge increase in homelessness in the United States between the late 1970s and today. For example, high poverty rates existed throughout the 1940s and 1950s, yet they were not accompanied by high rates of homelessness. Arguably then, the most important key to the causes of homelessness is a lack of affordable housing, which is a problem endemic to the post-1970s period. The elimination of single-room-occupancy housing in favor of expensive condominiums and luxury apartments from the 1970s onward contributed significantly to the rise in homelessness. There was also a dramatic reduction in boarding homes for the poor as well as inexpensive apartments. These changes provided an opportunity for developers to rehabilitate the housing market and appeal to baby boomers, who now wished to move to the cities in the post-1975 period (known as the gentrification of housing). Through the lens of conflict theory, nearly everything, including people, can be viewed as a commodity, so it makes sense that developers see no benefit in providing poor people with housing, because there is no profit. Landlords and housing developers were happy to gain high-paying tenants and buyers, and cared little about what happened to those in the cities who now had no housing. In fact, homelessness can be viewed as a natural by-product of the society that we are currently living in. Peter Marcuse makes this point succinctly: "homelessness in the midst of plenty may shock people into the realization that homelessness exists not because the system is failing to work as it should, but because the system is working as it must" (1988, p. 93). More specifically, the National Coalition for the Homeless estimates that between 1973 and 1992, 2.3 million units of low-income housing were destroyed (National Coalition for the Homeless, 2009). It must be kept in mind that the reduction in housing units came during a period in which the number of people in poverty rose from 25 million to 39 million (Levitan, Mangum, and Mangum, 1998). Like a game of musical chairs, 10 million families competed to find housing in a market that had now lost 2.3 million units. Another estimate, in 1995, noted an "affordability gap" of 4.4 million units, referring to the number of people who could not afford housing (National Coalition for the Homeless, 2009). During this period, the federal government declared that it was "getting out of the housing business" and reduced aid for housing programs, further complicating the plight of poor people.

There is also a rather unexplored link between deindustrialization and gentrification. As the old manufacturing industries were eroding, they were being replaced by finance, real estate, tourist, and high-technology industries as the nation's largest sectors. In the past few decades, there has been an effort by business and urban governments to take back the cities, particularly the central cities, throughout the nation, so that not only will employees of these companies have a place to live, but also tourists and suburban residents will be able to "safely" travel into metropolises, that is, not confront large numbers of poor people. In this way, the change from a manufacturing society to a service-information society has also changed the cities, with a new period of urban renewal occurring.[2]

Most analysts, and certainly conflict theorists, agree that the government's abandonment of the poor as recipients of social benefits is also key to understanding homelessness. Welfare benefits from the Aid to Families with Dependent Children (AFDC) program, local general-assistance programs, and disability benefits had already been falling in value for years prior to the election of Ronald Reagan. But in the 1980s, major cuts were made to social welfare that drove many off the AFDC, Social Security disability, and Supplemental Security Income (SSI) rolls; in addition, Section 8 housing vouchers were cut, and the Comprehensive Employment and Training Act (CETA) was abolished. Many states and municipalities dropped general assistance altogether (the only aid program available to those who are not single-parent families qualifing for federal aid), forcing the very poorest out of whatever housing they had. The general trend of cutting social benefits continued into the 1990s and 2000s. In 1996, for example, Bill Clinton signed the Personal Responsibility and Work Opportunity Reconciliation Act (that is, welfare reform), which pushed millions of families off the welfare rolls and placed time limits on access to welfare assistance. As part of this reform, substance users were denied SSI and Social Security disability, becoming still another group to be pushed to the bottom of society. It seems unlikely that there will be any return to the levels of social benefits seen in the 1970s.

Conflict theory contradicts the "common sense" notion that people who are homeless simply do not work hard enough or have personal deficits that keep them from being able to provide for themselves or their families. For if the main causes of homelessness lie in corporate and governmental action—the reduced wages available, the decrease in social benefits from government, and the higher rents demanded by landlords—then clearly homeless people are victims of broader circumstances. Of course, certain populations are more vulnerable to homelessness, and the declining conditions of life in the decades following the mid-1970s were not uniform for all people. Those already at or near the bottom of society—the poorest, including many members of racial minority groups, and many people who lived off low-wage industries and casual work—were the most affected. Certainly too, other vulnerable groups—the mentally ill, alcohol and drug abusers, and victims of domestic violence and child abuse—were significantly affected.

Despite the strengths of conflict theory regarding the causes of homelessness, the theory also has some weaknesses. First, social conflict theory, at least as applied in the United States, tends to be highly partisan and subject to convenient distortion regardless of the facts. As noted in Chapter 1, despite the fact that homelessness was highly visible in the late 1970s, both activists and many scholars insisted that the problem began later and was caused by Reagonomics. One can often see advocates shaping this "theory" to fit the agenda of the Democratic Party.[3] Few activists and scholars seem to have aimed as much criticism at "Carteronomics" or "Clintonomics." Second, some homelesss scholars have questioned the insistence that there was a "new" homeless population in the 1980s. They have argued that this is a distortion of the reality (Hoch and Slayton, 1987; Timmer, 1994). For example, the continued drumbeat about homelessness among families and women can obscure the reality that most homeless people are men. Nor in presenting this "new" homeless population have many conflict theorists or activists stressed the overrepresentation of African Americans.[4] It was convenient at times to present the population as female or as female with young children. Efforts were frequently made to attract allies, such as feminists, to the coalition against social welfare cuts and poverty, but at times distortions were made in this effort. Counts of homeless people sometimes included children (male and female) alongside adult women to achieve a more sympathetic reception. This is deceptive because, as homeless service providers know, homeless families, for the most part, are served much faster and better than homeless (mostly male) individuals.

But beyond stretching facts to fit politically correct propaganda, the broader issue is the failure of social conflict theory to explain its diagnosis and prescriptions to the average person, and the implicit assumption of many theorists and activists that homelessness, once explained, can be cured by adopting the perspective of conflict theory. This problem with conflict theory no doubt goes back to Marx himself, who was far better at diagnosing capitalism's faults than at moving masses of people into revolutionary action, as was his goal. In short, by ignoring the subjective aspects of the public's view of homelessness, social conflict theory repeats its analysis but does not necessarily convince a majority of observers. Nor does it seem to ever self-reflexively deal with this failure to convince a majority of observers to take action. Even if policy suggestions are made, they are often unpopular or difficult to understand. Social constructionist theory can help us better appreciate and understand the popular cultural consciousness about issues such as homelessness, and overcome the weakness of social conflict theoretical debate and analysis.

Social Constructionist Theory and Homelessness

As applied to homelessness, social constructionist theory is certainly compatible with social conflict theory (see Heiner, 2001). Social constructionist theory grew out of a variety of theories—phenomenology, symbolic interactionism, the sociology of knowledge, and the work of Peter Berger and Thomas Luckmann (1966). At its more subjectivist spectrum, social constructionism has some similarities with other recent theories such as postmodernism and deconstructionism. Essentially, social constructionist theory is interested in the definitional and attributional nature of human life—how and why we believe what we do, and how such beliefs change over time. Social constructionist theory deals more with culture and media than with economics. Although social constructionists do not all agree on how far to extend the social critique (after all, everything in life is socially constructed—meaning that everything in society is created by humans), in practice many social constructionists "bracket" parts of reality to look primarily at media, culture, political conflict, and activists and advocates.

Social constructionist research into social problems has helped puncture the conventional wisdom that problems rise to the surface in some "natural" or "logical" way, such as based on some new empirical evidence or new discovery. Rather, social constructionism usually attempts to show how a set of actors or "claims-makers" can convince the public to define something as a problem (even when empirical evidence is absent or questionable). Once a problem has been defined, various claims-makers will propose solutions to the problem—for example, Joel Best (1989) on the problem of missing children, Barbara Nelson (1984) on the problem of child abuse (1984) (see also Phofl, 1977), and Craig Reinarman and Harry Levine (1997) on the problem of crack cocaine. Many studies on the history of drug illegalization draw on social constructionist theory, particularly those drugs that are socially constructed as "demons." For example, Howard Becker (1973) famously described the single-handed efforts of claims-maker Henry Anslinger in securing the passage of the 1937 Marihuana Tax Act, which essentially made marijuana illegal. Stanley Cohen's (1972) early work on the "mods and rockers" showed how the "problem" of youth gangs was exaggerated and essentially constructed by the mass media in the United Kingdom. British theorists in particular have looked critically at crime and crime waves (Hall et al., 1978; Waddington, 1986). Some US sociologists too have looked at the elevation of crime as a news issue above many other equally or more important issues (Chambliss, 1994; Beckett, 1994).

Almost all social constructionists emphasize the mass media as an important transmitter of cultural definitions and values, as do politicians and government officials, advocates and social movements, and a host of experts, from scientists to scholars. As Herbert Blumer (1971) wrote, there are no natural social problems; they require legitimation by important elements in society to achieve the status of a "social problem."

Most social constructionist research has focused on noneconomic cultural issues (missing children, child abuse, hate crimes, drug use, crime, mental illness, sexual predators, stalking, etc.). It is not clear why issues related to the economy—unemployment, poverty and homelessness, attitudes toward accumulation of wealth, for example—have not been addressed by social constructionists. It is difficult to know whether social constructionists believe economic issues to be more "social facts" (that is, empirically self-evident, as opposed to "truth claims" made about crime or drugs) or whether, as is more likely, they simply prefer not to arouse controversy. After all, if many social scientists are at work establishing poverty as an issue, a social constructionist approach might appear, at first glance, to challenge the data and definitions that allow social scientists to argue without controversy about the rise or persistence or changes in poverty. There is obviously more controversy among the academic community about US drug laws, for example, than there is about the undesirability of poverty and unemployment. In fact, many sociological arguments (Nelson, 1984; Reinarman and Levine, 1997) often see the hidden underlying issues as being economic, or class- or race-based.

One of the few treatments of homelessness from a social constructionist perspective is Cynthia Bogard's *Seasons Such as These* (2003). Bogard looks specifically at the rise of homeless activism and policy in two of the largest cities in the United States—Washington, D.C., and New York City—cities in which the issue of homelessness, in her view, was primarily defined for the nation. Within these two cities, advocates and activists, mass media, experts, and politicians all played critical roles in determining how homelessness came to be viewed and, perhaps more important, in determining what types of solutions to this rising social problem could be found.

The issue of homelessness was constructed in very different ways in the two cities, and arguably neither effort was at all successful in "solving" the problem of homelessness or in creating major policy alternatives. In Washington, D.C., because of lack of opposition from political officials, homelessness as an issue was significantly defined in the late

1970s and early 1980s by advocates, particularly the charismatic Mitch Snyder of the Community for Creative Non-Violence. This group put pressure on the government using the mass media, which led to the first publicly funded homeless shelter in 1978. The CCNV used tactics such as occupying buildings, pressuring religious groups, and framing the issue as a matter of morality and social justice. The concept of framing (see Goffman, 1974) is crucial, because advocates attempted to transform an issue that was often portrayed as resulting from personal deficiency into a political and social issue. Claims-makers in Washington, D.C., drew heavily on concepts of charity and morality as reasons why something needed to be done about homelessness. They used strong visual images (such as images of "tent cities"—groups of homeless people and others moving into streets and public spaces and creating their own communities, sometimes clashing with authorities) as a tactic to draw media attention and thereby increase public knowledge and apply pressure to political leaders. These claims-makers brought the issue forward from the public to the government and proposed as a solution the creation of more social programs and public funding to help the homeless, including the building of federally funded homeless shelters. Still, as Bogard notes, Snyder's CCNV did not address in its demands the structural roots of homelessness, focusing instead on publicizing the issue and demanding shelters. The CCNV, through its ideological mix of Roman Catholicism and anarchism, tended not to engage government deeply in solutions, but seemed to prefer demanding that the homeless be empowered to take care of themselves.

In contrast, homelessness as an issue in New York City was brought forth by political claims-makers whose agenda was significantly different from that of their activist counterparts in Washington, D.C. Led by controversial mayor Edward Koch, and backed by the early coverage in the *New York Times,* homeless people were often characterized as "former mental patients" and "bizarre characters" in the articles on the subject in the 1980–1981 period. These actions contributed significantly to the long-present idea that homelessness is caused by personal deficiency (Bogard, 2003, p. 30). New Yorkers were bombarded with claims that the majority of homeless people were mentally ill, and that deinstitutionalization was the primary cause of homelessness. Despite the opposition of some, including New York's governor at that time, Mario Cuomo, who blamed housing policies, not mental health policies, the image of the homeless as mentally ill prevailed in New York City. While the "common sense" attitude toward homelessness may include notions of "craziness," it is unclear whether, absent the major push at the early stage of recognition of homelessness as a social problem (or more precisely, the *re*-recognition of the problem for the first time in forty years), the mental illness argument would have gained such legitimacy.

Although Bogard gives a creditable review of the social construction of homelessness in the two cities, she does not generalize much from her findings. What was the relationship between the struggles in Washington, D.C., and New York City and views on homelessness in the rest of the nation? What were the differences historically between the 1980s and previous periods of claims-making about homelessness and poverty? Although Bogard accepts conflict theory's general description of the causes of homelessness, she does not significantly link the economic, housing, and benefit cutbacks to her discussion. And finally, were there any alternatives to the claims-making and issue definition in this period that could have been employed?

Many of the issues that remain unaddressed regarding homelessness have been problematic to social constructionist accounts of other social issues. First, social constructionists tend to look at episodes in the defining of social problems, and with few exceptions do not look at historical patterns—similarities to and differences from other eras (work on illicit drugs may be a major exception here). Second, because their focus is on media, culture, movements, and politics, economic factors tend to be given shorter shrift. Another issue is the tendency of social problems to cluster or "bundle" together. As Philip Jenkins (1992) noted, social problems are interdependent. That is, one can study illicit drugs, but a case study may miss the coinciding cluster of moral issues, such as temperance movements (including drugs and tobacco as well as alcohol) as well as sexuality and even food habits (see Wagner, 1997). Jenkins identified issues of "moral panic" in the 1980s tied to children and sexuality and violence, greatly as a result of the changing family and conflicting cultural battles of the period. Homelessness was part of a broader parcel of issues linked to poverty, economics, government cutbacks, and also foreign affairs and AIDS that were taken up by the anti-Reagan coalition in the 1980s. Although each issue had its own dynamic, there was a strong affinity between anti-Reagan politics and support for addressing this broader set of problems. Another type of argument might be the reverse of "bundling." For example, an argument might be made that the Democrats' drift toward welfare reform in the 1990s contradicted the possibility of policies supporting the poor. After all, with welfare recipients being vilified, how at the same time could officials propose massive new programs for the poor? Finally, another criticism, made by Steve Woolgar and Dorothy Pawluch (1985), involves the stance of social constructionists, who are sometimes seen as standing above the fray and judging issues in their criticisms of claims-makers. As I have argued elsewhere (Wagner, 1997, p. 43), I agree with this argument to the extent that social constructionists may be obscuring their own values and political views by not making their priorities clear. That is, if we criticize the construction of the drug problem as a "moral panic" in the 1980s, we should be clear that most theorists do so not only based on some sense of empirical evidence, but also because they believe the wars on drugs have had profound negative consequences for US society. After all, the determination of what constitutes a "panic" is subjective, and some will always argue that fear and outrage are appropriate reactions. Similarly, if we criticize how homelessness is or was constructed, we need to be clear about the objectives and values we have in disagreeing with popular conceptions of homelessness. Readers will then be freer to support or reject the judgments we make.

Despite these criticisms, social conflict theorists need social constructionist theorists, and vice versa. Without the analysis of social constructionists, social conflict theorists leave us with causes of an issue from their point of view, but they cannot determine why the issue succeeds or fails in political and cultural life. Poverty in the United States, at least as it relates to homelessness, became an issue in the 1980s, but lost momentum in the 1990s and 2000s. Social constructionists concentrate on cultural and political representations, but often fail to provide the empirical evidence from social conflict theory that explains when issues occur and why (after all, homelessness was not created by claims-makers and could not have been an issue in 1970). Both social conflict and social constructionist theorists need to better develop their work within a historical context (and if possible also with an international context) so that better explanatory links can be made by comparison.

The Stages of a Social Problem

Much of the remainder of this book is devoted to developing a stage model for how homelessness was constructed as a social problem in the United States in the past three decades (approximately 1979–2009). Surprisingly little attention has been given to how social problems, particularly those involving the economy and the potential for redistribution of income, travel a route from enthusiasm to disappointment. While not every social problem goes through the same stages, there are some strong reasons to believe that major social problems—those that have a socioeconomic origin and a large economic cost—might parallel homelessness in their relative intractability.

In order to investigate a social problem, it is helpful to have some guiding theory and principles for making sense of the massive amounts of data that today's media culture provides on any issue. Herbert Blumer (1971), in one of the earliest statements on social problems from the constructionist literature, broke down the process of collective definition of an issue along the following lines: (1) emergence, (2) legitimation, (3) mobilization of action, (4) formation of an official plan, and (5) transformation of the official plan in its empirical implementation. In other words, a problem is not a social problem unless it emerges publicly and is legitimated by the major organs in society, usually a combination of the mass media, social experts, at least some politicians and bureaucrats, and sometimes social movements. A successful social problem has a constituency that demands action and some sort of an "official plan" (usually by government), no matter how inadequate. Blumer is quite right that this stage is only the beginning, as politicians, bureaucrats and administrators, and advocates and opponents will struggle around the plan, perhaps eventually emaciating it or perhaps improving it.

The work of Anthony Downs (1972), who coined the term "issue-attention cycle," and Barbara Nelson (1984), who applied Downs's stage theory to the history of child abuse and neglect in the United States, arguably provides an even better framework. Their stages maintain the need for a "discovery" of a social problem, but are less technocratic than Blumer's stage theory. It suggests that Americans are prone to excitement, at least for a short time, about an issue, but that such enthusiasm has negative as well as positive consequences. Further, it suggests that, inevitably, a social problem must become less exciting as the realization of the costs involved in remedying that problem cause a decline in interest. Both of these major additions to Blumer are important. They suggest a structured response of US politicians and media audiences that is on the one hand naively good-natured, but on the other hand firmly opposed to the means that would end many social problems, because they would require profound economic changes or changes in power structures.

The Pre-Problem Stage

The pre-problem stage is the period prior to the consensual realization of the social problem. For Downs and Nelson, this is perhaps the broadest stage, as it could be attached to an unlabeled and "undiscovered" social problem over hundreds of years (think about, for example, sexual abuse as an undiscovered social problem in the United States). To some degree, we can look at homelessness or even the lack of healthcare for all Americans as being in a perpetual pre-problem stage, with the media, advocates, and politicians all silent on the issue at times. We can draw on this pre-problem stage as a way to describe the years prior to the full "discovery" of homelessness in the 1979–1982 period. This is helpful because in the lead-up to the rediscovery of a social problem by the mass media, advocates, politicians, and others, we usually see hints of this rediscovery coming. With an issue such as homelessness, we have enough information to track the rise of the phenomenon prior to it becoming a major national social problem.

The Discovery Stage

There is wide acceptance among political scientists and sociologists that social problems, after lingering (even for generations or centuries), need to be "discovered" (or rediscovered) in order to be framed as major problems that require solution. Child abuse had its day briefly in the 1870s with the famous "Mary Ellen" case (a young adopted girl who was beaten by her stepfather in New York City in the 1870s), and returned to the public attention cycle in the early 1960s (Nelson, 1984). Poverty, though it has remained constant in the United States, is always being lost and rediscovered as a problem. Poverty was most famously rediscovered in the era of the muckrakers and Progressives in the early twentieth century, during the Great Depression, and in the early 1960s (see, for example, Ehrenreich, 1989; O'Connor, 2001; Stricker, 2007). One can give examples of innumerable issues that are lost and found in America. Downs captures Americans' combination of innocence and optimism when he writes of an "alarmed discovery and euphoric enthusiasm" that implies that "every problem can be solved . . . without any fundamental reordering of society itself" (quoted in Nelson, 1984, p. 53). Whether the social problem is poverty or child abuse, domestic violence or drugs, a combination of experts, politicians, mass media, and some of the public need to become enthusiastic about solving it.

The discovery stage is critical to how a problem is defined and shaped, and to its further career. At least in regard to issues that are economically costly or that may threaten power arrangements, the very optimism and superficial confidence of Americans, as led by political leaders, mass media, and sometimes advocates themselves, will inevitably end in disappointment. With homelessness, its presentation as a completely new and horrific condition in the United States that could be remedied presumably by charity and shelters and other superficial services laid the seeds for a failed solution. As Theda Skocpol (1996) has written about the defeat of Clinton's healthcare reform in the 1990s, serious failures in the policy arena have a boomerang effect in the sense that progress can be completely arrested for many years or at least considerably weakened by defeats. These swings are probably critical to political discourse in the United States, where enthusiasm, after surging in preparation for election years or during election periods, then declines into disappointment and skepticism during postelection periods.

Of course, with time, all issues lose some interest among the public. Issues decline for all sorts of reasons. AIDS, for example, was initially portrayed as a sickness of the deviant, but later became a national media sensation, particularly after Rock Hudson revealed that he had the disease (Albert, 1989). Later, with the development of some successful treatments for the disease, and with the wider spread of AIDS in Africa than in the United States, for example, coverage of the issue declined. For problems that require immense economic change to solve, the failure to reveal these facts to the public is in many ways a "setup" for failure—it does not provide the public with the proper solutions to problems nor does it warn against the odds of the problem being "solved."

The Sober Realization and Loss of Interest Stages

In their account of issue careers, Downs and Nelson note that, partly in response to the "alarmed discovery" of naive optimism, a period follows in which a "sober realization" emerges in which at least some of the public (and presumably political and policy leaders) begin to realize that "progress will be costly not only in terms of money but also in terms of social stability" (Nelson, 1984, p. 53). In her case study of child abuse and neglect, Nelson argues that the passage of mandatory-reporting laws for child abuse in the United States, while not without value, could never solve the issue of neglect and abuse for a wide variety of reasons, including the embedding of abuse, and even more so neglect, in the economic structure of inequality in the United States (poverty creates the conditions that result in maltreatment of children). There are also limits to the degree to which the state can police families, again for a variety of reasons. With homelessness, the presence of large numbers of homeless people and the increasingly disruptive nature of the problem, both politically and socially in terms of crime control, resulted in anger. The realization that most homeless people were not downwardly mobile middle-class people but usually poor people to begin with may have also affected the career of this issue, which advocates struggled to present as almost universal ("it can happen to anyone").

It is not clear that Downs's "sober realization" and "loss of interest" stages are always conceptually separate (as may also be the case with the post-problem stage). Downs sees the "loss of interest" stage as involving a loss of media and public interest in a social problem due to its intractability, and resulting from lack of support for redistribution or social reordering. With homelessness, the mass media certainly continued coverage of the issue during the "sober realization" stage, and press coverage did not begin to decline dramatically until 1993. However, the sequence of these two stages might be transposed. For example, where an issue becomes centered in a particular policy and piece of legislation (such as healthcare reform was in the early 1990s and is again today), we can see conceptually that sober realization and loss of interest could occur relatively simultaneously. Homelessness was less tied to a particular legislative agenda and hence did not suffer immediate backlash, as in the case of the failure of healthcare reform in 1993–1994 or in the perceived failure of the war on poverty in the late 1960s.

Because most issues are diffuse and clustered with other issues, it is likely that, at least for the mass media and advocacy groups, issues will continue to be given coverage even if interest in the broader policy fades. For example, over the past three decades, homelessness has gained new coverage through subdivision of the problem: homeless mentally ill, homeless women, homeless families, homeless elders, homeless youth, homeless middle-class people, homeless veterans, and so forth. Sometimes, parts of a problem generate greater interest because they tap the American view of "deservedness" more than does the broader problem as a whole. A good example is the problem of homeless veterans. Because the United States has fought several wars since the problem of homelessness reemerged in the late 1970s and early 1980s, this subset of the problem of homelessness continues to receive media coverage and advocacy at certain times of the year, given its fit with other social problems (in this case veterans) that Americans have more sympathy for. This media coverage does not necessarily lead to successful resolution, for a variety of reasons, but it continues nonetheless.

The Post-Problem or Institutionalization Stage

Downs argues that although issues lose attention and interest, they still remain institutionalized in government services: programs that were "once innovative and exciting . . . become part of the business-as-usual process of government" (quoted in Nelson, 1984, p. 53). Like the pre-problem stage, the post-problem stage is not without some ambiguity. Is this a complete loss of interest, or a waning interest relative to its high point? Institutionalization is a major part of the absorption of all social problems in the United States, as I (Wagner, 2000) and others (e.g., Morone, 1990) have argued. That is, almost as soon as a problem reaches the political system through a web of activism or advocacy, it is likely that some programmatic response will occur. Domestic violence, drugs, sexual abuse, poverty, healthcare, benefits for the elderly, and child abuse are just a few of an array of issues that are handled through social services, either directly provided by government or funded by government. In this sense, the institutionalization process of handling homelessness began quite early as local and state governments began developing an array of service responses to the issue. By 1987, when the federal government passed the Stewart B. McKinney Homeless Assistance Act, the national political system was moving to further institutionalize the issue. Not only does the issue become depoliticized by being shifted to routine social service (or criminal justice) responses, but also a variety of stakeholders gain a vested interest in the issue and in attending to it in a bureaucratic fashion. Administrators, from the head of the smallest soup kitchen to social workers and other employees, and also homeless and formerly homeless consumers themselves, become embedded in the weekly or monthly developments of funding, committee meetings, processing grievances, and engaging new clients. As James Morone (1990) argues regarding the incorporation of dissent in the workplace through the National Labor Relations Board starting in the 1930s, and its institutionalization from the streets to community action agencies in the 1960s, the issue of homelessness becomes a province of specialists. Academics, adminstrators, and experiential specialists (e.g., client representatives) are now likely to attend meetings or write budgets than demonstrate or protest.

Despite the ambiguity of the post-problem stage, it does fit with the post-1994 response to homelessness. While the backlash toward the homeless that started in the late 1980s is still apparent in some local efforts to incarcerate the homeless and in the increase (or at least increased reporting of) hate crimes, generally the issue has stabilized, with moderate media coverage clustered at certain times of the year (particularly between Thanksgiving and Christmas; see Shields, 2001) or in response to relatively predictable events (news conferences of the National Coalition of the Homeless or the US Mayors Conference, or Homeless Memorial Day in late December, for example). Coverage remains sympathetic and advocates and experts remain, but proposed solutions become ever more remote and unmentioned, and the problem ever more routinized.

* * *

In applying these stages, the exact years become somewhat fluid, because we cannot, even in retrospect, account with precision for all the vast political and other developments across different parts of the nation. There are those who believe (see Schneider, 1985) that stage theories can be misleading, because they overemphasize the differences and underemphasize the similarities between stages. This is a valid caution, but again note that the stages are meant to represent the predominant attitude of a period, not a total of all the attitudes in each period.

For this study of homelessness, the period 1979–1982 seems to best represent the move from the pre-problem stage to the discovery stage, though the period could arguably span to a year earlier or a year later. The period 1983–1988 seems to best represent the height of enthusiasm and alarm about the issue of homelessness, as indicated by charitable mobilizations ("Hands Across America," for example) and sympathetic mass media coverage. The "backlash" period of 1989–1993 (again, the period could span to a year earlier or later) seems to best correspond with the stage of sober realization. Finally, loss of interest and institutionalization of the homeless problem are most evident in the post-1994 period.

Notes

1. Although many advocates and those on the left have urged this view in the recessions of the past three decades, recessions seem to afford a very different environment than depressions. Not only are the downturns more concen-

trated regionally, racially, and in other ways than was the Great Depression, for example, but also the media and cultural environment in the United States have changed drastically since the 1930s.

2. I thank Pete White, codirector of the Los Angeles Community Action Network, for our conversations linking these phenomena.

3. This is certainly not to argue that there were no radicals who maintained their positions. More often, though, advocates and activists often spent most of their time denouncing Reaganomics, and at least implying that better days were ahead if the Democratic Party could win.

4. The dynamics of presenting gender, class, and race were quite different among advocates. The presence of women among the homeless was almost always mentioned, perhaps because women are historically seen as at least slightly more deserving of assistance than men and hence evoke sympathy. On the other hand, the fact that so many of the homeless were people of color and from poor or working-class families was much less emphasized, as it cut against the rhetoric of "it can happen to anyone."

3

A Brief History
of Homelessness

Homelessness, if defined as living without a closed-off structure that keeps out the natural elements, goes back to the beginnings of humanity. However, being without a settled, secure, and permanent abode is a concept that had little meaning in preindustrial societies (and this is still true, for example, of the Australian aborigines, who have no concept of a physical home, and of the Roma [Gypsies] of Europe, who also do not share the dominant Western concept [see Fonseca, 1996; Jackson, 1995]). Even in the United States for much of its history, those who lived without a walled-off home were not a recognized category of people; rather there was a somewhat different concept of having a "settlement."

Beginning with the Laws of Settlement, brought over from colonial England, a pauper on the road (as compared to a locally settled poor family or individual) who had no legally recognized settlement was subject to removal, "warning out," or in some cases even violence (see Deutsch, 1949; Katz, 1986; Trattner, 1984). However, being without a settlement did not always mean being literally homeless (for example, families or individuals were often on the road searching for work away from their home village), just as being settled did not mean that one could not be homeless (for example, a long-term settled family could well become homeless after a fire or accident). Most US cities and states developed very restrictive settlement laws, and even native-born residents who did not pay property or poll taxes for a certain period of time were not considered legally settled. Women held settlement only if their husbands or fathers held settlement in a particular town or city. Throughout US history, the ill treatment of the unsettled poor not only was a matter of social class prejudice, but also was entwined with preservation of religious, ethnic, and local traditions against the newcomers from abroad or other parts of the nation.

Homelessness arose as a modern issue only in the post–Civil War period in the person of the "tramp" (sometimes the word was used interchangeably with "bum" or "bummer" or "hobo"), a masculinized and feared figure who was often stigmatized as the bringer of social disorder and radicalism. Part of the origin of the modern stigma of homelessness lies in the development of this view of the rootless person. Although a counter-image that glamorized the tramp gradually developed in some radical circles, the majority of tramps were not necessarily without housing, for many took to the road looking for work. The Great Depression of the 1930s and its folklore, to some extent, changed the earlier social construction of the homeless as shiftless tramps, because of the perceived near-universality of poverty and the rhetoric of the "forgotten man." But even though images changed, treatment of people who were actually homeless was probably no different than in other eras. After World War II, when the United States entered a generally more prosperous period in the 1950s and 1960s, "homelessness" as a term and concept fell out of use, and was associated mostly with "bums" who lived in the so-called skid rows, the derelict areas of central cities where low-income housing was available.

These earlier images of homelessness are important not just as background, but also because our cultural scripts determine the way social problems are framed in contemporary and future eras. A great deal of rhetoric and campaigning around homelessness in the post-1979 period was shaped by this past, with activists attempting to break away from the older stereotypes of homeless people as "bums" and "tramps." Two lessons come from the history. The first is that severe and profound economic change, whether in the form of depressions or recessions, usually directs public attention to the very poor and homeless. Second, the portrayal of the issue of homelessness is often not so much primarily about the homeless, but about the public (generally the white middle class) and its fears about the future. It is far from clear, then, that increased attention to the very poor actually substantially improves the conditions of their lives; if there are any improvements, these are often peripheral to other policy changes and social agendas.

The Stigmatization of Poverty and Homelessness

Though a complete history of homelessness is beyond the scope of this book, it is important to understand that poverty and homelessness were not always stigmatized. In medieval Europe, the Catholic Church glorified the giving of alms—and how could there be great almsgiving without a large supplicant class? The ideals of Catholicism were often personified in Saint Francis of Assisi, who, in emulating the model of Jesus, gave away all his belongings and lived among the poor. Most medieval cities had large crowds of beggars seeking alms. Almsgiving was unconditional; it did not matter, as it would later, whether the supplicant was in fact disabled, a leper, or elderly, or whether he or she was an imposter who could actually toil all day. Not only for the Catholic Church, but also for noblemen who wanted to secure their place in Heaven, it was considered a great virtue to give to the poor, sometimes lavishly. In a notable example from Bronsilaw Geremek's history of poverty, a well-to-do townsman in Lubeck, Germany, left instructions that upon his death his wealth was to be distributed as alms among 19,000 people in the town (out of as many as 24,000 residents) (1994, p. 34). While many religious people still believe that through charity they can buy their way into heaven, in earlier eras this was held as literally true. Also, feudalism, with its basis in land and its settled classes of nobility, vassals, and serfs, did not need the specter of mass unemployment (as was later true) in which people faced starvation if they did not work. Theoretically, everyone knew their rights and obligations, including the "noblesse oblige," a belief that ensured the nobles cared for their own serfs from cradle to grave. Of course, in practice, as increasing social changes in European society occurred after the Crusades and Marco Polo's visit to China, movement out of the stable classes increased. Urban centers and ports began to emerge where traders and merchants (the future bourgeoisie) came into being as well as artisans and craftsmen. Freed or escaped serfs as well as runaways from the army and clergy left their ancestral lands and moved to the cities, as did children who lost out in the primogeniture system (in which the firstborn male inherited the land and the younger sons were excluded from inheritance and often forced to fend for themselves on the road; see Miller, 1991).

Feudalism was a harsh, hierarchical, and ultimately coercive system supported by the laws of nobility and church, and later by the growing power of the state. No one wanted to live the life of a poor wanderer or beggar. However, neither the economy nor the ideology of this era before the advent of capitalism and Protestantism supported a harsh view of poverty or an anti-poor ideology.

Treatment of the poor, particularly the most visibly unsettled—the beggars and wanderers—changed so quickly after the Protestant Reformation that its effects are still startling. Martin Luther, in his rebellion against the excesses of Roman Catholicism, declared emphatically that "he who would not work, shall not eat!" and the strictest religious radicals (such as John Calvin) reversed any semblance of the Catholic heroization of the poor in order to wage punishment, including violence, upon the poor. For example, in England in 1547, Edward VI, noting that "Idleness and Vagabonding is the mother and root of theft, robberies and all evil acts and other mischiefs," mandated that "every person not impotent and loitering or wandering and not seeking work *or leaving it when engaged* is to be apprehended and taken before a justice of the peace. He is then to 'mark' with a hot iron in the breast the mark of V [vagabond]" (quoted in Miller, 1991, p. 11; original emphasis).

Max Weber (1978) famously argued for the "elective affinity" of an emerging capitalist system and Protestant ideology. Protestantism, in its early form, relied on an ideology that stressed a "calling," a visible occupation—landowner, public official, merchant, farmer—that showed others that one was among the "elect" and thus on the road to Heaven. For those who had few or no material possessions, this was a sure sign of the reverse—that one was unworthy of Heaven and divine grace. Further, Protestant reformers saw the Catholic Church's unconditional support of a large retinue of poor people, including beggars, as corrupt, as much as simony and nepotism. For the Protestants, humans were to be judged by their deservedness, and particularly by their work ethic, not their capacity for asking alms or other forms of "free-loading."

Added to the religious arguments were the vast changes occurring in Europe, particularly in England, in the period between the sixteenth and nineteenth centuries. As land became more valuable, common lands reserved for the people were "enclosed" by a series of laws that annexed the land that they had previously used to graze their sheep or plant crops. This process, along with the collapse of many feudal manors, led to the impoverishment of millions of former serfs. No longer attached to their ancestral villages and assured of sustenance by their lords or even by a common grazing ground, poor people were everywhere—on the roads, crowding the squares begging, and sometimes acting in an unruly fashion. Some manors and even early factories were burned to the ground. Later in England, the new workhouses for the poor were also sometimes violently attacked. According to most historians who study this era, capitalism needed not only to punish and stigmatize the unruly poor, but also to make sure people understood that there was no option but to work at low wages in the emerging industries (see, for example, Polanyi, 1957). There was no more free lunch, so to speak. Factories, when they arose in the eighteenth and nineteenth centuries, were not popular places, and groups such as the famous Luddites actively sabotaged the factory system. Coercion was necessary to build a new society.

Perhaps understated in the accounts that focus on religion and capitalism is the role of the modern state in enforcing the work ethic, labor settlement, and mobility, and in putting down disorder. Capitalism was at a very rudimentary stage in which its power was limited, and its modern apparatus of work control was only just being invented. It was the powerful state in places like Great Britain and France that was able to control the poor, punish and discipline them, and develop laws that would allow Benjamin Disraeli, prime minister of England, to later declare poverty a crime (Piven and Cloward, 1993 [1971], p. 35; see also the work of Foucault [1977, 1980] on the "governmentality" and great changes of the bourgeois era).

The United States inherited the English laws developed under the Tudors and Stuarts, which both disciplined and assisted the poor. These laws were also intended to divide the poor into different categories.

The Division of the Poor

The English were the first to develop a public system of relief for the poor, under Queen Elizabeth, through a series of laws in the late sixteenth and early seventeenth centuries. These Elizabethan Poor Laws were the basis of the US system as well. The prime features were the granting of aid to those, and only those, who were settled in a local area (the Laws of Settlement), and the division of the poor into a "deserving" or worthy poor category and an "undeserving" or unworthy poor category. Of major importance was that all aid to the poor was local in nature, as determined by an official or group of officials called the "overseers of the poor." Eventually, in the twentieth century, overseers became known by more modern titles such as directors or heads of public welfare. Some small towns in both Britain and the United States continue to use the name "overseers" even today.

The context for the Elizabethan laws was dramatic poverty and social unrest as the old feudal society was unraveling. In many ways, this was "progressive" legislation in that it acknowledged, when other societies had yet not, the need for some public aid for people who were poor, disabled, ill, or elderly. However, this legislation also enshrined in Anglo and US law a set of prejudices, distinctions, and public stinginess amid local differences. First, since poor relief was a local expense based on the poor tax, each town and city in England (and then in the United States) sought to guard its own budget, and had incentive to argue that the potential recipient of charity was from another town or village. No doubt some overseers in the United States and in Britain were more generous than others; this provided for the ever recurring battles within and between towns over the possibility of being flooded with "paupers," with stricter towns believing that they could avoid being overrun by poor people. Later, when poorhouses were built in the United States, the same competition arose, with some towns viewing others as treating the poor too generously. Reformers constantly stepped forward, at both the local and state levels, pledging to minimize costs either by treating the poor more harshly or by forcing other states and localities into paying their bills. These debates have lasted now for hundreds of years, and continue to this day.

Paradoxically, particularly in the United States, a country built on immigration and residential mobility, the Laws of Settlement exerted a powerful deterrent against being considered an outsider ("from away") and receiving aid. Some aspects of the settlement laws actually lasted in the United States until 1969, when the Warren Court overruled long and unreasonable residency requirements for welfare programs. Settlement laws in nineteenth-century New England, for example, often required five years of residency through payment of property and poll taxes, with women acquiring settlement status based on their father's or husband's residency (Wagner, 2008b). In the United States, as early as the 1820s, towns were spending as much money fighting each other over settlement (in arcane legal cases, seeking to prove that applicants had been born in one town or another) as they actually spent relieving poverty (see Katz, 1986). Settlement laws, in the context of widespread immigration, reinforced xenophobia, as the presence of people "from elsewhere," whether determined by visible characteristics (race, ethnicity) or by legally traceable foreignness (for example, those who were captains of ships had to certify by bond they were not releasing paupers onto the shore), was a constant concern. Obviously, however, as the nation grew, it became impossible for major ports to police their entrants, and cities like New York, Boston, Philadelphia, and Baltimore filled with paupers. To control and (to some extent) aid these paupers, large numbers of poorhouses, and some workhouses (where paupers were required to work or do work that was not really needed or productive), were built in the United States in the first half of the nineteenth century, both as a financial expedient (it was usually cheaper to aid the poor in a house or institutional setting than at home) and as a way to at least mitigate some of the distress. The British embraced workhouses in a much larger way in the mid-nineteenth century, and built thousands of the morbid and dark institutions made famous by Charles Dickens's novels. In the United States, despite the settlement laws, the growing employers' desire for labor as well as the increased availability of land allowed people to move about, with only the unlucky forced to face the consequences of the settlement laws.

In addition to having to prove one's residence, the built-in legal concept of "deservedness" formalized Protestant morality by legally defining categories of deviance. Although each overseer could do as he pleased, ordinarily certain groups of people were clearly considered more "deserving": widows, orphans, elderly people, and most physically disabled people (although, just as AIDS is stigmatized in our times, venereal disease and tuberculosis were often exceptions to the rule, and those with these diseases were sometimes banished from town). Men who were able-bodied were viewed as the main category of potential "malingerers," who later came to be known as "vagrants" and "tramps." To the suspicious and unscientific eyes of these overseers, many men who today would be acknowledged as having mental disabilities—not to mention problems with substance abuse—were dealt with very harshly (see Deutsch, 1949). Women who were single or widowed but still sexually active were dealt with harshly as well. As Mimi Abramovitz (1988) notes, while men were held rigidly to an idealized work ethic, women were rigidly judged by their adherence to a family ethic that moralized loyalty and subservience in the roles of wife and mother. Although children who were well behaved and simply poor were aided, those judged delinquent or runaways were considered undeserving. One example of this determination of undeservedness comes from the nineteenth-century laws of Connecticut, Massachusetts, and Maine, where incarceration or "indoor relief" in a poorhouse, workhouse, or house of correction was prescribed for the following categories of people:

> all rogues, vagabonds and idle persons going about in town or country begging or persons . . . feigning themselves to have knowledge in physiognomy, palmistry, or pretending that they can tell fortunes, or discover where lost or stolen goods may be found, common pipers, fiddlers, runaways . . . common drunkards, common night-walkers, pilferers, wanton and lascivious persons . . . common railers or brawlers . . . as also persons under distraction and unfit to go at large. (See Deutsch, 1949; State of Maine, 1833)

Although it might seem amusing to twenty-first-century Americans to equate homeless wanderers ("vagabonds and idle persons . . . begging") with fortune tellers, palm readers, musicians ("pipers" and "fiddlers"), sex workers or prostitutes ("night-walkers") and others considered to be sexually deviant ("wanton and lascivious persons"), the mentally ill ("persons under distraction"), and belligerent people ("railers or brawlers"), the phrasing here is important, because it shows how certain forms of poverty and even mental illness were equated with moral crimes against the citizenry. For most of US history, deviance and the treatment of the deviant—the "insane," "feeble-minded," "drunk," or "criminal"—were dealt with under the Poor Law system.

Although we can see here the obvious basis of our modern prejudice against some categories of people who are deepest in poverty, and particularly the tie between not being local and being mistreated, homelessness was rarely a national issue prior to the 1870s. An elderly man who lived all his life in a town could lose his house in a fire and receive aid from the town to rebuild and avoid homelessness; many widows and children lost their homes and were aided; and as veterans gained more "deservedness," they too might become a category of people to be aided even if homeless. But those who were homeless and not from the town were cast off as outsiders, and those who may have been from the area but who were considered to be "distracted," "rogues or vagabonds," "malingerers," or other such categories of "undeserving poor" were refused aid. In other words, the status of not having a roof over one's head did not itself propel hostility or anger, as this condition was shared by many who were immigrating and migrating, and by people of many different ages and conditions. It was rather the prejudice against the "unsettled" that would change into a prejudice against homelessness, with the assumption, often made still today, that homeless people are not local, but come from afar to drain local "hospitality."

The First Homeless Crisis:
Tramps, Bums, and Hobos in the 1870s and 1880s

Even well after the Civil War, many Americans felt that this country would still become exceptional, that the social problems and social stratification of Europe—with its slums, proletarians, and poverty—would not happen in the United States. The great American writer and poet Walt Whitman illustrated this well when in early 1879 he reported:

I saw today a sight I had never seen before . . . and it amazed, and made me serious; three quite good-looking American men, of respectable personal presence, two of them young, carrying chiffonier-bags on their shoulders, and the usual long iron hooks in their hands, plodding along, their eyes cast down, spying for scraps, rags, bones, etc. . . .

This sight of respectable Americans without work gave testimony to grim and spectral dangers long familiar in the Old World but unknown here. Is the fresh and broad demesne of America destined also to give them foothold and lodgement, permanent domicile? . . . If the United States, like the countries of the Old World, are also to grow vast crops of poor, desperate, dissatisfied, nomadic, miserably-waged populations, such as we see looming upon us of late years—steadily, even slowly, eating into them like a cancer of lungs or stomach—then our republican experiment, notwithstanding all of its surface-successes, is at heart an unhealthy failure. (Quoted in Trachtenberg, 1982, p. 70)

It is important to keep in mind that, like Whitman, Americans were shocked at the dramatic pace of industrialization in the decades after the Civil War. While no doubt most citizens had seen poor people before, the United States prior to the Civil War was still an agricultural nation and in many locales the sight of beggars and poor men roaming was novel. In the aftermath of the North's victory, industrialization boomed along with the vast expansion of rail transportation, making distant travel possible, and the nation's communication system expanded rapidly. Prior to the advent of the railroad, mass-circulation newspapers, and a virulent media campaign against tramps in the 1870s and 1880s, few people knew that what they were seeing in these wandering poor people were "tramps" or "bums" or "hobos." A massive, nationwide depression beginning in 1873 and lasting through 1877 made the issue of poverty, want, and crime even more visible. Finally, the association of radicalism with wandering poor men also placed these people within the "dangerous classes" that writers such as Charles Loring Brace (1967 [1872]) were warning about.

The origin of all these pejorative terms and the origin of the attack on the wandering (mostly) men are a bit obscure. Historian Ken Kusmer traces the term "bummer" to the *New York Times* as early as 1868, when the newspaper used the word as a synonym for "vagrant" (2002, p. 37). The term "bum" or "bummer" or "bummer element" would remain in usage afterward as a generally derogatory label for any poor or deviant person or group who committed antisocial acts or was judged capable of inciting social unrest. The term "tramp" by the mid-1870s seemed to replace "bum" as a specific noun for the wandering unemployed. The *New York Times* claimed that "he (the tramp) is at war in a lazy kind of way with society and rejoices at being able to prey upon it" (quoted in Kusmer, 2002, p. 8). The *New York Tribune* said that "they are like barbarians who came down like wolves upon Rome!" (quoted in Kusmer, 2002, p. 43). Social scientists similarly attacked the tramp. In a paper presented at the American Social Science Association in 1877, Yale Law dean Francis Wayland announced that the term "tramp" meant a "lazy, incorrigible, cowardly, utterly depraved savage" (quoted in Trachtenberg, 1982, p. 71). Other opinion-makers were so vehement in their denunciation of these poor men that they advocated (if perhaps tongue-in-cheek) violence against them:

> The simplest plan, probably, where one is not a member of the humane society is to put a little . . . arsenic in the meat and other supplies furnished (for) the tramp. This produces death within a comparatively short period of time, is a warning to other tramps to keep out of the neighborhood, keeps the coroner in good humor, and saves one's chickens and other . . . property from constant destruction. (*Chicago Tribune,* July 12, 1877, quoted in Cresswell, 2001, p. 9)

> A wrecked train car invariably means a dead tramp, Wrecking trains provides an expensive, but effective way of getting rid of a very undesirable class of nuisances. (*St. Louis Journal,* 1879, quoted in Cresswell, 2001, p. 10)

Of the three terms "tramp," "bum," and "hobo," the latter was used (at least initially) the least in this period, though when it did appear it became nearly synonymous with "tramp." Later the "hobo" came to be regarded as more the "home guard" poor person who stayed in the skid rows, often called "the main stem" of major cities, where these people picked up day or seasonal work, as opposed to the more stigmatized wanderers called "tramps" and "bums."

There is little dispute in the historical literature that vast numbers of wandering men began appearing all over the nation in the decades after the Civil War. Eric Monkkonen, in his book *Walking to Work,* suggests that these numbers were so vast that by the last two decades of the nineteenth century, between 10 and 20 percent of all families included a transient male member (1984, p. 8). Monkkonen, as well as other scholars, note that "tramping"—moving from place to place—was a rational response to the cycle of unemployment and uneven industrialization in the nation. For example, as Tim Cresswell (2001) points out regarding the Great Lakes area, tens of thousands of jobs required mobile work—for example, railroad building, crop harvesting, and lumberjacking. But throughout the United States, and especially when depressions enveloped the major cities, building and construction work, casual farm labor, mining, tree felling, ice harvesting, and fruit picking remained available, in some areas even plentifully. Although some workers moved with their entire families (the "settlers" or "migrants"), few of these jobs were secure or lucrative enough to support a family. It made more sense for the male worker to travel and return home with some cash in his pocket or to send home some of his earnings. Another reason for not returning home or bringing a family to a new locale was the settlement laws. If a Boston worker left for a year to mine gold in California, he lost his settlement rights in Massachusetts. But in his absence, his wife and children may well have been supported by relief. Of course, the man who struck it rich had no problem, but for those who failed, they now were ineligible for any aid. If a New York City worker arrived in Oklahoma and had no work, not only would he not receive relief, but also he was likely to be arrested under the vagrancy laws. A new class of people, the mobile transient—men without a home, always moving—was created. This large class was produced by the needs of industry and the nation to build the infrastructure of the vast expanding frontier, but at the same time, agents of the state, social science, media, and others vehemently opposed the presence of these men, whether they were working or not.

The response to the presence of "tramps" was harsh. Vigilante groups formed in many towns to drive out poor wanderers by force, sometimes under threat of lynching. States vied with each other to pass harsh vagrancy laws. Massachusetts, as early as 1866, had anti-tramp legislation for "idle persons who, not having visible means of support, live abroad without lawful employment . . . or place themselves in the streets, highways, passages, or other public places to beg or receive alms." These men were forced into houses of correction for six months of forced labor (Montgomery, 1993, p. 84). By 1876, nineteen states had passed laws rewriting their vagrancy statutes as tramp laws. In Connecticut, for example, "any act of begging or vagrancy, by any person not a resident of this state, shall be *prima facie* evidence that such a person is a tramp." Excluded from the provision were females, minors under the age of sixteen, and blind people (Cresswell, 2001, p. 52). As Amy Dru Stanley notes, the US legal presumption of innocence was reversed in the case of tramping. Suspects were presumed guilty unless they could rebut police testimony with a "good account of themselves." Indeed, Stanley quotes a contemporary saying that one "could find himself behind prison walls without his knowing even upon what charge he had been put there and without having made the slightest defense" (Stanley, 1992, pp. 1278–1279). By 1877, there had been 1 million arrests for vagrancy in the United States. Eventually, forty of the forty-four states at that time enacted anti-vagrancy statutes, and some allowed mandated imprisonment in a house of correction or workhouse for as long as two years.

These laws were certainly not without critics. Henry George, a social critic and political radical, associated the "material progress" of capitalism with the worsening of conditions for the worker, including the label of "tramp" and the destination of the almshouse (see Fink, 2001, p. 21). The incipient labor movement vehemently opposed vagrancy laws. One labor newspaper quoted in Sherri Broder's study of the latter nineteenth century criticized vagrancy laws "as the first step to enable the employers of labor to say to a man 'you must take the wages we offer you; if you don't, we will discharge you, and if you dare to go away you will be arrested as a tramp and sent to prison to work there for forty cents a day'" (2002, p. 22).

When American Federation of Labor leader Samuel Gompers testified before the US Senate during an 1883 investigation and the term "tramp" was used, he said: "I should call them, workingmen, who for a time have become superfluous in society, men rather, whom the employing class has made superfluous" (quoted in Montgomery, 1993, pp. 87–88). The *Washington Craftsman,* a labor newspaper, responded to the Connecticut tramp law by observing in 1885 that, "had Christ lived in Connecticut, he would have been imprisoned for asking for a drink of water" (quoted in Montgomery, 1993, p. 88).

Not all responses to tramping were negative. Police stations began opening their doors to homeless people. Numerous etchings of the nineteenth century show a sea of humanity crowding into these makeshift shelters. Some local reformers created their own charitable institutions, such as lodging houses, soup kitchens, and employment agencies. In Boston, for example, charitable agencies opened the Boston Wayfarer's Lodge in 1879. However, even in these privately run social services, though they may have been better than workhouses or almshouses, reformers believed that only forced work would discourage tramping, and that by forcing the poor to chop wood or perform other tasks, "they would repel the truly dangerous tramps" (Cresswell, 2001, p. 42). The large number of unemployed males, particularly in the depressions of the 1870s and 1890s, forced the entire social service system (or charitable system, as it was then called) to move entire categories of people, such as women, children, and the physically and mentally disabled, out of almshouses and into specialized institutions (asylums, orphanages, homes for wayward women, for example) in order not to contaminate the more "deserving" poor (or at least the more vulnerable poor, in their eyes) with the "undeserving" poor.

If social conflict theory (see Chapter 2) explains the effort of employers to keep wages low and to develop a large pool of unemployed or seasonally unemployed workers, what explains the vehement hostility of the media, state officials, charitable officers, and the middle class to tramps? Kusmer argues (2002, p. 11) convincingly that in every historical period, working-class and poor people are far more sympathetic to the plight of the homeless than are the middle class and wealthy. There are countless stories, some passed on to this day, of houses marked by small signs or symbols indicating that they would feed wandering people. But class conflict cannot fully explain the moral panic and hostility toward the homeless; a social constructionist view is necessary.

Some authors stress the impact of the Civil War and the railroad on the rise of panic about tramps. No doubt, the end of the Civil War left in its wake many hundreds of thousands of demobilized soldiers. At the National Conference of Charities held in Saratoga, New York, in 1877, the Reverend Everett Hale claimed that military life had "produced men who were hardened to life outdoors, used to living off the land and disposed not to thinking too far into the future" (quoted in Cresswell, 2001, p. 34). At the same time that large groups of men were unemployed, accustomed to traveling and surviving together, the major mode of transit shifted from horse and wagon to train. Most scholars do note that the public emergence of the "tramp" coincides with the emergence of the railroad. According to some sources, bands of men would jump onto trains together and refuse to pay; in some areas, these men commandeered the trains and terrorized passengers. Whether these stories are true or not, an ongoing battle between the railroads, through their employees and hired security, and those riding the rails for free would continue for many decades, including into the Great Depression. Cresswell (2001) recounts many stories of tramps and hobos being literally thrown off moving trains, with as many as 5,000 tramps and hobos killed annually by train employees. Local towns and cities that had been victimized by the appearance of the unsettled poor furiously blamed the railroads for disturbing their peace. But in turn the railroads argued that the towns should enforce their own vagrancy laws.

While no doubt there was an increase in tramping, and while perhaps some of the tramps became increasingly resistant to law and order, these factors still do not appear to explain the amount of vitriol and outrage manifested against tramps by the major newspapers, social scientists and other intellectuals, and railroad employers. Rather, as Kusmer convincingly argues, it may have been the atmosphere of the time: during the 1870s, the Red Scare, beginning with the Paris Commune, led some observers to conflate fulmination against subversives with images of the criminal, the labor agitator, and the tramp. Despite studies that showed the overwhelming number of tramps to be American-born, observers insisted that the tramps were recent immigrants, their heads filled with "crude ideology that somehow managed to combine socialism with burglary" (quoted in Kusmer, 2002, p. 49). From the 1871 Paris Commune on, newspapers and opinion leaders associated the "rabble" with political disorder and insurrection. More and more in the United States, the fact that most socialist and anarchist organizers were Central or Eastern Europeans added ethnic prejudice to the mix.

It is not coincidental that 1877 was the year of the most virulent media attack to date on tramps and one of the largest arrests of tramps. It was the year of the massive railroad strike that some authors believe was the closest the United States has ever come to a social revolution. The strike began with wage cuts at the Baltimore and Ohio Railroad in West Virginia and escalated into mass riots in cities across the Midwest and the Middle Atlantic states. Thousands of strikers and their allies were fired upon by federal troops after several state militias and city police refused to shoot their fellow citizens. Mass anarchy seemed to take over for at least six weeks as violence reigned, millions of dollars in damage was done, and possibly a hundred or more people were killed. The National Guard armories were actually started as a result of this national strike (Bruce, 1959). Although obviously many of the "rioters" were rail workers and other employed people, both the media and intellectuals singled out the "tramp" and unruly poor as the villains. The *New York Times* blamed the "bummer elements" for the riots. Henry Ward Beecher, the famous abolitionist minister, charged that "socialist theories were interfering with the natural laws of capitalism and evolution" and, in a statement that he would later regret, wrote: "I do not say that a dollar a day is enough to support a working man, not enough to support a man and five children if a man would insist on smoking and drinking beer. But the man who cannot live on bread and water is not fit to live" (quoted in Applegate, 2006, pp. 460–461). Another progressive, Franklin Benjamin Sanborn, condemned the rioters as "misguided, often vicious and dangerous" (Sanborn, 1878).

The association of "tramps" with presumably radicalized foreign-born men on the loose would continue to be a dominant theme throughout US history. Such examples included the Haymarket "riot" of 1886, where radicals were hanged after a bomb killed Chicago police following a strike for the eight-hour day, and the Sacco and Vanzetti case of the 1920s, in which worldwide protests arose against the sentence of execution for two foreign anarchists accused unjustly of murder. It is not exactly clear at what point the image of the "bummer" or "tramp" became disengaged from the stigma of rebellion, foreignness, and radicalism. After all, the depression of the 1890s was a massive blow to the economy of the United States and included a variety of protests, such as the famous mass march (including many "tramps") known as Coxey's Army, and the much maligned national Pullman rail strike of 1893–1894, yet historians believe that, by then, the majority of fear of the tramp had receded. Some of the ferocity of the earlier campaigns returned in the 1910s when the radical Wobblies (the Industrial Workers of the World) who opposed World War I were condemned as "bums" and lynched and even burned in boxcars in the West. After World War I and the Bolshevik Revolution, during the infamous Palmer Raids, thousands of foreign radicals across the nation were attacked, jailed, and deported. Yet unlike the 1877 rail strike or the condemnation of the Wobblies (who glorified the transient poor with songs like "Hallelujah I Am a Bum"), other strikes as well as the radicalism of foreigners deported in the Palmer Raids do not seem to be linked to transience.

The Great Depression and the Emergence of the Transient

Although US history has been rife with depressions, the Great Depression, given its number of victims, national impact, and longevity (1929 to 1940), is no doubt a unique event. While some scholars greatly overstate the impact of the depression as de-stigmatizing homelessness (Kusmer, 2002), the 1930s did mark a sharp break in the way homeless people were discussed and viewed by many, and led to a temporary (two-year) period in which the federal government sought to innovate in caring for the very poor, but only to abandon the effort and dump responsibility for the "transient" back onto the states and local governments.

Two sharp differences during the Great Depression compared to the 1870–1930 era were the language used to describe the homeless, and the end of the association of homeless people with radicalism and foreignness. The label "tramp" began to recede in the 1930s, presumably as the average worker, and perhaps even news editors, began to become aware of the widespread nature of want in the United States, including the lack of shelter. Immigration to the United States had been severely curtailed with the passage of the Immigration Quota reforms following World War I. These reforms considerably neutralized one of the major bugaboos of the previous half-century or more: the foreign poor. "Hobo" came to be more prominently used, and later the even more neutral "transient," the latter probably originating with the terminology of the federal government. Many of the disruptive events of the 1930s did include the homeless and very poor—the marches and councils of the unemployed, which were often founded by radical organizations in major urban areas, and the Bonus Army March of 1932, in which thousands of veterans assembled in Washington, D.C., lived in tents, and were later forcibly cleared out by the US Army, under General Douglas MacArthur. Nevertheless, the specific fear of the homeless or transient worker as a breeder of radicalism did not appear as great as in the pre-depression era. Henry Miller notes that the "huddled figure of the man selling apples . . . became a national symbol of despair and hopelessness" and that "shame and indignation was probably a more typical attitude of the homeless" (1991, pp. 55–56). David Snow and Leon Anderson, in their brief history of homelessness, write that there was "little collective organizing at the time," noting "one observer's lament that it was 'pathetic to see beggars where rebels once shouted, sang, and whored'" (1993, p. 15). Although these assessments may have some truth, it is more likely that the general surge in disorder that occurred between 1931–1932 and 1937 was more associated with working-class people and with visions of communist-influenced organizers and activists. The new "bogeymen" were not necessarily foreigners or homeless people, but more disciplined radical organizers, longshoremen, teamsters, autoworkers, and other blue-collar workers who were involved in the visible social unrest of the 1930s.

Despite what would come to be seen as a lessening of stigma, the approach of the nation to this new crisis of homelessness (estimated to be as high as 1.5 million people a day by sociologist Nels Anderson (cited in Crouse, 1986), was harsh or even harsher than before the depression. Most communities simply refused to admit homeless people, and some states and locales again set up patrols to keep out the "unsettled." California, for example, in 1931 increased its residency requirement for settlement status from one year to three, and Colorado from sixty days to six months. Outside Tucson, Arizona, large signs greeted newcomers: "Warning to Transients: Relief Funds for Local Residents Only Transients, Do Not Apply" (Miller, 1991, p. 63). Joan Crouse, an expert on New York State's treatment of transients, notes some of the typical headlines of the time—such as "37 Men Seized in Subways" and "23 Jobless Sent to Jail"—and characterizes the huge shelter set up by New York City at the South Ferry Terminal Annex as the "largest bedroom in the world, with beds lined up side by side and head to head in an attempt to fit as many people as possible in the shelter" (Crouse, 1986, pp. 71, 74). Still, the nonsettled poor were limited to stays of one night per month. People who stayed at the large shelters complained that the housing accommodations were "like nothing else under the sun, perhaps a scene from Dante" (Crouse, 1986, p. 74). Not surprisingly, in a pattern remarkably familiar to that of the twenty-first century, many homeless people preferred sleeping in shantytowns (then often known as "Hoovervilles") to the indignities of the shelters.

Despite the terrible times and poor treatment of the transient, financial collapse at the local level and mass pressure on the Franklin Roosevelt administration led to brief experiments with radical change. When the Federal Emergency Relief Administration (FERA) was set up in 1933, it had an unparalleled mission, as noted by Elizabeth Wickenden, an aide to relief czar Harry Hopkins: "there was one concern—to distribute as much money as possible, as fast as possible to as many people as possible" (quoted in Piven and Cloward, 1993 [1971], p. 75). This brief period of financial redistribution—with no attention to the distinction between the "deserving" and the "undeserving" poor or to an employment test—helped spur Hopkins's innovative founding of the Federal Transient Services (FTS). With $15 million, Hopkins declared that "needy persons who have no settlement in any one state or community" would be provided for (Kusmer, 2002, p. 210). Much of the FTS money did go to localities to finance the same (or expanded) shelters, soup kitchens, and other programs that were already present, breaking down the division between the local poor and the nonlocal, who had formerly been considered ineligible for aid. Most innovative was the creation of hundreds of "transient camps" in rural areas across the nation. The innovation of the camps was in their inclusive capacity (as many as 700,000 individuals were served in the two years of the program's existence) with no questions asked, provision of free physical examinations and routine (but not hospital) medical costs, free clothing, free meals, and presumably an opportunity to work, though at only a dollar a week.

Because of the depression; the isolated nature of some of the camps; and, no doubt, as documented by scholars, the continued community opposition, the camps did best when they could find work for their residents. For example, most camps developed their own newspapers, with names like *Nomad, Highway Citizen,* and *Quaker City Trumpet* (Kusmer, 2002, p. 215). Transients worked as barbers, tailors, cooks, and clerical aides, essentially keeping the camps running with their own labor. Some camps even offered college-equivalency courses. Hopkins would tout the federal program as having "pulled men and women by the hundreds of thousands from the despair of aimless wandering, misery, and the complete neglect of health, back to self-respect and their place in the world of working people" (quoted in Kusmer, 2002, p. 218).

But even prior to the sudden abandonment of the program in 1935, Hopkins's rosy assessment was somewhat self-serving. Although the image of transient men running their own camps and publishing papers is reminiscent of some of the more radical protest–type gatherings in history, from the Bonus March of 1932 to the many "tent city" and "Justiceville" or "Reaganville" protests of more recent decades, the effectiveness of government strategy is debatable. Most transients stayed at the camps only a short time, perhaps a week or month, and then kept wandering. Why? The same reason these transients did not remain in almshouses and poor farms in the nineteenth and early twentieth centuries: they wanted real jobs at fair wages. This the FTS could not provide, given the program's more "palliative" approach. Interestingly, the FTS's own client-run newspapers critiqued the removal of the thousands of urban homeless away from the cities and into rural camps. After all, the rural areas were nowhere near jobs. As one FTS transient of the time explained: "they shunted us away from the cities into isolated camps on the fringe of civilization, when most of us are city workers and city dwellers," while camp newspapers called out: "Why isolate us as a group and call us transients? Are we not citizens of the United States?" (quoted in Crouse, 1986, p. 169).

The ideological separation of the homeless or transient from the worker, even during the New Deal, made the return to the status quo inevitable. Even early programs such as the Civilian Conservation Corps (CCC) had excluded nonresidents. In the minds of policymakers, there were the workers laid off due to the depression and blocked by unemployment from their usual work (coded as "blue-collar"), and then there were those who had not been perceived as employees, although they were. Just as African Americans and women were often blocked from New Deal reforms by continuing cultural prejudices and norms that made them ineligible for help, workers who were mobile or lost their settlement status were not perceived as deserving or even eligible for full-time work. So when the Roosevelt administration closed down the transient camps as part of an overall departure from relief-without-work programs, it implicitly was reaffirming the exclusion of the transients from the benefits of the New Deal. As Crouse (1986) notes, the second pillar of the New Deal (the first being work programs) similarly blocked transients (and most racial minorities and women) from the income benefits of Social Security and Unemployment Insurance because of its reliance on past work credits and its exclusion of large numbers of groups such as agricultural workers, who were among the poorest in the land.

In the summer of 1935, when the FTS was ordered "liquidated," nearly 350,000 people remained under its care. Realizing that these and other transients would simply be dumped back into local communities with no reimbursement, Washington, D.C., was besieged by petitions from across the nation urging Hopkins to reconsider. Crouse points out the irony of the many areas that had initially opposed having the transient camps in their backyard now calling on the government to save the camps. Unfortunately, convinced that only a program of work relief would succeed in the United States, the New Deal refused. Most transients, though certified to the local boards of the Works Progress Administration (WPA), were never called to work. As Crouse notes, the math in part made it inevitable: at least 10 million people were out of work, but there would be only a little over 3 million jobs. Local residents with skills received preference. Nels Anderson found that the hiring of transients into the WPA was "so rare as to be conspicuous" (quoted in Crouse, 1986, pp. 210–211).

Life went back to usual for the transient in the United States. States raised their legal barriers to settlement and many increased their residency requirements for settlement status. Iowa and North Dakota, for example, returned to "warning out" as practiced in colonial times. In the winter of 1935 and 1936, Florida and California started border patrols to make sure nonsettled poor did not enter their territory. Most notorious was the Los Angeles Police Department, whose infamous border patrols violently loaded transients into vehicles and dumped them in the desert across the border (Crouse, 1986, p. 225). As Crouse notes, the transient were often greeted with "the hospitality of the police station, the 'two meals and a flop' in a municipal lodging house or second rate mission, the curt 'move on, you!' of the sheriff at the county line or actual arrest and sentence to the workhouse or chain gang" (1986, p. 224).

A more ambitious program to reform assistance was advocated by leading social workers and many states and localities at the time. They sought to add a fourth category to the Social Security Act amendments that would require local welfare (with matching federal funds) for the childless, non-disabled people who were not covered by the work credits of the Social Security pension system. Though the proposal never passed, it might have enshrined the aid that some local governments give as general assistance (usually to single people), including to the nonsettled.

Various reasons are suggested for the quick drop of homelessness off the agenda. Kusmer argues that much of the attention to homelessness came from the revelation early in the 1930s that large numbers of young boys were on the street, and that with the drop in attention to this issue in the middle to late 1930s, interest dwindled (2002, p. 222). He also notes that, early in the depression, middle-class people were often most upset by the presence of "their own" (such as clerks and professionals) in the bread-lines (p. 209), perhaps indicating that empathy does not transcend the involvement of one's own class. No doubt the resistance to the transient camps and to aid to the poor generally did not help. For Roosevelt, the key groups to be politically appeased were the southern Democrats, on the one hand, and the growing labor movement in northern urban areas, on the other. At that time, even more than now, because of the presence of the poll tax, the poor were not able to vote.

So while from a social constructionist viewpoint the image of the homeless person changed in a positive way from tramp to transient in the depression era, the actual gains for the poorest were not very great, and quickly reverted to the status quo. The homeless were a symbol of the "forgotten man" made famous by Roosevelt, but critics suggest that the transient remained mostly forgotten. Even when the nation was confronted with sympathetic images (the photographs of Dorothea Lange, the famous novel *The Grapes of Wrath* by John Steinbeck), this in itself was not enough to change policy, except for the more powerful groups who gained indirectly from the sympathetic portrait, such as the organized elderly with work credits.

The Postwar Decades and the Skid Row Bum

The impact of World War II in finally ending the Great Depression and ushering in full employment led naturally to a long end to concern not only for the homeless, but also for the poor generally. When Michael Harrington wrote his famous book *The Other America* in 1962, Americans, whether liberal, conservative, or moderate, were shocked at the numbers of poor people in the United States. It was not that poverty (or likely homelessness) vanished in the postwar period, but that, for several decades of relative US prosperity, poverty was greatly confined away from the view of the affluent and even the middle and working classes. The mass movement of Americans to the suburbs in the postwar period gradually depleted the cities of some of their white ethnic populations. The poorest areas—the skid rows and the ghetto regions inhabited by nonwhites—received very little publicity in the late 1940s and 1950s. Rural poverty was extremely high, but lacked media attention and advocacy. As I noted in my study of the county and city homes and city farms that still existed in the postwar period (Wagner, 2005), many people were still "out of sight, out of mind," relegated to the old poorhouses (now called city and county homes), particularly the elderly who were not eligible for pensions; the physically and mentally disabled, including the developmentally disabled; and many other groups, such as unmarried mothers, who had been stigmatized and rejected as deserving of welfare assistance.

The stigma of the "skid row bum" was a reaction to the most visible of its occupants, the older white male who appeared drunk and sometimes mentally ill. There were significant signs of change in the skid rows that the public was unaware of. In one of the first studies of homelessness undertaken in the 1980s, for example, Ellen Baxter and Kim Hopper (1981, pp. 45–46) cited demographics from New York's Bowery district (one of the most famous skid rows in the United States) indicating that, since 1968, users of shelters had been growing younger and less white, with racial minorities becoming more prominent. In the heady 1960s and 1970s, many young people, and some middle-aged people as well, joined the counterculture and "lived rough." Those who stayed on the streets were labeled "street people" but were not taken seriously as a homeless group.

It can be argued that, in addition to the booming economy for the middle and working classes in the postwar era, spatial separation and housing availability kept homelessness in check as a social issue in the early to mid-1970s. The public could avoid skid rows, ghettoes, and slums, as well as the city and town farms or homes. Images of people on the street were limited to places like skid rows and later to areas like Haight-Ashbury or other areas where "street people" mingled with the counterculture. Additionally, in historical retrospect, the availability of relatively cheap rentals in the 1950s and 1960s afforded the possibility of "crashing," or what is today called "couch surfing," in a way that became difficult later. People in low-income areas and within racial and ethnic pockets who lived many to an apartment, as well as wanderers like the "hippies" of the counterculture, were able to easily avail themselves of temporary housing from nonaffluent friends. Because of all these factors, as well as the rather blind embrace of the American Dream that captured the postwar period, homelessness and even poverty remained hidden issues.

4

Recognizing and Naming a Crisis, 1979–1982

When does an issue become a social problem? That is, when does an issue become known to the public as a clearly defined problem that must be remedied? This is always an extremely hard question to answer. Those closest to the realities of an issue may notice changes far earlier than the mass media or social scientists. But prior to an established name and category being established for a problem, there will always be some mystery as to its origins retrospectively. This is similar to what Joel Best (2001) calls the "dark figure" of the unknown cases. Many recently named problems, such as hate crimes, for example, were not routinely reported in the past. Even for longer-known issues such as rape and domestic abuse, it is difficult to know whether these problems are increasing or decreasing, because before the 1970s they were often not reported to police or other agencies to the extent they are now. Homelessness prior to the early Ronald Reagan years of 1981–1982 existed in this nether land. There were certainly people without homes, but what they were called remained unclear. In searching media databases, we must include labels like "vagrants," "bums," "derelicts," "hobos," "transients," "destitute," "bag ladies," and "street people," not just "homeless."

One clear finding in contrast to the research of Cynthia Bogard (2003) is that the activism and advocacy in Washington, D.C., led by Mitch Snyder's Community for Creative Non-Violence, and in New York City, led by Robert Hayes (what would come to be known as the Coalition for the Homeless), was not critical to the issue development. As important as this activism and advocacy may have been, it was not very influential across the nation in defining the issue of homelessness. The national broadcast media did not cover homelessness at all until March 11, 1981, when *ABC News* made reference to the issue (see Vanderbilt Television News Archive). The next mass media reference did not occur until December 1982, long after Snyder and Hayes began their activism. Snyder's first network television appearance was in December 1982, while Hayes did not appear on national television until December 1983. The *Los Angeles Times, New York Times, Chicago Tribune,* and *Boston Globe* made only scattered references to Snyder or his CCNV. The *New York Times* did begin covering Hayes by at least 1981, but only as a local story.[1] The other newspapers provided only minimal coverage of Hayes and the New York City consent decree to shelter the homeless. Thus it was not activists and advocates who initially seem to have defined the issue of homelessness as much as a combination of journalists and editorial writers as well as social service, mental health, and shelter (mission and secular) administrators. Later, as the issue emerged further, advocates and some political leaders began to more clearly gain media coverage in their quest for public support for the homeless.

First Media Stirrings of the Homeless Crisis, 1979–1980

The relatively small number of news articles (including letters to the editor and editorials) on homeless people in this pre-problem stage divide interestingly into those that were highly prescient in terms of the issues and problem definitions that would emerge later, and those that appear anachronistic at least in their terminology and uncertainty on what the "new" problem was.

In the first four months of 1979, for example, the only references to "vagrants" (or similarly named people) in the *New York Times* appeared in two prominently placed articles on a "shopping bag lady" who was murdered and turned out to have significant savings and assets and even owned land (Daniels, 1979a, 1979b). Somewhat sensationalistic, the articles wondered about other people roaming the streets with thousands of dollars in savings. The issue was sufficiently well covered that several other news articles and even the first official report on homelessness (Baxter and Hopper, 1981, p. 12) sought to counter this image, noting that most "bag ladies" and other "vagrants" did not have large amounts of money tucked away. On the other hand, as early as January 1979, a letter to the editor in the *Los Angeles Times* noted a widening "division into an affluent few who live splendidly . . . and the desperate, homeless individuals who cannot keep pace" (Fitzgerald, 1979, p. C6). The letter noted a low 2 percent vacancy rate around the Los Angeles area and blamed the government for failing to help provide housing.

Whether the phenomenon of people "on the road" was new or not was also a matter of dispute and wonderment. In a fairly long article on August 4, 1979, in the *Los Angeles Times,* Kenneth Bunting reported on the large numbers of people on the road (Bunting, 1979, p. 8). Titled "Nomads on the Road to Nowhere," the article cited "old hitchhikers" and countercultural types whom one would associate with the travelers along coastal California. Then there were the "modern vagabonds"—the panhandlers, some of whom made money, according to the author. And yet, as the article unfolds, Bunting mentions a veteran, a man on Social Security disability, and a woman complaining of police maltreatment. It is unclear how many of the subjects of Bunting's piece resemble what would come to be called the "new homeless," or were simply new incarnations of the older category of "street people." The ambivalence toward defining who these people were was also clear in two earlier *New York Times* reports: "Facilities for 'Shopping Bag Ladies' and Battered Women Are Planned," by Anna Quindlen, on May 26, 1979, and "Homeless Given Help on the Streets," by Tony Schwartz, on September 1, 1979. Both are, on the one hand, news pieces about helpful services being offered to evidently recalcitrant people ("they generally refuse services, but we're going to make an attempt to help them," reported New York City's head of Human Resources Administration, Stanley Brezenhoff, in the first article [Quindlen, 1979, p. 23]; and the second article noted that the mission of a new outreach program in New York "is to aggressively seek out people who have dropped out of the social service system—shopping-bag ladies, alcoholics, ex–mental patients, senior citizens—and help them get help" [Schwartz, 1979b, p. 21]). Both articles, to different degrees, touch on at least some social and political issues raised by what could be called the homeless problem. Quindlen quoted Brezenhoff as asking for support in raising basic welfare allowances to help the poor (p. 23), while Schwartz, in talking with workers from Project Reachout in New York City, noted that

> the greatest need is housing. . . . [The Human Resources Administration] reports that there has been a 30% drop in the last five years in the number of hotels specializing in single room occupancy—partly as a result of the tax incentives granted to builders in order to encourage

them to tear down old and decrepit structures. . . . [T]he vacancy rate
has dropped from 25% just four years ago to 5% today. "I never realized how hopeless it was" (a worker opined). "Many of these people
have been kicked out of buildings that are being converted." (p. 21)

One divergence, beginning in the fall of 1979 and continuing into
1980, was the tendency of the *New York Times* (and, to a lesser degree, the
Boston Globe) to give more weight to the issue of mental illness as a cause
of homelessness than did the *Los Angeles Times* (and later the *Chicago
Tribune*).[2] The coverage of mental illness and deinstitutionalization in New
York was no doubt influenced by the highly public dispute between New
York City's vocal mayor, Edward Koch, and two New York governors,
first Hugh Carey and later Mario Cuomo, over who was to blame for homelessness. Koch's perception that many of the homeless had psychiatric
problems led him to blame New York State's policies of deinstitutionalization of mental patients. Koch's argument was a highly advantageous
one for the city, as he asked for funding to track discharged mental patients, which would increase New York City's share of the state's Medicaid
funding. On the other hand, Governor Carey denounced Koch's position by
noting that the decline in housing in New York City had occurred under
Koch's watch, and that the City's J-51 tax abatement policy was "the single
greatest cause of increased numbers of homeless" (Herman, 1980, p. B1).
This policy gave a tax break to owners of single-room-occupancy hotels
who converted their properties to luxury buildings.
     While not entirely endorsing either the mayor's or the governor's
views, the *New York Times* wrote three editorials in 1980 and 1981
stressing the presence of the mentally ill homeless and the need for New
York State to step up to support the city. On October 24, 1979, the *Times*
editorialized that "[disturbed people] permeate some areas, particularly
Times Square and parts of the Upper West Side with their own weird am-
bience" ("Careless of the Mentally Ill," p. A30). Two months later, on
December 26, after a discharged mental patient named Adam Berwid followed through on his threat to kill his wife upon his discharge, a *Times*
editorial called in strong terms for control over patient discharges and
again linked the issue to homelessness ("The Danger of Dumping the
Mentally Ill," p. A26). A year later, on December 20, 1980, the *Times*
again charged that "hundreds, maybe thousands have been living literally
on the streets" because of deinstitutionalization, and pushed Governor
Carey to provide some emergency relief. The paper suggested that the
issue of homelessness was also a housing and single-room-occupancy

issue but still remarked that "many former patients have been allowed to drift away from their squalid hotels of first resort. And some roam the streets in ways that alarm city residents" ("Patients Left out in the Cold," p. 24). In one *Times* report, Mayor Koch claimed that the former patients were creating a "climate of fear" and "often carry their problems out onto the street with them, sometimes submerging our parks, subways, and public places in an atmosphere of danger and anxiety. . . . The City," he warned, "can no longer afford to have its neighborhoods used as mental wards and its police officers used as orderlies" (Haberman, 1980, p. B3).

Still, even as the political battles over deinstitutionalization went on, mental illness was by no means mentioned in all of the slowly growing number of news articles. In December 1979, Robert Hayes, along with another Legal Aid attorney, won the first of the court decisions affecting the responsibility of New York City to house the homeless (*Callahan v. Carey,* later *Callahan v. New York City*). The coverage in the *New York Times* was surprisingly buried in the newspaper, and no reasons at all were mentioned for the large numbers of homeless people in New York City (Kaiser, 1979, p. 81). In a December 28 article, "50 SRO Tenants Charge Harassment," in which landlords were charged with using violence and threats against tenants, Tony Schwartz noted how critical the need for housing in New York City had become, explaining the loss of 10,000 single-room-occupancy rooms and pointing to the tax incentive for luxury housing (Schwartz, 1979a, p. B3). In March 1980, a long article about homeless people living in the subway tunnels near Grand Central Station (an article that was reprinted elsewhere through wire service coverage) appeared. The residents of the tunnels were very varied, some veterans, some suffering from problems with alcohol, and a number complaining of having lost their housing or being unable to afford rent. Mental illness was not even cited as a factor (Bird, 1980, p. B1).

The confusion nationally about naming the issue and its causes was reflected in an August 1980 article after the Democratic National Convention was held in New York City and a protest demonstration related to homelessness was staged. The article noted New York City's "effort to rid the area around Madison Square Garden of 'shelter-seekers, drifters, hippies, vagrants, prostitutes, bums, beggars, weirdos, tin cup wavers, curbside musicians, and sidewalk speakers'" (Weinraub, 1980, p. 9). This odd and varied list suggests much uncertainty about what homelessness was or what cause was even being demonstrated about.

While the *Los Angeles Times* almost completely handled the still relatively few stories about homelessness as a housing issue, the *Boston*

Globe in its first year of coverage[3] alternated between human interest stories that tended to evoke housing and income problems and a series of articles by columnist Jean Dietz that covered complaints by the head of the Pine Street Shelter (Boston's long-standing shelter that existed well before the homeless crisis of the 1980s) about mentally ill patients. A short article in July 1980 noted a vigil organized by an activist group, the Coalition for Human Needs, that "was designed to draw attention to the problems of families left homeless by the system" ("Joan Ford and Her Six Children," p. 1). This piece noted rising rents, as did an article on August 1 about the large number of homeless people in Cape Cod, Massachusetts, when summer tourists arrived and rooms became more pricey (Dietz, 1980c, p. 1). Topics of other short *Boston Globe* articles in 1980 included a family who was living out of a car because there was a fire in their apartment and they had no money for another one, two homeless families living in a parking lot because they were unable to afford rent increases, and a disabled homeless man in the suburb of Weymouth who protested: "I worked all my life until the accident, but I never know when I'll black out, so I can't work. I'm no bum, I'm a citizen. I vote. I joined the Marines when I was 17" (Rubin, 1980, p. 1; "Some Offers of Help Extended," September 18, 1980, p. 1; and Quill, 1980, p. 1).

In an August 26 article, Jean Dietz first reported on an overflow of homeless at the Pine Street Inn. According to the inn's director, Paul D. Sullivan, "mental patients, who need more than we can offer, are driving out the people we were established to serve" (Dietz, 1980f, p. 1). In a November 4 follow-up, Sullivan, as well as the state mental health commissioner of Massachusetts, Robert L. Okin, worried that, as the latter said, "we are racing against the weather. The immediate thing is to make sure that people do not freeze" (Dietz, 1980b, p. 1). Later that month, a building in the Boston State Hospital complex, scheduled to be closed, was opened (Dietz, 1980a, p. 1), and still later a building at the Boston Trade School complex was opened for the homeless (Dietz, 1980d, p. 1).

In a later article, Charles Mahoney, head of the Massachusetts Office of Human Services, blamed mental health commitment laws: "People have assumed this is a problem of deinstitutionalized patients. It would be more accurate to say that the situation reflects a change in our commitment laws (in 1971) limiting commitment to those deemed dangerous to themselves or others, and recent court decisions banning forced medication" (Dietz, 1980e, p. 1). Compared to New York City, the mental health issue in Boston brought relatively little recrimination, nor was it linked to broader causes for the homeless crisis. In fact, in a

Christmas Day editorial in 1980, the *Globe,* while mentioning the mentally ill, seemed to lump many situations and groups together:

> There are estimates, really only guesses, that on any given night there are in Boston up to 10,000—yes, ten thousand—people who are without shelter. Over the course of a year, you will see some of them and occasionally read a newspaper story about some of them. There are families, whole families, who live in wheezing old station wagons in which they camp out like gypsies, except that there isn't much romance to it, in the dark back corners of parking lots. There are street kids, many of them really only children, runaways from home or tossed out, living their short, unhappy days, and long, dangerous nights as prey. There are now also the former mental patients, released from the cheerless institutions by an act of good social policy that has been thwarted by budget cutters and inept planners. And there are the "bag ladies," true symbols of homelessness as they trudge from shelter to soup kitchen, day after day, lugging their pitiful belongings in the shopping bags that give them their name. ("After the Lights Are Packed Away," December 25, 1980, p. 1)

This editorial is a good example of the media's growing discovery of homelessness by the end of 1980. Those covering the issue still lacked an agreed name, with the press using "transients," "vagrants," "bag ladies," and "hobos," as well as "homeless" and "street people." They also lacked descriptors that would unite the various groups, and lacked a solution or policy frame for this new concern. By 1981, however, the labels "homeless" and "homelessness" would begin to stick, and a consensus that there was a "new" crisis of homeless would begin to take hold. Solutions remained a more elusive and less unified part of the policy frame, but a consensus was building around a compassionate response to homelessness that focused primarily on charity and the building of temporary shelters. Gradually, in the early 1980s, the issue of opposing the policies of the newly elected Reagan administration and its budget-cutting policies became another unifying point for most of those who identified and constructed the homeless crisis.

The Crisis in the Early Reagan Years, 1981–1982

The election of conservative Republican Ronald Reagan to the presidency by a fairly wide margin in November 1980 had a strong impact on how homelessness as an issue was presented to the public by claims-makers. Although Reagan triumphed over the relatively conservative Democratic administration of Jimmy Carter, the strong ideological tenor of Reagan and his aides and congressional allies sent a shockwave through not only Democratic Party stalwarts but also much of the nation's social service and advocacy organizations. Indeed, in lightning fashion, Reagan succeeded in 1981 in securing his objectives of large tax cuts, a major defense buildup, and deep cuts in social services, passed in the Omnibus Budget Reconciliation Act of 1981. Among the many changes for the poor was the "block granting" of fifty-seven previously separate programs that had been categorical (that is, they were now folded into funds that were at the discretion of the states, and some programs, such as the Comprehensive Employment and Training Act job program, were completely abolished). Also, deep cuts were made to Aid to Families with Dependent Children, Food Stamps, Medicaid, and other such assistance programs, including housing assistance (see Jansson, 2004). The strong defense of the morality of cutting welfare programs by aides such as Budget Director David Stockman made for an ongoing confrontation between conservatives and liberals, with even some moderate Republicans drawing away from Reagan's harshness. The events of the early 1980s were compounded by a severe recession that arrived in the 1981–1982 period. As one measure of what had been the deepest economic downturn since the Great Depression, official unemployment climbed to 10.8 percent nationally in 1982.

While the changed political and economic climate would strongly affect the presentation of homelessness, it did not do so in one fell swoop. Nor is it clear how the issue's career might have been different in the absence of Reagan. The Community for Creative Non-Violence held the first homeless demonstration back in 1978 (*Los Angeles Times,* "Indigents Ousted at Visitors' Center," December 10, 1978, p. C6). As noted, the *Callahan v. Carey* case (which was the landmark case regarding sheltering the homeless) was launched in New York City in 1979, and sources had already cited an increase in homelessness in New York City before Reagan (see, for example, Baxter and Hopper, 1981, the first official publication on homelessness to appear in the United States). Also, articles in Los Angeles and Boston about the increase in homelessness had already appeared in the late 1970s. Nor can events that occurred in fiscal year 1981–1982 be blamed on government cuts, as budgets work prospectively and did not have major effects until implemented well after passage of the Omnibus Budget Reconciliation Act. It is hard to know, had Jimmy Carter had won the 1980 election, whether the target of outrage would have simply shifted to his administration or whether major differences in social welfare funding would have become apparent.[4] In any event, presentation of the homelessness problem and strategies to address it often centered on Reaganomics.

Another complexity that at least initially may have limited the completely partisan nature of the issue was the differences among officeholders who were Democrats, including the nation's mayors, who were on the front lines of the issues of poverty, crime, drugs, and other problems associated with urban decline during this time of recession. Mayor Edward Koch of New York City, for example, a Democrat, continued to take a hard-line position against homelessness, as evidenced by his unsuccessful attempt to gain authority to detain homeless people for seventy-two hours (*New York Times*, "The City: Koch Revises Plan on Aiding Homeless," March 28, 1981, p. 2). In January 1982, the bishop of New York City's Episcopal Church, Paul Moore Jr., took both Reagan and Koch to task about their suggestions that each church and synagogue house a number of homeless people to solve the crisis. He charged that both men were being at best naive in their beliefs that the voluntary sector could solve the problem (Moore, 1982, p. 21).

It took a number of years for Democratic officeholders, as opposed to the early advocates and activists, to fully embrace homelessness as an issue, especially symbolically in opposition to the "heartless" Republicans. Of those early comments that did originate from politicians in this period, most were from African American mayors or left-leaning Democrats rather than from major party leaders.

For example, in 1981 and 1982, there were uneven spurts of coverage of homelessness that took a political spin, but they were not yet consistent. Interestingly, shortly before the inauguration of Reagan, Governor Robert Graham of Florida seems to have been the first public official to visit a shelter and soup kitchen, in which he actually served food. In the same newspaper article that covered Graham's shelter visit, the author praised Washington, D.C., mayor Marion Barry for opening up government buildings to the homeless on very cold nights to avoid further deaths in the capital (there had already been four deaths). Though the article was silent on the strong and continual pressure exerted by the D.C.-based CCNV that led to Barry's decision, it nevertheless shows some movement on the part of political leaders (McCarthy, 1981, p. 1). In March 1981, as the national administration was preparing its historic budget cuts, an *ABC News* broadcast, in presenting the first national network story on homelessness, covered administration officials, Democratic Party liberal opponents Shirley Chisholm and Pete Stark, as well as a protest song against Reagan and Budget Director Stockman that had been written by the activist group CCNV (Vanderbilt Television News Archive, March 11, 1981).

However, between these examples and the end of 1982, when the first congressional hearing on homelessness since the Great Depression was held, it was activists and advocates who held political protests. Alongside the activist CCNV, coalitions for the homeless rapidly emerged in many states, and in May 1982 the National Coalition for the Homeless was formed. But other activist groups whose missions involved other issues besides homelessness played a role in local protests, including the Association for Community Reform Now (ACORN), a national activist group; Jobs with Peace, an activist group formed in the early 1980s to link peace and social justice issues; and local unaffiliated groups in many cities.

Regarding grassroots protests, the *Los Angeles Times,* for example, reported on a squatting movement that was particularly active in Philadelphia, where as many as a thousand of the city's abandoned homes were being occupied. The paper quoted the "chief Robin Hood," Henry DiBernardo, who was associated with Project Aegis. The squatters, who were taking over Housing and Urban Development (HUD)–owned buildings, "were mostly poor, black inner-city residents on welfare" (Linder, 1981, p. 2). Given far more coverage nationally (squatters' movements would continue on and off for many years with often minimal coverage) was the Community for Creative Non-Violence's erection of tents and sleeping-out near the White House in a "Reaganville" protest against homelessness and federal budget cuts, during which Mitch Snyder of the CCNV and others were arrested. The erection of "tent cities" and other encampments to protest homelessness would become one of the prime tactics of the next decade (see, for example, *Los Angeles Times,* "'Reaganville' Protest Ends with 6 Arrests," 1981, p. A2).

In 1982 there were a number of additional protests. For example, the *Boston Globe* reported a rally in May of about eighty participants led by Jobs with Peace and the South End Project Area Committee (SEPAC), a local Boston group. The rally also featured the construction of a mock city of cardboard shacks and an old green truck laden with junk and garbage called "Reaganville." A leader noted: "What we're trying to do is make the connection between what is happening here in Boston and other cities with respect to displacement and unemployment and how the Reagan Administration's policies have affected us." The rally drew the participation of left-leaning Democratic state representative and later mayoral candidate Mel King (Lewis, 1982, p. 1). In October 1982, a series of "tent city" protests, seemingly led by ACORN, were staged in fifteen cities, with protesters planning to stay in place "until Election day to denounce the Reagan administration" (*Los Angeles Times,* October 26, 1982, p. 4F). In December, for the first time in Chicago, the *Chicago Tribune* reported on a major protest involving 150 to 200 demonstrators that included a statewide coalition of social service organizations. The demonstrators converged on Chicago's City Hall and the State of Illinois Building and presented a "Christmas list" of demands to representatives of Mayor Jane Byrne and Governor James Thompson (Houston, 1982, p. 11).

By the holiday season of 1982—with the period from Thanksgiving to Christmas, including the beginning of the winter, always being a key focus for homeless issues (Shields, 2001)—media coverage reached a new high. The US Mayors Conference, which would become a major claims-maker on behalf of homelessness (as well as other urban issues) in the 1980s and 1990s, called for immediate emergency aid for the homeless in a pre-Thanksgiving statement (*Chicago Tribune,* "Mayors Ask Aid for Needy This Winter," November 23, 1982, p. 7). The conference warned that "the winter of [1982–1983] poses a deadly threat to the many homeless and hungry people in cities across the country." Mayors from Newark, New Jersey; Denver, Colorado; and New Orleans, Louisiana, gave estimates of the numbers of homeless people in their cities and also spoke of the "new" crisis. The Mayors Conference also appeared on a December 11, 1982, CBS program with Lesley Stahl warning of the dangers ahead for that winter (Vanderbilt Television News Archive).

Congress's hearings on homelessness in mid-December 1982 brought an array of publicity, with all three major networks covering the issue. Both Mitch Snyder of the Washington, D.C.–based CCNV and Robert Hayes of the New York City–based Coalition for the Homeless were quoted on television, and even New York mayor Edward Koch moved away from the mentally ill as a topic, declaring the issue "a national problem" and calling for jobs (Vanderbilt Television News Archive, December 15, 1982, NBC). As part of the hearings, advocate Mitch Snyder issued his well-publicized but much disputed estimate that there were 2 million homeless people in the United States at any given moment. Later Snyder admitted that the estimate was overly broad. The hearings, while unsuccessful in accomplishing anything immediate, did succeed in spreading the word about the issue of homelessness, and gave birth to a second, emotionally impactful book on homelessness—the CCNV-published *Homelessness in*

America: The Forced March to Nowhere (Hombs and Snyder, 1983), which included a forward by activist priest Daniel Berrigan and testimony from many cities reporting on the problem and its causes. Like other statements by this time, the book centered the crisis on a heartless government that had abandoned its people, aiming blame and solutions more at the federal level than at either the private sector or state and local levels. Interestingly, the almost sole focus on Reagan's policies gave little recognition that a new period of economic decline was occurring in the United States, which would last well beyond his administration.

The Creation of the "New Homeless"

A key element of the social construction of homelessness in the 1980s is that it was a new phenomenon that should not be compared to the homelessness of the 1950–1970s, nor should it be associated with skid rows of the urban centers. It was in the 1980s that advocates and activists, the media, and others were trying to shape a message that was still uneven and unclear. Who the "new homeless" were (there were also claims of a "new poor") ranged from modest statements to a vast universalization of the problem that was not always supportable.

Interestingly, Ellen Baxter and Kim Hopper's 1981 report, *Private Lives/Public Spaces,* which received wide attention, claimed only modest differences between the new and previous homeless. Baxter and Hopper noted that two new populations had increased in the homeless shelters even in the 1970s: the mentally disabled, and younger men, particularly racial minorities, in contrast to the earlier prevalence of older white men. Leo Srole, a Columbia University professor of medicine who wrote the introduction to the report, made a more general claim: "the homeless include no small number of rather respectably attired people who do not fit the tattered 'derelict' and 'bag lady' stereotypes. Nor by any means are they all chronic 'psychos' or 'winos.' Many are 'displaced persons' of the 1970 generation" (quoted in Baxter and Hopper, 1981, p. i).

These relatively modest claims swung wildly between cautious advocacy, which warned against portraying the homeless as deviants, particularly as alcoholics and the mentally ill, and generalized claims that homelessness could happen to anyone. The key issue that all advocates certainly were struggling with was the age-old battle of the "deserving" versus the "undeserving" poor, which goes back to English and early US history (see Katz, 1989). Enshrined in the Poor Laws of the past, but still very much alive today culturally and in social welfare law, is the different treatment poor people receive based on their perceived deservedness. Those perceived as "deviant" (substance users, criminals, the mentally ill) are rarely regarded as deserving. Moreover, as the homeless crisis grew, the assumption was also made that the nearer the homeless were to the American majority (white and middle class or former middle class, for example), and the greater the presence of women, children, and families among the homeless, the more deserving the population. This logic was consistent with US history back to colonial days.

Boston Globe reporter Timothy Dwyer, for example, noted the presence of "a former beauty queen" on the streets and then followed this news with the statement that "some are alcoholics, some are former mental patients. But there are also doctors, lawyers, and college professors who somehow lost their way" (Dwyer, 1981, p. 1). An even more specific *Globe* report by Richard Higgins described a soup kitchen line: "High school dropouts and former members of the brass section of the New York Philharmonic. Men who wear three threadbare sweaters and some who wear hooded, cotton-filled parkas. Alcoholics and teetotalers and glue-sniffers and sailors, proud dignified men in neat but soiled suits and foul-smelling men who have let their bodies go" (Higgins, 1982, p. 1). In an article describing a plea for the homeless from the US Mayors Conference in late 1982, Armando Atencio, manager of the Denver Department of Social Services, characterized the new homeless as having "doctoral degrees and masters degrees but just out of luck" (*Los Angeles Times,* "Mayors Seek Winter Help for Homeless," November 22, 1982, p. A2).

This universalization of homelessness as affecting Philharmonic musicians, doctors, lawyers, and professors was of course well-meaning. But none of the many surveys conducted in the 1980s, 1990s, and 2000s have documented much evidence of professionals or more highly degreed individuals becoming homeless.[5] Like the 1980s portrayals by Robin Williams as a homeless professor in the film *The Fisher King,* and actor William Daniels as Dr. Craig, a wealthy neurosurgeon who is forced to go to a homeless shelter in the television drama *Saint Elsewhere,* such accounts are more likely to be urban legends. More recently, when portraying African American homeless people, Hollywood has offered a medical equipment salesman (*The Pursuit of Happyness*) and a Juilliard graduate (*The Soloist*). Certainly anyone who spends time at a homeless shelter, a soup kitchen, or on the streets will find few people who resemble these characters.

The *Los Angeles Times,* whose early coverage of the homeless was among the most liberal, developed the concept of "deservedness" in a much different way by highlighting former industrial workers and construction workers who had fled from the Rustbelt looking for jobs. In a 1981 article, staff writer Bob Secter found that this was "a growing phenomenon" in Los Angeles' Skid Row, "traditionally a refuge for drunks or the elderly whose paltry pension checks run out quickly. More and more, however, the area is being besieged by clean cut men in their teens, twenties, and thirties who had the misfortune to believe in a southern California that exists mostly on the Late Show" (Secter, 1981, p. A3). An article about a year and a half later by staff writers Judith Michaelson and Louis Sahagan supported this portrayal by profiling examples of "economic refugees" such as Tom and Mary McGuire: "they could have passed for tract neighbors next door, both young and energetic, attractive, clean-cut, he a draftsman, she with a major in fine arts. . . . [But] four months ago, although Tom still had his job at a subsidiary of IBM . . . they became part of the newer wave of people without homes, or as various agency officials have begun calling them, 'economic refugees.' Blaming the severe recession as well as cuts in social benefits, the 'new homeless' includes carpenters, cement workers, painters, looking all over for work" (Michaelson and Sahagan, 1982, p. A3). These articles, though of course slanted toward the "deserving" homeless, are at least closer to reality than portrayals of the homeless as doctors, lawyers, and professionals.

The *Chicago Tribune* initially presented the new homeless as a kind of vast mishmash. For example, in 1981 the *Tribune* carried a UPI article that portrayed "urban nomads" as being "now a permanent fixture" of the country. These included "bag ladies, . . . the elderly who can't afford their rent and urban renewal, . . . youngsters kicked out of their house, . . . Vietnam vets, . . . mental patients [who have been] deinstitutionalized," and so forth (United Press International, "The Street Walkers: Why?" p. 1). Gradually, though, the *Tribune,* like the *Los Angeles Times,* began to emphasize the recession and economic factors: "Chicago, once shunned by traditional derelicts because of harsh winters, now finds its emergency shelters doing a brisk business. They include the 'economically displaced' in the Sunbelt cities and unquestionably the single greatest cause of this human tragedy is the lingering national recession that has brought severe unemployment to many areas" (Coakley, 1982, p. 5).

The paradox of advocates portraying the possibility of homelessness happening to anyone is that it undermined the more relevant argument that deindustrialization, gentrification, and other social changes primarily impacted working-class and poor people. In fact, the people hit by the new crisis were not doctors, professors, Philharmonic musicians, or medical equipment salesmen, but low-level industrial and other marginalized workers. Further, the plea for help for the "new homeless" rested on a complex mix of guilt, sympathy, and, for those who presented the homeless and poor as being downwardly mobile (from the middle class), potential self-interest, given the assertion that homelessness could happen to anyone. But it does not appear from polls or other evidence that the vast majority of Americans ever accepted the possibility that *they* could become homeless. Thus a broader frame for the problem did not seem to attract action or support from the middle class.

Finally, another issue that would later become prominent—gender—made only a tentative entrance at this time. The first book on the subject, consisting primarily of photographs of homeless women, was Ann Marie Rousseau's *Shopping Bag Ladies,* published in 1981. It discussed, for the first time, the stigma of being a woman on the streets and the "invisible" nature of much of female homelessness due to societal prejudice (Gregory, 1981, p. K5). In 1982, a conference was held at the University of California at Irvine with a focus on homeless women. The special needs of women were stressed, given the dominantly male design of shelters and other services. Importantly, the increased "feminization of poverty" (a term coined by Diana Peirce) was featured (McLellan, 1982, p. F1). As the years passed, coverage of homeless women, as well as homeless youth and homeless families, would notably increase. The "new homeless" discussion would continue to increase in volume with some media and advocates insisting on universalizing homelessness and others simply focusing on cases that were "deserving" or were particularly touching because of downward mobility or other factors. But, more importantly, people began to see homeless people more regularly in their neighborhoods and their perceptions began to differ from portrayals of homelessness presented by the media and advocates.

"Gimme Shelter"

One of the important ironies of the initial discovery of homelessness in this period was the absence of solutions to the problem other than temporary shelters and associated services such as soup kitchens. By the mid-1980s and increasingly thereafter, advocates, activists, and even some political leaders would begin to stress the need for permanent affordable housing, job programs, and, to a lesser extent, other social policy solutions. Many homeless activists themselves would later denounce the efficacy of shelters. In fact, in late 1982, leading advocates Robert Hayes and Mitch Snyder themselves would denounce the efficacy of public shelters (though they would frame the alternative as being smaller, private shelters).

The typical pattern that emerged in this period was that the media noticed homelessness in a particular city, and then subsequently a plea was made for more shelter beds. In Massachusetts, for example, liberal state representatives Jack Backman and Joseph DeNucci, who cochaired the state's Human Services Committee, both said that they would draft a bill for more shelters. Backman stated in April 1981 that "the shelter is an important partial step toward solving the problems of many people who were shipped out from state mental institutions with no programs or help. It's a way to enable people to make it without being institutionalized again" (quoted in Dietz, 1981, p. 1). In February 1982, Backman was identified as a supporter of "the Parker Street concept," which involved erection of temporary shelters by the Salvation Army; he was in support of Massachusetts providing such shelters in each of its seven regions (*Boston Globe*, "37 Who Died on the Streets," February 19, 1982, p. 1). By the end of 1982, the Massachusetts Coalition for the Homeless began to support the idea of more shelters, as did longtime advocate Kip Tiernan. As the *Boston Globe* reported:

> With temperatures beginning to fall outside, politicians and people who work with the homeless gathered yesterday to call for more shelters to house the city's growing street population. Boston currently has 643 beds in public and private shelters for homeless people, Carol Johnson of the Massachusetts Coalition for the Homeless said, with an additional 120 beds to be added by the end of January. But Johnson said the figure still falls short of the 2000 people the coalition estimates are currently without a place to live. Last year, according to statistics compiled by the coalition, 37 homeless people died in Boston. "There was an emergency five, six, seven years ago when the homeless first started coming to us," Kip Tiernan, founder of Rosie's Place, a Boston shelter for women, said at a press conference. "Now it's chronic and chaotic." ("Group Seeks More Shelters for Homeless," December 17, 1982, p. 1)

In Chicago at this stage there did not appear to be coordinated advocacy or political pressure, but several *Tribune* news articles in 1981 and 1982 had cited the need for more public shelters. Joye Brown, for example, bemoaned the lack of shelters for an estimated 12,000 homeless in Chicago and stated that public officials had no place to put the homeless; two successive articles characterized the shelters as "overflowing" and city officials as not knowing how to provide for the homeless (Brown, 1981, p. N1; Coakley, 1982, p. 5; Brown, 1982, p. 5). In response to this coverage, the *Chicago Tribune*'s first editorial on the issue, in 1982, called for more shelters for the homeless:

> Chicago is worse off than other cities in literal homeless because we have less provision for unsheltered people. . . . [T]he need is unusually severe, thanks to the current combination of high unemployment, a groggy economy, slashes in welfare funding and a lack of affordable housing. We call [on the] alderman to set aside two million dollars for the 1983 budget to fund and supervise shelters for the homeless throughout [the] city. ("Chicago's Thousands," p. 18)

The opposition of community members to shelters that was later enshrined as the "not in my backyard" (NIMBY) movement (and also came to describe the opposition to the placing of many controversial populations in neighborhoods) gained considerable attention at this time. Community resistance was apparent even before major shelter-building programs got under way. In November 1980, for example, the *Los Angeles Times* reported that when the Orange County Rescue Center (a traditional mission for the homeless) moved to a new neighborhood, it attracted a picket line of sixty residents of a Santa Ana neighborhood. Interestingly, the protesters were largely minority-group members who felt that many such institutions had already been placed in their area (Bunting, 1980, p. A1). In Chicago in January 1982, as part of this early public reaction to the homeless problem, a conflict broke out in Chicago's uptown area over the opening of a Residents for Emergency Shelter (REST) storefront during the previous November:

> Members of the powerful Uptown Chicago Commission sounded their objections, contending that the location was improperly zoned for a first-floor shelter and worrying that it would attract vagrants from across the city. . . . "Uptown already has had enough unfortunate people dumped here. Our community needs a little R and R. We don't need street vagrants attracted from all over the city," said a representative of the Uptown Chicago Commission. (Frantz, 1982, p. N1)

The most bitter of such early community battles over homeless shelters erupted in New York City. In response to successful litigation starting with *Callahan v. Carey* in 1979, the city signed a consent decree in

1981 to house homeless people in shelters that had to meet certain minimal requirements, with the zoning changes to be approved by community boards. In reaction, major battles erupted throughout the boroughs of New York City:

> [East Side, Manhattan, 1981] "Since the program opened, this has been a disaster area," she [head of community board] wrote. "Our brownstone steps, doorways and vestibules have been invaded by derelicts and bag people—and their urine and their feces. Some of us have been physically attacked by the more violent of the church's clients. A bag person couple were seen fornicating on the church steps one afternoon. Some of their male clients lie on our sidewalks exposing their genitalia. All of this, and there is more, is not only disgusting and dangerous to our adult population, but we have young children living here as well." (Carmody, 1981, p. A1)

> [Brooklyn, 1981] Some area residents remained unalterably opposed to the Gateway proposal, and City Councilman Leon A. Katz said: "This is nothing more than a foot-in-the-door tactic by the city, which is under the mistaken impression that it can import derelicts and vagrants into our community. There is no way we are going to let this happen." (Campbell, 1981, p. 27)

> [Noho, Manhattan, 1982] "We are besieged with far more than our fair share of social service agencies," said Star Sandow, president of the NoHo Neighborhood Association. "How can they add another shelter to an area that is already inundated with them? We don't even receive minimal support services from the city to keep this growing community from falling apart, but they keep turning it into a ghetto for the homeless. This is a very serious problem," he said of the homeless. "[The Human Resources Administration] dumps 1,100 people on us every day—and that's in addition to an entire subculture of homeless people here. They are aggressive and, at times, psychotic. It is my No. 1 priority for foot patrol in this precinct. If we have an available man, that's where he goes." (*New York Times,* "Noho Residents' Opposition Kills Plan for Homeless Shelter," December 26, 1982, p. A46)

Communities across the nation began opposing the homeless "in their backyards" just as in New York City, despite later polls showing abstract support for aid to the homeless. These battles continue today, decades since their inception, with such NIMBY groups continuing to stigmatize and stereotype the homeless and other marginalized groups.

But why was temporary emergency shelter, often undertaken in large, congregate group quarters that provided no more than cots, seen as a solution to homelessness to begin with? This is a complex question, and will be returned to throughout the book. There are a number of reasons, some historical and cultural, and some specific to the events of the 1980s.

First, on a broad level, solutions to social problems tend to follow prior historical patterns. Although it is true that homelessness in the United States had been relatively forgotten by the 1980s by many citizens, still the skid rows of most US cities usually contained several mission shelters run by churches or nonprofit groups such as the Salvation Army. In areas like the Bowery district of New York City and Skid Row of Los Angeles, missions provided food or clothing to lines of usually destitute men. This residue of the first 150 years of homelessness in the United States, as well as the still-existing boardinghouses, lodging houses, and single-room-occupancy hotels, remained the most available solution to policymakers and the public. As with soup kitchens and surplus food for the hungry, Americans tend to look at problems at their most limited level, not addressing (at least not immediately) the causes of homeless, and instead focusing only on its symptoms.

Second, as Michael Lipsky and Steven Smith (1989) argue, when social problems are treated as "emergencies," in many ways the response tends to reinforce their superficiality. Because few people expected that homelessness would exist for decades to come,[6] this meant that social policy, as developed by politicians and policymakers as well as advocates, stressed immediate, easily implemented, and quickly fundable solutions. Most cities either used existing public spaces (armories, closed schools, or institutions) and converted them into shelters, or contracted with religious organizations to provide shelters. These were low-cost and relatively low-commitment programs that, no doubt, many policymakers and advocates sincerely believed would be beneficial. Interestingly, in the 1930s, most efforts to help the poor were also described as "temporary."

There were also, however, more proximate reasons why the early 1980s was not a favorable time for structural approaches to policy issues such as homelessness. First, the election of Reagan in 1980 and the cuts in social welfare promulgated in 1981 were clear signals that plans for progressive social change were not on the agenda. Throughout the period, and arguably since, advocates, activists, and academics mounted a rearguard action to protect aspects of the "welfare state," such as it is in the United States, from complete dismantlement rather than stressing new and expensive social programs. Local leaders realized that the possibilities of federal reimbursement for their homeless services were low, and that without raising taxes, a highly unpopular move at this time, local funding was unlikely.

Second, the New York City consent decree of 1981 seemed to reinforce the idea that the courts would not interpret "shelter" as an actual permanent residence, but as a bed at a large, congregate institution. It is not clear when, in negotiations between attorneys and the city of New York, the solution in terms of shelters and not real housing became set in stone. In retrospect, Robert Hayes, leader of New York City's Coalition for the Homeless, who addressed a class of mine in 1993, said that if he could have done it again, he would not have agreed to the consent decree. Another contributing factor against permanent housing may have been the court's rejection of another suit that attempted to force New York State to provide housing (unspecified) to the many former psychiatric patients whom the state had discharged. Justice Richard W. Wallach (a judge who monitored and enforced the consent decree) rejected a suit filed by Hayes, saying that it was not the court's job to second-guess public officials and that the remedy for their failure was legislative (Shipp, 1982, p. B8).

Finally, the early advocates for the homeless, in New York City and Washington, D.C., at least, countered the idea of large public shelters with a proposal for smaller, privately run shelters. Already by March 1981, Baxter and Hopper had criticized the efficacy of public shelters (which were already being avoided by many of New York City's homeless), but rather than stress permanent housing, they offered as a model the small shelters run by various religious groups, from the Catholic Workers to the Franciscans. Similarly, Mitch Snyder's fight in Washington, D.C., was for a resident-run shelter. He noted that "government shelters are run like prisons," and said that private shelters were usually more humane (Muth and Morehouse, 1981, p. N6). Hayes, too, joined his colleagues in these preferences, as the *Los Angeles Times* noted:

> While government may have the ultimate responsibility for the homeless of our society, governments tend to throw the homeless into huge barren institutions that breed psychiatric disturbances and violence. . . . Now while still insisting that government cannot abdicate its responsibility for the homeless, Hayes sees better results when government enters into humane and economical partnerships with voluntary religious and charitable organizations. (Peirce, 1982, p. 11)

In many ways, the sentiments of Baxter, Hopper, Snyder, and Hayes are understandable. Large, barren armories had a long reputation of crowding, violence, and stigma that would in fact worsen in the 1980s. Small shelters can be more homelike, and the auspices of some small shelters (though hardly all; see, for example, Dordick, 1997, and Marvasti, 2003, for contrary examples) can encourage more independence and less stigma. However, as a policy solution for the huge numbers of homeless people, these statements did not support what later would become the mantra of the advocates, as frequently voiced by Hayes himself (see, for example, *Newsletters of the National Coalition for the Homeless* 7, no. 9 [December 1988]), that what the homeless needed was "housing, housing, housing," clearly meaning regular permanent housing. It seems in the initial construction of the homeless problem that the religious backgrounds of some of the advocates and their admiration for groups who had long worked with the poor directed them somewhat away from major preventive and redistributory strategies.

Although some aspects of the social construction of the homeless problem worked well for a while in gaining heightened attention in the short term, the very way the problem was characterized during the "alarmed discovery" stage—with the centrality of Reagan and Reaganomics, the "deservedness" of most homeless people in terms of cultural stereotypes, and the solution of shelters, whether private or public, small or large—served only to compound the problem over the decades that followed.

Notes

1. The *Chicago Tribune* made only one reference to Hayes through 1982 and none to Snyder. The *New York Times* made its first references to Snyder on November 27 and November 28, 1981. The *Los Angeles Times* made one reference to Snyder and the CCNV, in 1981, and one to Hayes, in 1982. And the *Boston Globe* made only three references to Hayes, the first in December 1981, and two to Snyder, the first in November 1981. With the exception of the *Chicago Tribune*, the laggard of the group, the other three newspapers had begun printing a considerable number of articles about the homeless by 1981–1982.

2. There were no references at all to homelessness in the *Chicago Tribune* in 1979 and 1980. However, once articles did begin appearing in the *Tribune* in 1981, the coverage of mental illness was fairly minimal, as in the *Los Angeles Times,* reflecting the judgment that most homeless people were economic victims of the recession. Although the political battles between Mayor Edward Koch and Governors Hugh Carey and Mario Cuomo of New York would not dominate coverage of the homeless for long, the question of mental illness among the homeless was still most dominant in the *New York Times* compared to the other three newspapers.

3. The *Boston Globe* has no available archive before 1980.

4. All demographic statements about the homeless are subject to at least some dispute. However, surveys done by advocates have not differed dramatically from those of government and academics in terms of the demographic char-

acteristics of the homeless as opposed to gross numbers. All agree that most homeless people are between the ages of twenty and forty, that more are male than female, that more are members of minority groups than white, and that most have an average education of high school equivalent or less. There are some surveys that count each member of a homeless family to arrive at a higher number of females or a higher percentage of families. There is also the possibility of prejudice, not only because of what target populations are visible and available for counts, but also because even survey sampling focuses on urban areas. There are homeless people in rural and suburban areas, and it is possible, though probably not likely, that comparatively more white and middle-class people might be found outside cities. The best early demographic accounts include Rossi, 1989 and Burt, 1993. The National Coalition for the Homeless consistently uses data from the US Conference of Mayors (see www.nch.org and *Newsletters of the National Coalition for the Homeless*).

5. Although Carter did not run on promises of massive budget cutting, in the last years of his administration significant budget cutting and increases in defense spending occurred. This is partly the reason why Ted Kennedy challenged Carter in the reelection primaries, which of course Kennedy lost. It is not at all certain that the homelessness issue would have had less of a scope had Carter been reelected.

6. In 2009, I interviewed Gary Blasé, one of the chief advocates of the homeless in California, as well as Michael Stoops, a longtime official at the National Coalition for the Homeless. I also spoke years ago with Robert Hayes, founder of the Coalition for the Homeless. All three immediately confirmed that the possibility that homelessness would last for years, much less decades, had never occurred to them or to fellow activists involved in the early days of the movement.

5

Modest Victories,
1983–1988

As homelessness became a broader public issue in the 1980s, a number of different political and social positions, or policy frames, became evident, most of them consistent with the previous history of homelessness in the United States. Despite protests in some quarters that efforts to help the homeless were far too generous or far too minimal, on the whole the political approach to homelessness during the 1980s can be characterized as somewhere between liberal and centrist, with compassion dominating the public debate and an apparent acceptance of the liberal argument about the "new homeless" being vulnerable members of society who needed help (see Hoch and Slayton, 1987, for a similar view). Such help consisted primarily of emergency assistance such as shelters, soup kitchens, and other services consistent with the traditions of US history. By about 1984, most advocates and activists were predicting that such aid would not end homelessness. In 1987, the signature piece of federal legislation for the homeless, the Stewart B. McKinney Homeless Assistance Act, was passed.

Policy Frames and Homelessness

Social constructionists and other social scientists have adopted Erving Goffman's earlier concept of a "frame" to describe how political or social problems are constructed along certain predictable paths (Snow, Anderson, and Benford, 1992; Goffman, 1974). Though the concept is helpful in clarifying the intentional nature of how issues are developed in the public arena, it tends to privilege intended action on the part of advocacy groups, experts, political actors, and social movements, while other potential frames that are historically and culturally available (see Chapter 2) are sometimes minimized. That is, available cultural frames—that the homeless are "bums" or that all people deserve charity regardless of who is to blame—do not need as much intentional policy framing, since they already coincide with the viewpoints of much of the public. There are four major policy frames that came to envelop homelessness as an issue in the 1980s, but perhaps the more successful ones were not necessarily intended by advocates or political supporters of aid to the homeless.

The Social Justice Frame

As noted in Chapter 4, advocacy groups for the homeless (such as the Community for Creative Non-Violence and the Coalition for the Homeless) quickly developed the "plight of the homeless" as a symbol for the failures of the Ronald Reagan administration, and at times for the failures of the broader political and economic system. By the mid-1980s, advocacy groups would be joined by grassroots protest groups composed of homeless and other poor people and their allies who would at times go much further in their critique, including criticism of the advocates themselves. In the context of the Democratic Party being out of power, gradually some politicians on the liberal side of the party—for example, Boston mayor Raymond Flynn, Chicago mayor Harold Washington, New York and Massachusetts governors Mario Cuomo and Michael Dukakis, and presidential contender Jesse Jackson—would reflect at least some of the rhetorical frame of the advocates and social justice movements. The increasing amount of mass media coverage devoted to homelessness in the mid-1980s, including interviews with advocates, newspaper coverage and television footage of homeless protests, and sympathetic receptions from groups such as liberal church and synagogue groups and Hollywood actors, certainly reinforced this frame. However, the social justice frame always had considerable problems succeeding in the political arena because the more specific its demands were, and the more separate it was from the charitable assistance frame (see below), the more it was rejected by national and local politicians and policymakers, and by the public. For example, as long as the social justice frame was used to embrace the development of remedial or charitable institutions such as shelters or provision of unspecified government or private funds to "help the homeless," the advocates and homeless protesters retained wide support. However, when advocates or homeless people sought to demand permanent low-cost (or no-cost) housing or other major social structural reforms, they may have lost much support from the liberal and charitable activists.

The Charitable Assistance Frame

Americans of many political and ideological stripes and of many social classes have historically supported aid to the poor and homeless under certain terms. In fact, as during the Great Depression, poverty at times moved the public to wide sympathy. A further important point is that Americans enjoy the process of giving aid directly, particularly when they can see tangible results in their own communities (see Wagner, 2000). The development of homelessness as a popular issue by the early to middle 1980s spurred many voluntary efforts through churches, fraternal organizations, liberal cause groups, and even individuals and families, efforts that dominated the news media in many cities. In fact, the National Coalition for the Homeless and many of its affiliates, as well as groups run by the homeless, turned to direct service provision themselves. While the notion of compassion and the call to help the vulnerable was similarly seen in the social justice policy frame, the charitable assistance frame did not endorse social conflict as an appropriate strategy to aid people, nor did it endorse widespread governmental intervention, much less radical redistribution of resources, to end homelessness. The overlap between these two frames may have made the homeless issue more popular at first than in later years when support for the homeless diminished. Perhaps one way to put this is that liberalism in one respect is symbolic (holding certain stances and sensibilities such as a desire to aid the poor and homeless), but is also ideological, as is certainly the case with leftism, in its specific support for social welfare and for redistributive economic measures.

The Mental Illness "Expert Support" Frame

Many experts and writers, primarily academics and working professionals, argued that large numbers of the homeless were mentally ill or substance abusers, or both. Although some of the methodologies of these claims-makers were questionable, overall there is no reason to believe that they intended to oppose the social justice and charitable assistance frames. Depending on the particular issue, mental health experts and advocates supported mild political and charitable efforts, such as provision of shelters and more social services to aid the homeless. However, when the claims of the more radical social justice advocates became louder, certainly some of the mental illness and substance abuse experts firmly rejected the social justice view, using the issue of deinstitutionalization, for example, as the key policy frame rather than linking to the downturn of the economy or the Reagan-era budget cutbacks as causes.

The "Bum" Frame

As described in Chapter 3, there is nearly a century and a half of history when most viewed people without homes as "bums," "tramps," and "hobos," as impolitic as these terms may be. Such a view does not mean those who tended to frame the issue in this way were not at times sympathetic toward the plight of the homeless, nor does it mean that they necessarily opposed charitable assistance. But generally, much of the public was not influenced by the creation of the "new homeless" as an issue, the calls for compassion, and the solutions of government and other interventions to assist the homeless. Interestingly, in the initial years of advocacy, the negative "bum" view was not often represented in the mass media. Perhaps, in fact, the negative reaction of the media and others to comments by Reagan and, for example, his attorney general, Edwin Meese, on the homeless may have initially discouraged opposition. Nevertheless, by the mid-1980s, a significant (if still minority) amount of news coverage began to show conservative politicians and think tanks objecting to aid for the homeless along with newspaper editorials that were hostile toward the homeless and a growing number of "not in my backyard" movements against shelters and other homeless services. The public also began voicing the sentiment, even if they did not use the word "bum," that most homeless people were mentally ill or substance abusers, therefore undeserving of aid.

* * *

Because so much of the literature on homelessness as a social problem has focused on efforts of advocates (part of the social justice frame) and to a lesser extent on the opposition of government and conservatives to advocacy efforts (the "bum" frame), we turn now to further exploration of the centrist-liberal charitable assistance policy frame. Though the charitable assistance frame sought to help the homeless, in other ways it created a dilemma for advocates and social justice supporters in their portrayal of homelessness as a symbolic issue.

The "Euphoric Enthusiasm" of Charity and Shelters

For many Americans of all walks of life, the opportunity to aid their fellow humans helps them meet religious and other spiritual obligations, meets their own needs for fulfillment and community involvement, and even makes "help" pleasurable. The appeal of aiding those "least among us" is a deeply American trait, and has been conditioned by a unique history in which Americans have not only privileged voluntary activity over public entitlement, but also preferred quick good deeds over lengthy (and more thoughtfully considered) policy debates.

A review of the newspaper and television coverage of homelessness in the 1983–1985 period—even prior to major nationwide charitable efforts such as "Comic Relief" and "Hands Across America"—shows significant individual, religious, entertainment, and civic undertakings for the homeless, as well as events that combined political figures with private-sector figures to raise funds for the homeless.

Frequently the press highlighted the actions of individuals in aiding the homeless. The *Los Angeles Times* in 1983 profiled a man named Todd Waters who was vice president of an advertising agency in Minneapolis. Waters decided to "dramatize the plight of the homeless" with an eighteen-day trip from New York City to Los Angeles. Along the way, he sought a one-penny pledge for each of the 3,082 miles he traveled. He donated this "Penny Route" money to the local homeless shelters he visited along the way (Walker, 1983, p. C1). In another story the following year, the *Los Angeles Times* featured Robert Dalgleish, a farmer who started a one-man harvesting operation in the state of Washington. Dalgleish collected onions, potatoes, fruits, vegetables, and other crops and distributed them by truck to food banks across the Northwest. Dalgleish's "First Harvest" was the beginning of the idea of donating "excess goods" (those considered "less than perfect") to the poor, and by 1984 sparked a national model (Kunzl, 1984, p. 10).

In the Northeast, the *New York Times* increasingly aimed its annual "Neediest Fund" at the issue of homelessness as the visibility of large numbers of street people in its namesake metropolis grew. Many donors wrote in to the newspaper, some with poignant messages. As a reporter noted: "New York residents feel a special responsibility and compassion for their impoverished, homeless neighbors." He then introduced a bit of verse sent in by Ben Steinberg, an eighty-year-old Brooklyn resident who had contributed in the past. Alongside his donation of $25, Steinberg wrote:

> He searches the silent wind-swept street,
> For some scraps of food and a place to sleep
> For him too, no room at the inn,
> He has no friends, perhaps no kin.
> As many enjoy the holiday cheer,
> Will they remember the lonely and homeless this year?
> (Waggoner, 1983b, p. B2)

Heidi Meller of the Bronx, who donated $100, wrote:

> I am a resident alien who has spent seven happy years in New York, but from year to year I observe more and more sadness and misery in the streets surrounding me. Therefore I would like to contribute to your fund and hope that someone else, less fortunate, will be able to enjoy life in this city a little more. (Waggoner, 1983a, p. B7)

Ruth Linn of Plainview, Long Island, sent in a $25 donation with the following words:

> From the warm comfort of my home, I wish to offer my token of help—and wish that it could be much more—for those who are suffering and homeless. Perhaps they will be provided a bit of hope, knowing they have not been completely abandoned by society and our Government. (Kennedy, 1983, p. A56)

Not surprisingly, religious institutions were at the core of much of this assistance. Sometimes the assistance was more symbolic than material, as when the *Chicago Tribune* headlined the successful appeal of a West Side church to Mother Teresa to send nuns to Chicago to help the homeless. In an impoverished area with a 60 percent unemployment rate, the four nuns spoke of providing help for "spiritual impoverishment," but it was unclear what this would entail ("Four Nuns Coming Soon to Aid the Poorest of Poor," January 24, 1983, p. 1). But often churches embraced setting up shelters for the homeless, enthusiastically casting these efforts as a return to their original mission of charity. In New York City, St. George's Episcopal Church, on East 16th Street, opened a shelter and recruited eighty volunteers. The Reverend Thomas Pike called the effort "a profoundly spiritual experience" that strengthened the church's roots in the neighborhood "and quicken[ed] the church's teachings in the lives of its members. Words like mercy, forgiveness, and kindness take on a new meaning when you are in a program like this" (Austin, 1983b, p. A42). At St. Finbar's Roman Catholic Church in Brooklyn, the Reverend Anthony J. Failla proudly displayed the work of his parish volunteers, who had turned a former meeting hall into living quarters for fourteen homeless people. "I think it's the positive side of a negative situation," said another clergyman, the Reverend James E. Gunther of Transfiguration Lutheran Church, on 126th Street in Manhattan. "We are being forced to feed the hungry, clothe the naked and do the things we are supposed to do" (Austin, 1983a, p. A47).

Almost from the start, Hollywood actors as well as other celebrities began to take on the homeless cause. In California, actress Marsha Hunt decided to contact all honorary mayors of each community in the southern part of the state (these were figurehead leaders, some famous, appointed by town or city chambers of commerce) and invite them to attend meetings to try to establish shelters for the homeless. A liberal activist, Hunt urged the group to mobilize volunteers (McGarry, 1983, p. V1). In 1984, when a shelter for fifteen to eighteen homeless families opened in the South Bronx, there was "a star-studded news conference" including actors Jeremy Irons and Candice Bergen and directors Penny Marshall and Mike Nichols. These celebrities helped lead a fundraising campaign by the private nonprofit agency Women in Need (Kelley, 1984, p. 1). Songwriter John Stewart called homelessness the "cause of the '80s, where civil rights was the cause of the '60s," and organized a benefit concert through his Homecoming Records label under the banner "Homecoming for the Homeless" (Hochman, 1985, p. 7). Soon much bigger stars were at the center of the charities; in 1985, Ted Koppel of *ABC News* did a show on Bruce Springsteen's fundraising for the homeless, and in 1987, Peter Jennings, also of *ABC News,* did an entire show on celebrity involvement in the homeless cause (Vanderbilt Television News Archive, August 30, 1985, and March 4, 1987).

The homeless cause provoked a rapid sequence of collaboration, with political leaders, church leaders, civic leaders, celebrities, and volunteers taking collective action. The following headlines reflect a three-month period in Boston:

[April 25, 1985] RULING THE ROAST—A benefit culinary tour of some of Boston's hotel and restaurant kitchens will be conducted Saturday, May 11, with proceeds going to Horizons, a shelter for homeless women and their children. Uncommon Boston, a tour service, will run the event, which will leave at 9:30 A.M. from the Women's Educational and Industrial Union on Boylston Street. (Levy, 1985, p. 77)

[May 5, 1985] "WALK FOR HUNGER" TO BE HELD TODAY—Gov. Michael S. Dukakis and Cardinal-designate Bernard S. Law planned to join an estimated 10,000 Massachusetts residents today in the annual "Walk for Hunger" to help raise money for soup kitchens and homeless shelters. (Associated Press, 1985, p. 35)

[June 2, 1985] SHORT CIRCUITS—Boston Harbor has been used as a backdrop for many an upscale publicity extravaganza—waterfront condo development, tourism, environmental cleanups, fun in the sun and the like. Now comes a new twist to the old PR game: a harbor cruise to benefit the homeless. On Wednesday, Gov. Michael S. Dukakis and his wife, Kitty, will host a $50-a-head evening cruise aboard the *Spirit of Boston,* proceeds to benefit the Fund for the Homeless. The voyage will include dinner, dancing and entertainment, plus a raffle for a two-week trip to the Orient, a Nantucket getaway and more. The homeless should be so lucky! (*Boston Globe*, 1985c, p. 25)

[July 24, 1985] AN APPEAL FOR THE NEEDY—David Samuels, an intern in Sen. Edward M. Kennedy's office who will be a freshman at Harvard this fall, plans to sleep in a shelter for the homeless tonight. He is one of eight organizers of Intern Summer Project '85, a bipartisan group on Capitol Hill that wants to focus attention on the plight of the poor, the homeless and the illiterate in America, and to ask that the government do more to help these people. To publicize the effort, Samuels and up to 45 other interns—depending on how many spaces are open—intend to sleep in a shelter tonight, and to hold a rally on the steps of the Capitol tomorrow. (Pertman, 1985, p. 3)

Although this charitable mania of the 1980s was well intentioned, it often lacked clarity and accountability in terms of funding and measurable results. In the following two examples, taken from California, we see a kind of "disconnect" between the solutions proffered by leaders and the real needs of the homeless, particularly on a long-term basis. First, in early 1983, the county government of Los Angeles decided (as was typical at this time, during which 3,500 new shelters opened; see Jencks, 1994) to inventory property held by the county that could be used as shelter for the homeless. In July, with the help of a closed ward at Long Beach Hospital, a shelter opened with a two-week limit for each client. Additionally, clients were allowed to stay only if they sought work. Despite the admittance and residency limits, the reporter who covered the story seemed exuberant: "Now they [homeless people] have a place to stay, three meals a day and help they need to rebuild their lives. Most of them seem to sense that the worst of their troubles are ended. They can relax while they are here and gradually regain some sense of hope about the future" (Overend, 1983b, p. F1). Jim Graham, the shelter manager, also seemed ecstatic: "the Long Beach community has pitched in with donations of cash, food and clothing as enthusiastically as [I] had hoped it would. It will be nice when the county gets some other shelters opened up. It's working better here than we imagined, and it can work anywhere where all the different elements of the community are involved" (Overend, 1983b, p. F1).

Ignored in the enthusiasm was not only the fact that many homeless people would demur at going to shelters at all, but also the unrealistic expectation that homeless people or families could completely "rebuild their lives" in two weeks. Nevertheless, the politicians, advocates, and organizers spoke enthusiastically of their achievement.

In a second example, the conservative city of San Diego, which came relatively late to shelter development despite its reputation as a "haven for the homeless," celebrated its "first Christmas" in which there was a place for the homeless to sleep (for all of three days). *Los Angeles Times* staff writer Tom Greeley applauded:

> Thanks to what many described as an unprecedented outpouring of public support, for the three days of Christmas weekend anybody could—without questions asked—spend the night in Golden Hall downtown on a cot donated by the Marines, using linens—given by Mercy Hospital—and eating food provided by a number of restaurants and hotels. . . . Scores of people also made impromptu visits during the weekend to drop off food, toys, and other gifts. (Greeley, 1984, p. 1)

County supervisor Patrick Boardman expressed enthusiasm as well: "I was truly startled by the reaction in San Diego last week—the outpouring of ideas and help. It's so easy for most of us to forget about the homeless because they are not in the mainstream of consciousness. It's time for that to change" (quoted in Greeley, 1984, p. 5).

As in the Los Angeles County story, the enthusiasm in San Diego over so little suggests some of the difference between the charitable assistance frame and the social justice frame. Even when far stronger demands were being made by advocates, the incipient homeless movement, and even some liberal politicians, the excitement about raising money for shelters continued. Few fundraisers looked at the long-term structural and socioeconomic issues related to homelessness that needed to be addressed. The widespread embrace of charity on the one hand and political symbolism on the other hand put social justice advocates in an ambivalent position.

"Hands Across America": Charity for the Homeless Goes National

Perhaps no other event better exemplified the symbolism of charity in the United States than the one-day (actually fifteen-minute) handholding campaign called "Hands Across America" on May 25, 1986. A brainchild of Ken Kragen, who promoted the 1984 "USA for Africa" charitable campaign made famous by the song "We Are the World," the "Hands" campaign also followed the well-known celebrity-studded event "Farm Aid" the previous year. The very vagueness of the idea of raising money for the homeless and hungry through voluntary pledges by corporations, actors, politicians, and millions of ordinary Americans seemed to have great appeal. Originally proposed as a way to raise $100 million (later reduced to a goal of $50 million, with less than $16 million ultimately raised), the handholding line would start at New York City's Statue of Liberty and was envisioned to stretch across the entire country to Long Beach, California's Queen Mary dock. Backed by such corporate giants as Coca-Cola and Citibank and celebrities such as Glenn Close, Bill Cosby, Jane Fonda, Tina Turner, Olivia Newton-John, and Lily Tomlin, "Hands" also gained the backing of President Reagan, who signed a proclamation declaring "Hands Across America Day." Accused of ignoring and worsening the homeless problem, the president declared: "By joining together in this way, in cities and towns, along the back roads and mountain highways, from sea to shining sea, the people of this blessed land are reaffirming their willingness to sacrifice so that adequate food and shelter are available to all" (quoted in Weinraub, 1986, p. 1). In an interview with one of the organizers of "Hands," Fred Droz, a former advance man for Jimmy Carter, the *Boston Globe* captured "the politics of the event," which had been organized "along the lines of a grass-roots presidential campaign, with offices in each of the 16 states." As Droz said, there was "something in it for every constituency. Yuppies see it as a return to '60s values, old folks see it as a return to neighbor-to-neighbor, Democrats see it as grass-roots activism, and Republicans see it as private sector initiative. Parents see it as a way to bring their kids back together again, and kids see it as the biggest party in the world" (Bradlee, 1986, p. 1). Paradoxically, the very enthusiasm of wanting millions of people involved—variously estimated as 6 to 8 million—led "Hands" organizers to waive what had previously been a minimum $10 pledge to take part, which (compounded by the failure of some participants to fulfill their pledges) led to considerably less money being raised than originally projected.

What was the response to the giant human chain that stretched (if unevenly) across the nation, and whose enthusiastic attendees sang "America the Beautiful," "We Are the World," and the less remembered namesake song "Hands Across America"? To those who attended, coming from a variety of stations of life and political perspectives, there were feelings of optimism, enthusiasm, and hope. As described in the *New York Times:*

> "Everybody must grab hands or this is not going to work," said 6-year-old Amy Sherwood of the Bay Ridge section of Brooklyn, whose family of seven had been homeless for most of the past year. . . . She stood at the head of the line in Battery Park, the line's East Coast terminus. Near her were Helen Hayes, Harry Belafonte, Yoko Ono, Mayor Koch, Governor Cuomo, Senator Alfonse M. D'Amato, and other celebrities and officials. From the Battery the line stretched up West Street, the West Side Highway and the Henry Hudson Parkway to the George Washington Bridge, south through New Jersey, Philadelphia, Baltimore and Washington D.C., north and west to Chicago and south and west from there to the Queen Mary, docked at a pier in Long Beach, California. "This is the richest country in the world," said Ben Vereen, the entertainer, standing in the line in Long Beach. "There is no excuse for hunger." If the line was a statement from America's heart, it was also a show of vast proportions. Over New Jersey, skywriters traced the line's path with a white streak against a blue arc of sky. Covered wagons stretched along Main Street in Dallas. Kenny Rogers, the singer, straddled the Texas–New Mexico border near Glenrio, Texas. One mile of line in Albuquerque, N.M., was made up of multicolored hot air balloons tethered into line. Forty-three miles west, at the Laguna Pueblo reservation, the line was filled with 1,377 feet of paper dolls sent by New York City school children, local organizers said. In Phoenix, a section of line was made up by guests at a reception for 13-year-old Sol Berger, who was celebrating his bar mitzvah. (Kerr, 1986, p. 1)

The *Chicago Tribune* described similar scenes of enthusiasm:

> Marilyn Pickers, standing in front of the Jiffy Lube on La Grange Road in La Grange Park Sunday, thought it was beautiful. "I think this is the most worthwhile thing I have done in my whole life," she said. Hands Across America didn't exactly resemble the organizers' slick promotional film footage when it snaked through Illinois. But that did

not prevent an emotional charge from surging along the line from South Side to North Side and down into the state's rural areas when the switch was pulled at 2 P.M. for the fundraising spectacular for the nation's hungry and homeless. . . . Never have so many people—perhaps half a million in Illinois, about 5 million nationwide—stood so happily in line. So moved were they in this unmoving queue, they burst into song, even if some couldn't remember the words to such new anthems as "We Are the World" and "Hands Across America." "Our whole staff felt it," said Jane Missimer, an organizer for the event in Illinois and a link in the chain on Michigan Avenue near Washington Street. "I had a grandmother come up and hug me with tears in her eyes. . . . It's about time they did something in America for Americans," said Susan Springer, a Chicago area resident who stood along La Grange Road. Her son and mother-in-law had taken a bus to Alton, Ill., to link hands, and the boy's father, who lives in California, was planning to take a spot in line out there. "We'll all be connected, even though we're thousands of miles apart," she marveled. . . . Martha Whelan, executive director of Deborah's Place . . . an overnight emergency shelter that houses about 30 homeless women a night, is hoping she'll get some of that money. She brought two carloads of women from the shelter to join the line at Cullerton Street and Michigan Avenue. "It's nice to have recognition of the issue," Whelan said. (Seigenthaler et al., 1986, p. 1)

Yet perhaps surprisingly, the event drew much criticism. Many newspapers quoted homeless people observing the event with cynicism. In Chicago, a thirty-two-year-old man named Stanley who was staying at the Pacific Garden Mission told the *Tribune* he was unimpressed: "A lot of people come out for it, but ten minutes after it's over they go back to whatever they were doing," he said, adding that he has been homeless for years. "I think the whole thing is like Christmas: It comes once a year and then it's over. People are nice for one day" (Seigenthaler et al., 1986, p. 1). In a relatively rare slap at charitable work for the homeless, Robert Hayes of the National Coalition for the Homeless complained: "The trouble is, Sunday's extravaganza is without content. There seems to be no recognition that several million Americans are homeless as a result of deliberate public policy decisions" (quoted in Kerr, 1986, p. 1). In terms of international criticism, the Soviet Union attacked Reagan for his support of the event, accusing him of participating only to improve his image. *Radio Moscow* said that Reagan had refused to deal with "the now-disastrous problems of hunger and poverty" in the United States (quoted in Kerr, 1986, p. 1).

But perhaps more surprising than the criticism from Hayes and the Soviet Union was the criticism from the media. Ben Bradlee of the

Boston Globe called the "Hands" event "the latest of the splashy, one-day mega-relief projects . . . [that] has taken on a God-and-country aura and a carefully crafted nonpolitical image that has won it the endorsement of the 16 governors whose states the human chain is to cross, as well as an abundance of corporate sponsors who see in the event both a noble cause and an opportunity for excellent public relations" (Bradlee, 1986, p. 1). Steven Daly, a columnist for the *Chicago Tribune,* critiqued the event three days before it happened:

> No one wants to be put in the position of being seen as pro-hunger, but it seems that this hippest of variations on doing good may have worn thin its welcome. The realization that famines cannot be cured in a single dosage, that the plight of the American farmer cannot be made right in riotous musical assembly, that the making of a joyful noise, at $10 a head, will not make it so may have soured our citizenry on Hands Across America. From the beginning, the danger in every modern-day helping-hand marathon from the concert for Bangladesh to Live Aid was the implicit belief that one move, one expression of concern, one afternoon or evening devoted to world hunger would somehow suffice. Many of the people involved in these projects believe, and not without good reason, that governments are not much interested in the hungry, the powerless and the disenfranchised. . . . The benefits raised much money and, we hope, did much good. But the fund-raisers were unable to come to grips with the political and logistical problems in Ethiopia. They were unable to alter the harsh reality of America's farm belt, and five million pairs of hands across the continent on a single afternoon will not change the face of poverty in America. The argument here is not that the organizers of Hands Across America ought not to try to aid the homeless. It is simply that symbolic acts, fueled by T-shirts and celebrities, have become cheap currency. Linking hands with Bill Cosby and Pete Rose and Kenny Rogers says more about our own psychological needs, and theirs, than the real needs of the hungry and homeless. There is smugness in the air, and the inability of "Hands" organizers to find the more than 5 million dues-paying volunteers required for Sunday's demonstration may be the giveaway. The success of USA for Africa was held up as proof that the Me decade was over, that a healthy concern for the travails of others was, for want of a grander description, back in fashion. That seems less certain as Hands Across America stumbles toward fruition. Fashion may indeed be the operative word in these endeavors, which too often fall into a self-congratulatory pose, particularly by the celebrities. By definition, fashion comes and goes. (Daley, 1986, p. 1)

Columnist Joan Beck, three days later, picked up on the self-righteousness theme: "Well, we've all done our bit for hunger and homelessness. We've held hands and taken a stand, just as we were asked to do. We've sent out the message loud and clear that Americans don't want people to be hungry or homeless. Now we're entitled to an afterglow of euphoria and self-congratulations. Right?" Arguing that Americans had become lost in symbolism, she wondered what would really be achieved for the poor and hungry:

> Hands Across America presumably did raise money—millions of dollars, probably, and still counting. No doubt it will do a band-aid bit of good for some of the hungry and a few of the homeless. But hand-holding, singing, good intentions, kind thoughts, T-shirts and even dribbles of money won't solve the fundamental problems that cause hunger and homelessness. That will take minds as well as hearts and hands. And tough-minded thinking is precisely what's missing from those extravaganzas of mass emotion that give participants the feeling they are solving complex social problems without really having to come to grips with them. That $50 million that Hands Across America intended to raise can help fund a few temporary shelters for the homeless and keep some soup kitchens going for the hungry. Some of the money can be funneled to agencies and social workers who deal, hands-on, with the needy. That's all commendable and relatively easy. Those whose $10 and $35 pledges go for this work do get brownie points. But holding hands, no matter how heart warming, won't get at the basic reasons why some Americans are hungry in a land of chronic agricultural surpluses and why the homeless have fallen between the cracks of ever-growing, multibillion dollar welfare programs. (Beck, 1986, p. 8)

The criticism of "Hands" grew far noisier when it became known that the event had raised far less money than expected, that much of the money went to pay for its own costs, and that no money had been distributed even many months after the event. Moreover, disputes arose over how the money would be distributed (see De Atley, 1986, p. 20). Columnist Sally Sommer, in an article in the *Los Angeles Times* in 1987 reflecting on these problems, wrote of the physical, social, and emotional distance between the event's offices in Century City and Skid Row in Los Angeles where the homeless gathered in soup lines. She wondered whether the organizers had any "conception of poverty, of what it is like to wait, as the homeless spend so much time waiting, for food, for the county's $247 [a month] relief check, for a place to sleep." Commenting on another charitable drive, Sommer declared: "I can't help wondering exactly what the motives are. How can they ask for more money when they have not yet succeeded in distributing what they received from the public almost a year ago? Is this just more hype for corporate images, as it often seemed to be during the heyday of the Hands project last spring?" (Sommer, 1987, p. 5).

The controversy over "Hands" suggests how the "alarmed discovery" of homelessness varied between, on the one hand, the many volunteers, politicians, actors, and do-gooders who participated in the event and, on the other, the more thoughtful critics and advocates, not to mention homeless people themselves. A deep split was already developing between those who responded with simple charity and those who worked on the homelessness issue as part of a social justice agenda, let alone others who simply opposed assistance for the homeless and those convinced that homelessness was caused by personal problems. The broader issue of homelessness as a social policy question was now at stake and would eventually become even more polarized.

The Social Justice Frame, Part 1: Advocates, Protest Movements, and Liberal Politicians

Three different sets of actors—advocacy groups, homeless protesters themselves, and liberal politicians—sometimes allied and sometimes just tensely tolerating one another, attempted in the 1980s to move the issue of homelessness beyond charity to demand a public response that would help address the roots of the problem as a social issue. Although none of the groups were very large in number, their skillful use of the media and political tactics, together with the apparent public support for compassion for the homeless and the very poor, helped them achieve legitimacy.

The most visible of the advocacy groups were the National Coalition for the Homeless (formally founded in May 1982) and the Community for Creative Non-Violence, based in Washington, D.C. (founded in 1977). Although these groups received much publicity, they were fairly small and, in the case of coalitions, were often divided politically among themselves. By 1983, a number of protests broke out around the country, most of them led by local activists seeking support for the indigenous poor, but often joined by local coalitions, national groups like ACORN, students, and other activists. The first national effort to actually organize homeless people as a group was the National Union of the Homeless, founded in 1986 in Philadelphia. Protests complicated life for advocacy groups such as the coalitions, which were primarily composed of professionals, students, and other advocates who themselves were not poor. They sometimes shared the protesters' objectives but not their tactics. As well, a small number of political leaders in the Democratic Party were particularly active in confronting the issue of homelessness. But these leaders, such as New York governor Mario Cuomo and Boston mayor Raymond Flynn, despite their eloquent statements about homelessness and social justice, often faced criticism at the local level for not following through on their own broad pronouncements. Moreover, at a time when state and local budgets were being cut, political leaders, even those from more liberal states, faced a strongly negative environment in terms of social spending. Ultimately then, for these leaders to succeed, they had to keep the support of the majority of their voters, not the poor or homeless or their organizations.

One dilemma of the social justice movement was the extent to which emergency shelter, as opposed to more permanent solutions to homelessness, should be emphasized, the latter of which, by the late 1980s, came to center on housing (and, to a lesser degree, income and jobs) as the banner of the movement. By the late 1980s, protesters had unified behind slogans for housing, not shelters.

But the issue was more complicated on a number of levels. First, some groups, such as the Community for Creative Non-Violence and its charismatic leader Mitch Snyder, though radical in tactics and ideology, aimed primarily at the goal of emergency shelter in their protests. Snyder, known for his frequent hunger strikes, became locked into a long battle with the federal government about the extent of shelter in Washington, D.C. Groups such as New York City's Coalition for the Homeless were committed to litigation, because of their legal responsibilities for consent decrees regarding housing. Finally, the needs of the homeless differed by location and demographics. Some US cities lacked homeless shelters entirely, and most non-eastern cities in the country lacked public shelters that were mandated to accommodate all homeless. Homeless protesters tended to be single men, racial minorities affiliated with the civil rights and other movements, and longer-term homeless. Less likely to be found among protesters were homeless families, people who were new to the streets, and people who were mentally ill. These groups may have most immediately needed and wanted a place to sleep for the night (for works on homeless social movements, see Cress and Snow, 1996, 2000; Noy, 2009; Snow et al., 2005; Wagner, 1993; Wagner and Cohen, 1991; Williams, 2005; Wright, 1997).[1]

But while the need for emergency services such as homeless shelters and soup kitchens was of course not incompatible with long-term proposals to end homelessness, it was the short-term emergency frame that often came to be understood by the public as *the* solution to homelessness, as it was both easier to achieve and more in harmony with US political culture than providing housing or income for people with no resources.

The Coalition for the Homeless, composed primarily of sympathetic professionals like lawyers and social workers, clergy, and students, was a diverse group that imposed no prescribed political line on its state affiliates. Its ideas of what it could do changed frequently, and some of its statements contradicted others. At its first meeting, in 1982, Robert Hayes had in fact urged "modest goals" and advocated "little more than a salvage operation" (*New York Times,* "National Group Formed to Help the Homeless," May 9, 1982, p. A14). But a year and a half later, at a conference in Chicago in which 200 delegates from sixty cities met, there was a "mood of political militancy marked by proposals for nationwide demonstrations." These proposals included a range of diverse strategies, such as a "memorial day for homeless, sit-ins at Congress and state legislatures, [and an] aggressive policy of political lobbying and litigation to establish a right to shelter," as well as the "defeat of Reagan in [the] next year's election" and the goal of a "statement on homelessness in [the] Democratic Party platform" (Overend, 1983a, p. D7).

Despite this militancy, the public was led to believe the need for shelters was the prime answer to homelessness. In Chicago, a city that at the time had no homeless shelters, Robert Adams of the Coalition for the Homeless called on the city to spend $2 million to create a set of neighborhood shelters (Houston, 1982, p. 11). In Los Angeles, Paul Selden of the National Coalition for the Homeless seemed to adopt a stage theory for homelessness, seeing the need for shelters as the first order of business: "The first thing needed is a shelter system. But that will take a growing awareness. In the end, everyone will have to get into the act" (quoted in Overend, 1983c, p. 1). And, of course, in New York City countless articles publicized the efforts of Hayes and the Coalition for the Homeless to demand shelters, although it would be Hayes who would later popularize the phrase that what was needed to end homelessness was "housing, housing, housing." Examples of the continued quest for shelter beds include:

> Charging that the city houses many homeless individuals in "grossly indecent shelters," a lawyer representing homeless men filed a motion with a State Supreme Court justice asking that he require the city to establish 1,000 new emergency beds by Christmas. He also asked that the city be required to bring another 1,000 beds in existing shelters into compliance with a 1981 consent decree setting minimal standards for sheltering homeless individuals. (Rule, 1983a, p. B5)

The coalition, in its report, charged that the city's capacity to shelter the homeless—in the face of rising numbers of homeless people—had "declined significantly" in the past year through the closing of some shelters, the failure to open new shelters and a lagging effort to move homeless people into alternative housing. (McFadden, 1985, p. A42)

Hayes was himself prescient enough to see that the significant spending of large amounts of money that did not help solve the problem of homelessness would backfire, and that patience among the public was limited. As the *New York Times* observed in late 1983:

The failure to provide permanent housing could lead to a backlash against the homeless, much as critics of national welfare programs have cited widespread waste and fraud as reasons for eliminating or reducing those programs. "I'm concerned that the city is spending 'bad' money, which will give the homeless a bad reputation," Mr. Hayes said. He said the city needed a housing policy, not a shelter policy. (Goodwin, 1983, p. A1)

As Hayes implied, if the short attention span of the public were squandered, the result, at best, would only be the establishment of homeless shelters, and not the end of homelessness.

The protest movement, on the other hand, almost always emphasized solutions other than shelters. In April 1983, a group picketed the Legal Aid Society in New York City, protesting a class-action suit that the society had filed against the city and the state on behalf of the homeless. Marcy May, a spokesman for the picketing group, said the suit misrepresented the concerns of homeless families by focusing on the need to improve temporary shelter rather than on the need for permanent housing (*New York Times,* "The City: Homeless Picket Legal Aid Society," April 8, 1983, p. B3). In 1984, a "tent city" protest in the Boston Commons also distinguished itself from other groups by noting in the words of spokesperson Allen Guerrini: "Our people want homes, not shelters, meaningful homes, and low-cost rooms." In fact, Guerrini noted, "my friends are against the temporary shelter system provided by the city and other private organizations and hope to focus public attention on their plight to gain either permanent housing or low cost rooms" (Andrews, 1984, p. 1).

It would not be long, for a variety of reasons, before protesters would find themselves on the other side of the issue from advocates, due to unsympathetic service agencies, newspapers, and liberal politicians. An example was one of the first major protests of the 1980s in Los Angeles.

It began as a "tent city" protest and later was dubbed a "Justiceville," which provided its own internal organization and leadership for its occupants. But as the protest continued, it received criticism from organizations usually known for sympathy: "I look out and see people living in shacks and I feel like I'm on the set of 'The Grapes of Wrath,'" said Catherine Morris of the Los Angeles Catholic Worker, which provided meals to the homeless of the city's Skid Row. "It is neither safe, nor decent, nor sanitary" (quoted in Clayton, 1985a, p. 1). This was a surprising comment coming from a group often known for its leftist politics and desire to serve the most needy. Several days later, amid charges of drug use at the camp, the police arrested the remaining protesters, and the *Los Angeles Times* wondered what should be done about "the hard core homeless" (Clayton, 1985b, p. 1; see also Ropers, 1988).

In Boston, a broadening protest and advocacy movement often came into conflict with the generally liberal *Boston Globe*. In 1986, when Boston's National Union for the Homeless began to organize, it came into conflict with the Pine Street Inn, a long-standing shelter. The NUH claimed that Pine Street had denied its members shelter as retribution for their organizing activities (Cox, 1986, p. 18). The *Globe* editorialized on the incident the next day, reminding the NUH of Pine Street's longevity and labeling the NUH's protest as "unexpected—perhaps even ungrateful" ("Pine Street Inn Under Fire," July 24, 1986, p. 14). A week later, the *Globe* took the surprising tack of criticizing a coalition of community, union, and housing groups who were seeking to make housing a human right by a popular referendum in Massachusetts. The *Globe* began to move from its liberal position of blaming the economy and other social ills for homelessness to blaming the homeless themselves: "There is a dangerous tendency for advocates to confuse a socially meritorious cause with broad interpretations of the common good. That tendency seems to have afflicted the advocates for the homeless. . . . For the great majority of the homeless, the problem is not one of 'habitable and affordable nontransient housing,' but of mental health care" ("A Constitution, Not a Catalog," July 31, 1986, p. 18).

In another conflict replicated in many parts of the nation, but interesting because it involved Boston's mayor, Raymond Flynn, a frequent spokesperson for aid to the homeless, the National Union of the Homeless occupied an abandoned building in the city's South End, which, according to the *Globe* in its initial reporting, had "the city's sympathy, if not total support." In addition to using the building for housing, the NUH proposed that it would set up a job-training program and a high school equivalency program (Negri, 1986, p. 13). Despite support from former mayoral candidate Mel King, the activist group Food Not Bombs, and the Boston Coalition for the Homeless, the police evicted the NUH the next day after it was determined by the city that the building did not meet safety codes and had no utilities (Mehegan, 1986, p. 38). The battle of words continued through December, with the NUH asserting that Flynn had promised it the building, or another similar building, while the city demurred.

By 1988, in the midst of what was then seen as a hotly contested national election between Massachusetts governor Michael Dukakis, who was known for his sympathy toward the issue of homelessness, and then-vice president George H. W. Bush, the *Boston Globe* was describing a split in the ranks of the Democratic Party over legislation. At the request of Mitch Snyder, Massachusetts representative Barney Frank had introduced a bill calling for $15 billion in new annual spending for affordable housing to be financed by taxes on tobacco, corporations, and wealthy individuals. As the *Globe* complained: "The rise in combative tactics and uncompromising demands has strained relations among some of the nation's leading legislative advocates of increased federal spending for affordable housing. And housing activists' insistence on an everything-now strategy has divided liberals into two camps: Those who favor a cautious approach to new legislation, with modest spending attached; and those who support bold action immediately" (Robinson, 1988, p. 3).

Congressman Joseph Kennedy II was scathing in his comments about the bill, noting it had no chance to pass: "What does it prove? The bill is not going anywhere." Representative Frank was apparently then taken aback when mass demonstrations were held in support of the bill, including on Capitol Hill. In an unusual rebuke, Frank said the demonstrations were "unnecessary, unwise, and unfair." According to the *Globe,* Mitch Snyder responded to Frank that he should stick to "legislating while the activists try to mold public opinion" (quoted in Robinson, 1988, p. 3).

As important as this conflict was on its own terms, in a broader view it is unclear whether most of the nation's citizens had an opinion on shelters versus permanent housing, and whether they noticed a split between moderate advocacy and more militant tactics (the media used the terms "advocate" and "activist" interchangeably, and also often spoke of "shelter" and "housing" interchangeably). A 1986 poll showed that most of the public was still leaning toward social pathology (unwillingness to work, drug and alcohol use, and psychological problems) as the cause of homelessness (Shipp, 1986, p. B3). Later polls, while showing increasing sympathy for the homeless, illustrated that many people had seen homeless people in their towns only relatively recently. In 1989, only 51 percent of those polled had seen a homeless person, as opposed to only 36 percent three years earlier (*Chicago Tribune,* "More People See Homeless in Their Towns, Poll Reports," January 23, 1989, p. 4). In such polls, the public was not even asked about housing as a solution to homelessness, but only given the broad options of blaming the economy or social pathology or both.

The possibility of meeting broader, more structural demands as proposed by radicals and some liberals to end homelessness— particularly by altering housing policies, but also through income and other social welfare changes—was remote in the 1980s, and remained so in later decades as well.

Of course, the most emphasized part of the social policy equation was the conservative domination of the White House in the 1980s and, de- pending on the particular years, the majority party in Congress as well. Since the 1930s, housing had become a federal responsibility with the Pub- lic Housing Act. Almost all other initiatives that followed, such as Section 8 housing assistance, came from the federal government as well. The scope of these problems, not only housing but also jobs, social welfare provi- sion, and other related issues, was simply too big for the states, which un- like the federal government were constrained by balanced budgeting and unable to borrow the needed funding. The major Democratic Party critics of Reaganomics, of course, frequently pointed this out, and waxed elo- quent on the federal government's abandonment of the poor.

However, the national administration is only one part of the complexity of social policy. The reality is that, first, few issues concerning poverty would succeed in the period after the early 1970s. No doubt a key factor was the deepening national split—often racially tinged—between many working-class people and the poor. This split also played out between increasingly conservative suburbanites and urban dwellers. These splits around social welfare were vastly deeper and sharper in the United States than in European and other Western societies, and involved an increased lack of concern of suburbanites and rural dwellers for urban areas. Second, a complex issue of equity and queuing exists in every policy. To those who worked most closely on the issue of homelessness, the deep suffering and utter desperation of those affected made homeless people a priority for any help. But to others in society and to rule-makers and policy specialists, this was not necessarily the case. If new housing is built, who should occupy it? Should homeless people jump those on long waiting lists for housing who are living in squalor or are potentially homeless? Or more broadly, is it politically feasible to focus on only the lowest socioeconomic groups in society? If welfare benefits are increased, who will be primarily affected, and, of course, who will pay? If jobs are to be created, then what type and at what pay, and who will finance them? All these questions involve equity issues requiring difficult decisions.

The Social Justice Frame, Part 2: Homeless Families and a Limited Victory in New York City

Few members of the homeless population received a more sympathetic response than homeless families, particularly homeless children. Although there had been homeless women in the depression of the 1930s and no doubt whole families, the nature of society was far different then. Often the "man of the house" who was unemployed left his wife and children to look for work and became homeless in the process. Many soup kitchens actually served only men, not children or women. The children and wives of these men on the streets often remained housed with other families or friends. Others were given residence in almshouses or county or city housing and orphanages. They were often out of sight, in other words. In the post-1960s world of single parents, many homeless families came from a population who could not survive on Aid to Families with Dependent Children in high-rent areas (many states simply froze rental allowances for years, if not decades), or came from the ranks of those who had been cut off from assistance for some reason. Although poor families in the United States, contrary to myth, are no larger than higher-income families, for each homeless mother (two-parent homeless families were a small minority), an average of two children became homeless.

No place had larger numbers of homeless families and children than New York City, which at one point, in 1988, was sheltering 5,218 families for a total of 17,746 people (Blau, 1992, p. 161). As with other aspects of homeless policy, New York stumbled along with emergency measures. Many families were found to be sleeping all night in the emergency assistance units of city welfare departments, on desks, chairs, and floors. As noted in one of the classic studies of homelessness of this period, Jonathan Kozol's *Rachel and Her Children* (1988), these families were like "human pinballs" being bounced between welfare and temporary hotels, which would evict them after twenty-eight days so they did not receive permanent residency. With a waiting list for public housing of eighteen *years,* the "lucky ones" were those who got into the squalid "welfare hotels" that Kozol chronicled so well in his book.

A combination of advocates and journalists (of course including Kozol) made New York City's shelter system a major issue in the 1980s, although no one disputed that New York did more than other cities. As early as 1983, the Legal Aid Society, in a lawsuit against the city, charged "that the families are frequently denied emergency housing or, if granted such housing, are placed in quarters that are dangerous and uninhabitable" (Rule, 1983b, p. A1). The lawsuit gave detailed descriptions of the plight of homeless families being forced to sleep on the streets or in abandoned buildings due to a lack of emergency shelter, or staying in "filthy, violation-ridden hotels" where children in these families were often exposed to violent crime, drugs, and prostitution.

The irony of the "welfare hotels" was that, despite their crumbling tile, nonworking plumbing, overpowering stench, broken elevators, peeling lead paint, and lack of sheets and pillows, they cost more than private housing. A large family could cost the city of New York $3,000 monthly to house, and many pointed out how ludicrous this was. The city's administration was also embarrassed when it was revealed that some of the hotel owners were political contributors to Mayor Edward Koch. Even President Ronald Reagan, when asked to comment on this practice, which was common in most urban areas, not just New York City, replied that, indeed, it would be less expensive to just buy homes for the homeless. Unfortunately, the president did not appear to know the rules of welfare, as Koch and his social service commissioner pointed out:

> "Under current Federal law," the Mayor said, "it's illegal to use Emergency Assistance to Families funds for construction of permanent housing." Federal funds pay half the cost of housing families in welfare hotels. The State Social Services Commissioner, Cesar A. Perales, said, "The fact that we have Federal rules that will allow us to spend this money on hotels and not on building housing for poor people is a disgrace." (New York Times, "Koch Gives Response to Reagan on Hotels," November 21, 1986, p. B3)

The public clamor over the issue mounted, however, and the New York City administration was forced to action. The results were another lesson in limited victories, as each had its problems. First, the city began giving preference to homeless families in its housing authorities. For a short time, families in hotels (some of which were closed) were put into housing units. This measure was not only temporary, but as Joel Blau reports, also extremely divisive, as thousands of residents in public housing were doubled up with their own families and friends (1992, p. 162). Koch also announced a $4.2 billion program of housing construction and rehabilitation in New York, but many of the units developed were hardly low-income and were only affordable to the middle class. This was particularly true of New York City's so-called in rem units, which were housing held by the city for nonpayment of taxes. To get these units off the city's budget, it was easier to invite developers to convert the units to higher-cost housing (Blau, 1992, pp. 166–168).

The combined efforts of advocates, journalists, and some New York City politicians (particularly the city council) did result in some improvement of the scandalous conditions in which homeless families were kept. However, absent a commitment to build low-income housing, each step created conflict among different parts of the population. In the end, most welfare hotels remained standing, and large numbers of homeless families continued to reside in welfare hotels in New York City and elsewhere.

The Mental Illness Frame

As noted in Chapter 4, from the beginning of the "new homeless" crisis in the late 1970s and early 1980s, many people attributed mental illness (and other personal problems such as substance abuse) as the primary cause of homelessness. On a general level, no one disputed that there was a percentage of the population on the streets who were mentally unstable (or used drugs), and in the early days of the crisis, advocates were as likely as anyone to raise concerns about the lack of social services and aid for the homeless mentally ill. As the crisis continued, however, mental illness came to be seen as the only cause of homelessness by some conservatives, a few politicians such as Mayor Ed Koch of New York City, and some claims-makers in the psychiatric professions. In turn, advocates tended to deny the universality of this assertion, and some research and critique suggested that proponents of the mental illness thesis may have overstated their case.

Generally, those who argued that mental illness was the cause of the new homeless crisis cited the decline in the number of beds available in psychiatric hospitals in the United States in recent decades due to deinstitutionalization. Since, however, it could not be shown that a large percentage of homeless people had ever been confined in psychiatric hospitals, the stronger case was that the absence of sufficient hospital beds meant that people who developed serious psychiatric problems beginning in the 1970s were no longer admitted to psychiatric hospitals or that, even if they were hospitalized, they could not be kept there for long. Not only had states sharply cut the number of beds by closing many institutions and downsizing others, but commitment laws had changed radically in most states from the 1950s to the 1970s as well. What had earlier constituted grounds for commitment, such as the vague assertion of "bizarre behavior" or the desire of parents, guardians, or relatives to commit someone who seemed a problem to them, was generally no longer adequate. In most states, commitment required proof of *immediate* harm to others or self certified by two psychiatrists. In New York City, where there certainly were violent incidents such as a mentally ill person pushing someone off a subway platform and a man killing people with a sword on the Staten Island ferry (see *New York Times,* "Why Was Mary Ventura Released?" June 21, 1986, p. 1; Glave, 1986, p. 3), there was a widespread belief that people who roamed the streets should be confined psychiatric hospitals.[2]

Claims-makers from the psychiatric professions split among themselves on whether deinstitutionalization itself was harmful or, as in the liberal critique of the movement, whether it was good in theory but flawed in practice. Most professionals blamed the failure of the federal government, which had set out an idealistic policy in the 1962 Community Mental Health Act, to ever follow up with promised funding and programming to track former psychiatric patients into the community. With a lack of good local treatment centers available as well as other services such as halfway houses and transitional residences and enough clinical personnel to counsel the mentally ill, former patients often failed to maintain their medication regimens or even remain in their apartments and jobs (if any) and found themselves on the streets.

Experts differed too on what should be done about the problem. Many among the psychiatric professions seemed to join advocates in simply making an issue of the homeless mentally ill, demanding services and shelters. For example, John Talbott, the president of the American Psychiatric Association, made several statements in 1984 that were not dissimilar to those of advocates:

> Saying America's homeless mentally ill have become the nation's "untouchables" Dr. John Talbott . . . yesterday called for a national policy to provide them with necessary treatment, food, shelter, and clothing. (Dietz, 1984, p. 1)

> APA president John Talbott "considers the situation a national disgrace
> and tragedy." He notes the need for treatment for [the] severely men-
> tally ill. He does not believe these people's lives represent freedom.
> (Dan Rather, quoted in Vanderbilt Television News Archive, Novem-
> ber 14, 1984, CBS)

However, as the problem continued, some cities, led by New York
under the Koch administration and supported by some ardent
conservative critics such as E. Fuller Torrey (see Torrey, 1988, 1991),
advocated new forms of institutionalization such as civil commitment
that could rest on much looser interpretations of commitment laws, and
gave rhetorical support for increasing the number of psychiatric
institutions and beds, although the latter proposal, given the fiscal
realities, never gained much traction. At least some people who
considered themselves liberal or civil libertarian began to support a
"tough love" approach to the seriously mentally ill homeless. For
example, Karl Fleming, a columnist for the *Los Angeles Times,* wrote:

> It's been fashionable among liberals in recent years to applaud the '60s
> move to "deinstitutionalize" the mentally ill—that is, turn them out of
> state hospitals and shield them against involuntary confinement. Thus
> many well-meaning liberals reacted in alarm and opposition when New
> York City recently began trying to take its more disturbed homeless
> people off the streets and forcibly put them into Bellevue Hospital for
> treatment. But as one who has been studying, and writing about, the
> homeless mentally ill for a long time—and as a fierce defender of
> individual liberty—I am not at all sure New York is wrong. In fact,
> with wet, colder weather upon us in Southern California, bringing with
> it the promise of a long and bitter winter for the homeless, this is a time
> for liberals, lawmakers and the mental-health Establishment to re-
> examine their supposedly humane position. (Fleming, 1987, p. 3)

Despite the fact that many supported the view that mental illness
was a primary cause of increases in homelessness, considerable study
and research often suggested an exaggeration of the causal nature of
deinstitutionalization and lack of sufficient beds in psychiatric hospitals.
First, there are considerable problems in a timeline that supports the
interpretation of mental health policy failure as a primary cause of
homelessness. After all, deinstitutionalization began in the 1950s. As late
as the mid-1970s, there were *no* widespread reports of homelessness,
though (as discussed in Chapter 4) some early reports noted an increase
in the number of mentally ill. But absent the gentrification of housing in

the late 1970s in cities like New York, which led to the wholesale dismantlement of single-room-occupancy (SRO) and boarding-room housing, and absent cuts in social benefits, which featured the mass cutoff of many psychiatric patients from the disability programs of Social Security and Supplemental Security Income, there is little reason to believe that a large number of people with mental illness would have been homeless. The cause was not deinstitutionalization alone or lack of services for the mentally ill, but the same factors that drove a variety of poor people onto the streets in the late 1970s and the 1980s. No doubt the mentally ill were among the most *vulnerable* to homelessness (this view was embraced even by most mainstream homeless researchers, such as Burt, 1993, and Rossi, 1989). Vulnerability to homelessness was also high among those just hanging on to housing and benefits, and to substance users, victims of domestic violence, veterans, and former prisoners, for example.

Others have raised questions about the quality of the research that suggested high numbers of mentally ill among the homeless (with from 25 to 50 percent of the homeless estimated as having a serious mental health problem, though some psychiatrists, for example Ellen Bassuk [see Peszke, 1985], estimate as much as two-thirds of the homeless are mentally ill; later estimates tended to settle by the 1990s at a range of about 25 to 30 percent). Most research did not sample the general homeless population, but rather sampled places like Bellevue Hospital's psychiatric unit (Arce et al., 1983) or only one shelter (Bassuk, cited in Peszke, 1985), or only studied homeless people who had been institutionalized and noted the number who then became homeless afterward (see, for example, Belcher and Toomey, 1988; Fuller, 1991). When research on the general homeless population on the streets was finally undertaken, questions were raised about their validity given the predominately upper-middle-class psychiatrists who conducted this research, which involved very brief interviews with poor people to determine their mental status. As Allan Horwitz (2002) has noted about estimates of the high prevalence of mental health disorders in the general population in the United States, there is a deep self-interest among mental health practitioners to conclude that large numbers of people are mentally ill; the fact that someone says they are depressed or sad on one particular day of questioning may hardly mean that they are seriously ill or will continue to feel this way for an extended period of time. And this process is much more complicated with homeless people, as is well described and critiqued by David Snow and colleagues (1986), who note many different barriers to making sound judgments. They and Ann Bradon Johnson (1990), among others, also question the cause-and-effect relationship between mental illness and homelessness. How do we know that depression and sadness, or even serious delusions or substance abuse, are not effects of living on the streets rather than causes? Some studies of homeless women (who constitute a large number of those diagnosed with mental illness) have argued that this group develops a functional, protective stance when homeless in order to prevent assault and rape, and that such behavior could lead people to view "bag ladies" as "crazy" as well as smelly and unattractive, despite the rationality of their actions (see Golden, 1992, for instance).

Surveys did show that advocates and researchers who criticized personal problems as causing homelessness made little impact on public opinion (as suggested in Chapter 2). Although few well-designed polls were undertaken early in the crisis, one from 1986 found many people citing a combination of "unwillingness to work . . . alcohol or drug problems, and psychological problems" among the homeless (Shipp, 1986, p. B3). Because the poll allowed the choice of multiple causes, there is difficulty in determining respondents' primary beliefs, but economic and housing issues alone were clearly not the dominant popular choice. In 1989, by which time polls on homelessness had become more routine, 50 percent of those surveyed assigned "a lot" of blame to alcohol and drug abuse by the homeless, and 44 percent of those queried in a joint poll conducted by the *New York Times* and *CBS News* blamed mental institutions for "releasing patients who aren't ready to lead normal lives" (*Chicago Tribune,* "More People See Homeless in Their Towns, Poll Reports," January 23, 1989, p. 4). In a poll of New Yorkers the same year, 60 percent said that psychiatric hospitals that released patients who could not lead normal lives were to blame for homelessness, while 49 percent said alcohol and drug abuse were to blame (Barbanel, 1989, p. A1).

The issue of mental health did have the potential to split the movement to help the homeless. An example was the participation of Ellen Bassuk (a Harvard psychiatrist who frequently wrote about the large percentage of homeless people who were mentally ill) in a Boston conference on homelessness. In March 1986, Bassuk's description of the homeless mentally ill caused a woman from the audience to interrupt her. "Don't label us!" shouted the woman, who had lived in Boston-area homeless shelters. As the *Globe* reporter suggested:

In that brief interruption, the woman hit upon a basic disagreement among the 600 persons at Harvard University this week who attended the first nationwide conference on the homeless: Those who consider housing the main issue are clashing with those who warn that mental illness is a problem homeless advocates must grapple with as an increasing number of American families face life on the streets. (Alters, 1986, p. 16)

Later that year, Bassuk's work came under more fire from service providers in the Boston area:

The reaction to Bassuk's study from human-services advocates was generally negative. Much of the criticism came from the men and women who run the homeless shelters in which Bassuk conducted her study and from other human-services workers. Katherine Mainzer of the Massachusetts Coalition for the Homeless said the essential problem with Bassuk's study was that it lost sight of the idea that the fundamental problem confronting the overwhelming majority of homeless families is economic, rather than psychological, emotional, or behavioral. Mainzer also believes Bassuk is simply wrong in her belief that most homeless families would be unable to live successfully on their own without an array of support services. (Kenney, 1986, p. 15)

But no event related to the mentally ill homeless in the 1980s was as dramatic in its newsworthiness as Koch's efforts to "clean up" New York City's streets by forcing at least some homeless people into psychiatric commitment. In 1987, Koch and city officials targeted an African American woman who had long lived on the streets of the fashionable Upper East Side. Known as "Billy Boggs," she was later identified as Joyce Brown. Initially, Koch's efforts seemed to generate positive support among New York City's citizens, despite protests by the Civil Liberties Union and chants at a December demonstration to "free Joyce Brown" (Lambert, 1987, p. B3; Barron, 1987, p. B3).

Interestingly, however, once Brown had been removed from the streets, "cleaned up," and medicated, she became an articulate, strong proponent for the rights of the homeless, and an ardent critic of Koch. As Brown spoke at major events and at elite universities such as Harvard, she pressed her case for housing the homeless, arguing that many "homeless people wind up on the streets because shelters are dirty and violent. Because these people have no permanent home, they soon are classified as mentally ill" (Daley, 1988, p. 86). Although Brown's activism may not have changed many people's minds, Koch's drive to remove the homeless from the streets also failed, and the episode caused much embarrassment for city officials. Brown herself later had a psychiatric relapse and was recommitted to a treatment facility.

While the social construction of homelessness as caused by mental illness can be considered successful if looked upon from the point of view of public opinion, it lacked specific policy objectives to distinguish it from either the mildly liberal, supportive policy frames calling for more shelters and services (as in the social justice and charitable assistance frames) or its co-optation by those who sought repressive solutions (as in the "bum" frame). As a result, the major policy result of the period (the Stewart B. McKinney Homeless Assistance Act, discussed later) incorporated mental health issues (and substance abuse) as a major component, but the mental health frame did not otherwise significantly shape the policies around homelessness.

The "Bum" Frame:
Critics, Conservatives, and Backlash

There were from the beginning of the homeless crisis a variety of dissenters and critics who to varying degrees rejected the idea that homelessness constituted a social crisis, that the causes were other than personal problems, and that the government had any role to play related to the issue. In the early to middle 1980s, this dissent was marginal, but later conservatives began more systemic criticism of the liberal construction of homelessness, and citizens as well as journalists questioned the "trendy" nature of the homeless cause. There was also an increase in reports of what later would be called "hate crimes" against the homeless by various youths in different parts of the country.[3]

Letters in the *Los Angeles Times* early on, for example, dissented from the view of homelessness as a crisis that required government intervention:

> [October 2, 1982] I dispute that there is a need for a government role of providing for the general welfare that includes those who have drugs [*sic*] and alcohol problems. Why must government be the ultimate provider for mental rehabilitation and/or incarceration? It is not only unfortunate but inappropriate that government should be construed as a panacea for society's ills. —Martin J. Paddio of Eagle Rock

> [November 6, 1983] Once again [columnist William] Overend has gone overboard to rescue street people who would rather be left to live (or die) but who have very suddenly been promoted to "Homeless People" whether against their will or not—one can only gather, yes, if it suits the

purpose of the political activists who are determined to use them one way or the other. There is no one who does not know that these activist quacks have never helped anyone and never will. —Wendell McKee of Los Angeles

[December 10, 1983] Why is spending billions more on hunger seen to help when so much hasn't? The liberal Democrats who push more of the same failed programs are those we should be truly outraged at. —Lynn Robert Davis of Granada Hills

In New York City, the backlash against homeless people often came from those who lived in close proximity to homeless people who were described as mentally ill. For example, Jane Kosarin, who lived at Sixty-third Street and Second Avenue in Manhattan, often heard a homeless woman screaming late at night, sometimes continuing for hours, shouting obscenities and intimate details about her life. Kosarin stated: "At first I felt compassion. After all, she's in the street and she needs help. But you can hear her with your windows closed and I haven't slept for nights because of her. It's affected my life and I'm on medication as a result" (quoted in Carmody, 1984, p. B4).

In a 1985 *New York Times* article that focused on West Eleventh Street in Greenwich Village, the negative influence of proximity on perceptions of homeless people was clear:

The presence of Harold and others like him on the block has prompted some spirited discussions among block residents, some of whom find their concern for the homeless heightened and others who now think "the homeless should be locked up," in one man's words. "It's different," said one passer-by, who stopped yesterday morning in front of Harold's [cardboard] box, "when they live in front of your house than when you see them on the TV news." A woman companion asked, "Why doesn't he get out of here and go to a shelter where he belongs?" There is, for instance, the matter of the absolute wild man who lived on the sidewalk for about two years who had the habit of waking the neighborhood nearly every night yelling loud, graphic obscenities. "The man's voice was unbelievably deep and strong," said Harriet Heyman, another resident. "It was like Walter Cronkite gone berserk." "It's a terribly uncomfortable position to be in," said Carl Stein, who owns a town house across from Harold's box, "to be sitting in your living room warm and comfortable and know a man is on your doorstep freezing." Mr. Stein said his 7-year-old daughter frequently had nightmares about the screamer. "For my wife and I," he said, "it's a real dilemma. If having homeless on the sidewalk is simply unsightly and an inconvenience, that's one thing. But when does an inconvenience become so great that it interferes with the way we live?" (Geist, 1985, p. 1)

While such reactions of discomfort are understandable, in some situations residents felt such strong distaste for the homeless that it bordered on hatred. A spirited "not in my backyard" rally in Chicago in 1985 included "Stop the Invaders" signs depicting a spaceship outside a shack surrounded by homeless people sitting around (Fuentes, 1985, p. 3). In 1985 in Santa Monica, California, in response to the large number of homeless people coming to the warm and liberal city, officials advocated that people make citizen's arrests of the homeless, particularly when they panhandled (Burbank, 1985, p. 1). Even more disturbing was a report on *CBS News* in November 1984 called "Community: Intolerance and Violence," which focused on Santa Cruz, California. Dan Rather reported on acts of violence, including the setting of a "transient" on fire, and on the popularity of "Trollbuster" T-shirts, which reflected the "local slang name for transients and street people" (Vanderbilt Television News Archive, November 26, 1984). Such violence and name-calling would become increasingly common across the entire country.

Initially, perhaps following the Reagan administration's general ignoring or minimizing of homelessness (as well as poverty), conservative activists were rather quiet on the subject. Even in the mid-1980s, these activists were not very well publicized in the major newspapers. The *New York Times* in 1983 quoted Thomas Main, a program officer at the private Smith Richardson Foundation, who authored an article in the conservative *Public Interest* criticizing New York City's homeless policy:

> The worst possible shelter policy is one that allows clients to adapt to the "life style" of homelessness. Apart from the moral questions such a position raises, the problem is that if more and more people adapt to homelessness, the demand for shelter will eventually rise to unacceptable levels. New York has locked itself into a policy not unlike the advocates', and which it may not be able to back away from, even as the limitations of such a policy become increasingly obvious. (Goodwin, 1983, p. A1)

Few voices were as prominent in attacking the homeless on the West Coast as that of Los Angeles police chief Darryl Gates, who would clash with other city officials because of his hostility and his frequent roundups of the homeless. For example, in 1983, Gates said:

> I don't question that there should be some additional temporary housing, but I think you have a lot of people out there who wouldn't use it if it was available. I think they're really happy just plopping on our soil.

That's what they want. While [the] Board of Supervisors moved in one direction, [the] City Council has moved an ordinance to ban people from sleeping in cars parked on streets and another being considered that would make it against the law to sleep on park benches. Gates wants to strengthen local trespass laws and have mandatory work programs for those found guilty of violating them. (Overend, 1983c, p. 1)

The Heritage Foundation, a major conservative think tank, was quoted by the National Coalition of the Homeless as opposing all spending on the homeless and as suggesting that "federal relief programs for the homeless will simply produce another coalition of bureaucrats and activists" (*Newsletters of the National Coalition for the Homeless* 3, no. 1 [July 1985]). In a column that was critical of homeless activism, *Chicago Tribune* reporter Stephen Chapman quoted a joint study by the Cato Institute and the Manhattan Institute (two other conservative think tanks) that had shown through "sophisticated statistical analysis" that of all the factors predicting homelessness, the strongest was the existence of rent control, a clear stab at liberal supporters of this policy (Chapman, 1987, p. 3).

The major opposition voiced in newspapers, and a particular theme in the more conservative *Chicago Tribune,* came through critiques of advocacy for the homeless as being a "trend" that seemed to meet the needs of the middle class and elite and to promote more government and other liberal agendas. For example, *Boston Globe* columnist David Wilson took on the idea of "affordable housing" as a vague and malleable concept that could be used by advocates and politicians to mean whatever they wanted:

Recently, advocacy groups have been marshaling their forces behind campaigns designed to raise public assistance entitlement levels to the federally designated poverty line and to amend the Massachusetts Constitution to establish a "right" to housing. This kind of demagogic overkill generates backlash from people who feel threatened by the poor. Worse, for people on welfare and without housing or in wretched housing, it encourages a belief that the government is going to make available to them a standard of living equal to that obtained by people who work, thereby rendering work undesirable and, indeed, contemptible. (Wilson, 1986, p. 15)

In one of several long critiques of homeless activism in the *Chicago Tribune,* columnist Raymond Coffey took on the "sleep out" efforts of young congressman Joseph Kennedy II of Massachusetts to publicize homelessness as a problem:

Young Joe Kennedy and a small herd of other political and show business celebrities and would-be celebrities spent one night this week sleeping out on some of the grates through which warmth rises from Washington's underground steam heat pipes. Their alleged purpose was to draw attention to the sorry plight of the homeless who spend every wintry night sleeping on those grates in the nation's capital and of the homeless everywhere. What they principally accomplished, though, was to demonstrate that epidemic brainlessness among the chic may be a greater blight on America than homelessness. The demonstration of alleged concern and compassion for the homeless was advertised as "The Grate American Celebrity Sleep out" (the pun on great passes for wit and cleverness among such people), and it was timed to coincide with congressional consideration of a $500 million homeless-relief bill. What it really amounted to, however, was yet another of those silly, phony, self-indulgent, self-serving, self-promoting exercises in which the oh-so-liberal well-off relieve their consciences and make themselves feel good—superior, even—by playing a one-night stand as St. Francis or Mother Teresa. . . . Did it ever occur to them, or their celebrity friends, that some of the homeless who spend every night on the grates might have appreciated it more if the Kennedys had invited them home for the night, for a hot bath, clean sheets, a warm bed and a big breakfast? With the kind of money he blew on his political campaign, Kennedy wouldn't even have had to take any of the wretched and unwashed into one of his homes. He could have put up the entire homeless population of Washington in a fancy downtown hotel for the night. . . . Now that "The Grate American Celebrity Sleep out" is over, the fundamental question is this: Who got more out of it, the miserable homeless or the "gosh, aren't we warm and wonderful human beings" celebrities and self-promoters who got their names in the newspapers and their faces on TV? (Coffey, 1987, p. 21)

Many of these critiques, of course, hit on some of the problems with advocacy for the homeless: its often symbolic, vague nature, somewhat detached from broad policy proposals, as well as its long-term class contradiction, with most activism for the poor in the United States (at least in recent years) being undertaken by elites and the wealthy rather than working-class or poor people (see Croteau, 1995, for an excellent discussion of social class and liberal politics).

Yet what is most striking in the criticism of journalists and conservatives, the negative editorials, the "not in my backyard" movements, and even the beginning of hate crimes and cruel satire of the homeless (in 1987, "bag lady dolls" made their appearance throughout the nation) is the lack of immediate impact on the relatively liberal and compassionate construction of homelessness. It is true that had prominent politicians and officeholders proposed radical reforms to end homelessness, they might have had to contend with serious opponents. But the vague sympathy that was shown by polls supporting at least some funding for the homeless (e.g., Shipp, 1986, p. B3; *Newsletters of the National Coalition for the Homeless* 1–3 [1988]) and the failure of the Reagan administration to mount a major effort to oppose all spending, as we shall see, led in 1987 to the first (and only) federal legislative victory for the advocates. Despite the important presence of the mental illness "expert support" policy frame and the "bum" argument, at this point the sympathetic appeal to compassion for the homeless was stronger. But the social justice and charitable assistance frames had limited power to significantly influence policy and would lose momentum when those who were less committed to spending large sums of money (or changing power relationships) no longer felt compassionate.

The Stewart B. McKinney Homeless Assistance Act: A Major Advocacy Victory

Both the success and the limitations of advocacy and public support for aid to the homeless were illustrated in the signature piece of legislation passed by Congress in 1987, initially titled the Urgent Relief for the Homeless Act and later named after Congressman Stewart McKinney, a Republican representative from Connecticut who died that year. The bill had its origins early in 1987 when Robert Hayes of New York City's Coalition for the Homeless offered to work with the Reagan administration and anyone else to pass homeless legislation (*Newsletters of the National Coalition for the Homeless* 4–5 [January 1987]), supported by protesters led by the Community for Creative Non-Violence, who camped out for seven weeks on Capitol Hill (Pear, 1987, p. A1). Perhaps most important, however, were the politics of the upcoming pre–presidential election year. Democratic liberals convinced Speaker of the House Jim Wright to make the bill a priority, hoping the issue would become popular at election time. Faced with this relatively small but "feel good" measure, most Republican representatives supported it, though a few tried to kill it with amendments. Nevertheless, early versions passed the House by a vote of 264 to 121 and the Senate by a vote of 85 to 12, followed by a vote of 65 to 8 in the Senate for final approval (Curry, 1987, p. 6; Lauter, 1987, p. 1; *Los Angeles Times,* "House Concerned About Cost," 1987, p. 4). Although President Reagan signed the bill on July 24, 1987, he did so in the evening, in an unusual move to signal his displeasure (Pear, 1987, p. A1).

The bill certainly was a victory for advocates, but, aside from additions and amendments in later years, it would be their last. Funding for the bill, nearly $1 billion over two years, was insufficient, and to the frustration of advocates and liberal supporters, neither Reagan nor his successor, George H. W. Bush, would ever authorize release of the full amount. Generally, through state and local governments, the bill established a variety of grants—some competitive, some allocated in blocks, some allocated by formula—to support emergency food and shelter programs and health services (including mental health), authorized the conversion of government property into facilities for the homeless, relaxed federal Food Stamp rules to allow homeless people to receive aid, provided grants for community agencies to undertake job training, authorized the Department of Housing and Urban Development to provide community-based housing and transitional housing for the homeless, and, finally, established the Interagency Council for the Homeless, which brought together the heads of fifteen federal agencies to "coordinate programs and to assess the true extent of homelessness" (Pear, 1987, p. A1).

Despite praise from Hayes and the Coalition for the Homeless (see Lauter, 1987, p. 1; Pear, 1987, p. A1; *Newsletters of the National Coalition for the Homeless* 7, no. 3 [May 1988]), the act resulted in few unqualified victories, with federal recognition of the problem of homelessness and increased availability of Food Stamp aid being the most obvious. Despite recognition of the need for housing, both transitional and permanent, the vast majority of McKinney monies would be used for shelters and food grants. The Interagency Council was judged a failure early on by advocates, as it did little to influence policy and exercised little leadership. It was abolished in 1993. When Joel Blau wrote his book *The Visible Poor* several years later, he praised the McKinney Act as a piece of "showcase legislation," but criticized its complexity, which created huge delays and bureaucratic paperwork for local providers that "entangled them in red tape" (1992, p. 113). Taking a broader view with the benefit of hindsight, Kim Hopper noted that the McKinney victory was purchased at the expense of miring advocates in "beltway politics" that "ensures a trap of its own making":

The McKinney Act made much possible, but for advocates it was a victory purchased on the installment plan . . . enormous energy and organizational resources went into making sure it was renewed, expanded. . . . In the process, advocates find themselves not only beholden to a growing constituency of programs dependent on federal funding but also bound to the state in a cross-cousin marriage of political convenience. Inconveniently, special-interest advocacy is one of those unendearing practices that pits potential allies against one another and works against broader movement building. (2003, p. 196)

Even at the time, at least some advocates were skeptical that anything but massive housing construction could solve the homeless problem. In a March 1987 *Chicago Tribune* article on an early version of the McKinney Act, an advocate, Barry Zigas of the National Low-Income Housing Coalition in Washington, D.C., remarked: "There's the sheer lack of availability and increased competition for housing. . . . At the same time, it's ironic that Congress is moving all this money out but not providing any real, permanent shelter." In the same article, George Stone, Chicago's first deputy commissioner for housing, remarked: "The Reagan administration suddenly discovered the homeless as a problem, but no one seems to want to talk about the basic problem—that there's not enough homes" (quoted in Curry, "House Oks More Homeless Aid," p. 6).

On the one hand, then, the passage of the McKinney Act reflects the ability of advocates and supporters, through vague notions of compassion and charity, to somewhat define the debate on homelessness in the 1980s and neutralize conservative opposition to the point where Reagan and conservatives fell silent. On the other hand, as with some other legislative victories under the George H. W. Bush and Bill Clinton administrations (such as the Ryan White AIDS Act of 1990 and the Family Leave Act of 1993),[4] Congress essentially provided a small amount of aid that would serve as a vehicle (intentionally or not) to entice service providers and advocates into an annual battle for money, and to divert some of the attention to "beltway politics." Passage of the McKinney Act also suggested a change in political approach that George H. W. Bush and later presidents (Clinton, George W. Bush, Barack Obama) would take regarding some of the liberal and leftist causes of the 1980s, which was to stop denying the existence of social problems and instead embrace solutions (though minimalist) to these problems. Ironically, however, for the problem of homelessness, the country would begin to suffer "compassion fatigue" and the issue would never regain the importance it assumed in the mid-1980s.

Notes

1. These citations and generalizations represent my own familiarity with the homeless movement. There may well be other correlations that can be made between those who pressed for shelters and those who criticized them.

2. Unfortunately, the "homeless mentally ill" became a major media construct in New York City. In media accounts, it is sometimes quite unclear whether an act of violence or bizarre behavior was committed by an actual homeless person (or simply a shabby-looking person) or whether the mentally ill person was actually homeless (as opposed to wandering away briefly from a family or a single-room-occupancy residence). The media tended to generalize about these acts.

3. The 1986–1988 period alone saw article titles such as the following: "Three Admit Beating Man to Death in Quincy" (*Boston Globe,* February 26, 1986, p. 34); "2 Held in Burbank Park Assaults; Boys Accused of Beating Homeless" (*Los Angeles Times,* July 16, 1987, p. 7); "Teens Accused of Torching Homeless Pair" (*Chicago Tribune,* August 30, 1987, p. 26); "Homeless Man Dies After Being Set Afire" (*Chicago Tribune,* January 18, 1988, p. 2); "Two Homeless Men Set Afire by Youths at a Bus Terminal" (*New York Times,* January 20, 1988, p. B2); "Woman Burned While Sleeping in Deserted Bus" (*New York Times,* July 7, 1988, p. B2); "Two Killings in Lowell Put Homeless on Edge" (*Boston Globe,* September 22, 1988, p. 39).

4. Similarly, the decision of Reagan and George H. W. Bush to support passage of the Americans with Disabilities Act (1988) was another example of the changing Republican reaction to some reform measures. While this act, because of its civil rights status, was more significant than other legislation, its vagueness led to considerable disappointments for disability activists and people with disabilities, who found the act, particularly in its workplace sections, extremely weak (see, for example, O'Brien, 2004).

6

Criminalization and Compassion Fatigue, 1989–1993

[There is a] backlash, a psychic numbing over the homeless. . . .
Politically, the issue isn't there; it's gone.
—Mitch Snyder, Community for Creative Non-Violence, July 1990

After the period of charitable concern for the homeless of the early and middle 1980s, the mood in the United States seemed to change profoundly, as Mitch Snyder noted shortly before his suicide in July 1990. Most observers began to talk about a "backlash" against the homeless and "compassion fatigue" among Americans. One clear indicator of such a backlash was the widespread use of police across the nation to clear the streets of homeless people, which in some cases (such as in the Lower East Side of New York City) involved violence, directed not only at homeless people but also at allies and advocates. Another was the cutbacks in programs intended to prevent homelessness or to assist the very needy, which struck particularly hard in the midst of the 1990–1991 recession. This change in mood fits the "sober realization" stage of Anthony Downs's (1972) issue attention cycle.

Criminalization: Rousting and Banning the Homeless

As discussed in Chapter 3, there was nothing new about using police to roust the "bums" and "tramps" and send them to jail; some cities and counties began using this tactic in the early and middle 1980s, and by the late 1980s and early 1990s this strategy had been widely reintroduced throughout the United States. Effectively, homelessness had become criminalized, and advocates were stunned by the change in mood. Although few US cities (and towns and counties) escaped the trend, the most newsworthy battles occurred in Miami and New York City, as well as several cities in California. Political consequences for officials who were perceived as supporting the rights of the homeless also became costly.

One of the first laws to bring widespread attention to the criminalization tactic was Miami's ordinance in 1988 to allow arrests of homeless people, under certain conditions, if they lived on the streets (Schmalz, 1988, p. A1). Street people were prohibited from sleeping, cooking, bathing, urinating, building temporary shelter, and disturbing public grounds or bushes. Those arrested would be booked, fingerprinted, held, and then released in an area other than the one in which they were seized. Police officials claimed to have received many complaints from businesspeople provoking them to act. Indeed, in Miami, one owner of a grocery store called the measure "the best law they ever proposed," claiming his business had declined 25 percent in two years because of homeless people. Noting that the city lacked public shelters and social services to assist the homeless, advocates charged that "Miami is to the homeless what Selma, Alabama was to blacks in the 1960's" (Bob Hayes, quoted in *Newsletters of the National Coalition for the Homeless* 7, no. 9 [December 1988]). Charging that the crackdown was aimed at clearing the streets ahead of the Orange Bowl festivities and the upcoming National Football League game, the American Civil Liberties Union took the case, but was refused an injunction (Kay and Conklin, 1989, p. 2).

Indeed, three years later, it was reported that 3,500 people had been arrested in Miami for sleeping in public or even for littering when they were found lying on cardboard boxes. Foreshadowing what Mayor Rudolph Giuliani would later do in New York City in his efforts to repress the "squeegee men" who cleaned car windows, Miami also passed laws that made approaching motorists to panhandle or wash windows an offense, punishable by a fine of up to $500 and a jail sentence of up to sixty days (Wilkerson, 1991, p. 3).

Interestingly, just as other municipalities, counties, and towns were adopting such strategies, in November 1992 a federal judge ordered the Miami law overturned and demanded that the city establish "safe zones" in which homeless people could freely eat and sleep without harassment or fear of arrest (*Los Angeles Times*, "Judge Orders Miami 'Safe Zones'

Where Homeless Won't Be Rousted," November 17, 1992, p. 17). Though this was seen by civil rights attorneys and advocates as a major victory, Miami had still successfully sent the message that the homeless should not come there or expect services, and would receive harsh treatment if they tried. This message signaled the growing conservativeness of the public regarding homelessness, crime, drugs, and related issues.

A series of bans on homeless people by New York City officials beginning in the late 1980s and continuing well into the 1990s made the changed environment more real. In two highly publicized but different moves, the city (first under Mayor Ed Koch and then under his presumably more liberal successor, David Dinkins) enacted laws to remove the thousands of homeless people from the transportation centers and subways where they lived, and also to remove homeless people and others from the city's parks, the latter of which involved skirmishes with members of a widespread squatting movement.

Removing homeless people from city transportation centers had begun earlier, at the major bus and train terminals, such as the downtown bus terminal, where fixed seats were replaced with narrow plastic "flip seats," which were difficult to sleep on. But in October 1989, an edict to remove homeless people from the subways—whether they were begging or simply sleeping in the trains—meant that thousands of people were to be thrown out of the underground. New York officials claimed to be reacting to a torrent of public outrage about begging and homeless people generally, and cited this outrage as a possible reason (though with no evidence) for a decline in ridership of the subway system. Interviewed by the *New York Times,* Lynette Thompson, a New York City Transit Authority official, said: "At the beginning of last year, the tenor of those letters [complaining about the homeless] was, 'Please do something to help the homeless.' But since August and September, they've been saying: 'Just get them out. I don't care. Just get them out any way you can.' It got worse, and people got fed up." Even riders who were sympathetic to the homeless complained: "There's just too much of it," said Diane Sonde, director of Project Reachout, which served the homeless mentally ill on the Upper West Side. "You can't get away from it. People are tired of going to their neighborhood bank machine and [encountering] someone asking for money." Paula Dubrow, a freelance graphic designer who worked at a homeless shelter at a synagogue on the Upper West Side, said she gave money to people on the street. But she had come to dread riding the subway, because of the parade of panhandlers working their way through the cars (quoted in Rimer, 1989, p. 1).

As advocate Keith Summa of the Coalition for the Homeless had earlier predicted, in this case the scope of the action was so great that it would not easily succeed: "They really aren't going to be able to get people out of the subway. Overall, it's a waste of resources. We have real crime in the subway, and I think most commuters will agree that it would be better to use our police resources on [that]" (quoted in Curry, 1989, p. 6). Indeed, in January 1990, district court judge Leonard B. Sand overturned the New York City Transit Authority edict as unconstitutional, ruling that panhandling was a form of free speech (Sims, 1990, p. 1). But even in May of that year, when the US Court of Appeals ruled that the New York City Transit Authority could ban begging, interviews with police officers indicated considerable ambivalence and reluctance to exercise their new role:

> "My mother always told me never to kick a dog when he's down," said one officer at the Union Square station, who, like other officers interviewed yesterday, asked not to be identified. "Well, these are people not dogs, and I would have difficulty kicking some of these people out of here." A transit officer on patrol at the West 72nd Street station said: "To whom and when does this ruling apply? I don't know. Do we arrest people who are sitting on the ground with a cup and aren't saying anything?" (Quoted in Sims, 1990, p. 1)

The difficulty in enforcing this broad law in the city that was home to the largest homeless population in the country did not prevent angry citizens from applauding the policy: "A dirty, smelly, disgusting person with his or her hand out is the last person I want in my face after a busy day in the office," said Joyce Tucker, an executive secretary from Queens and frequent commuter on the N train. "I am sorry that they are destitute, but I work hard to pay for my ride on the subways and deserve something a little more civilized" (quoted in Sims, 1990, p. 25). Former mayor Ed Koch also applauded his successor's policy: "[Homelessness is] destroying our society, it's destroying our subway system, it's destroying our parks. It's an imposition on the traveler to have to walk in an atmosphere where he or she feels threatened or the place just stinks because of people urinating or sitting on the floor in filth. They should be removed" (quoted in Tye, 1990, p. 1).

If New York City officials believed they had a hard task on their hands in banning panhandling on the subways, the battle over New York City's parks would be even harder. For unlike in the subways, many homeless people in the parks had bonded with nonhomeless people and allies. Particularly problematic was the Lower East Side (and the East Village), which was undergoing a wave of gentrification that was displacing thousands of people, an assortment of squatters and other poor people, leftists including anarchists, and even "punk rockers and drug dealers," according to the police chief, who stood shoulder-to-shoulder with the homeless (quoted in George, 1988, p. A1). When the city tried to enforce a park curfew of 1 A.M., hundreds of protesters at Tompkins Square Park in the East Village clashed with mounted tactical police, which led to many arrests and injuries and charges of police brutality (McFadden, 1988, p. A1; see also George, 1988, p. A1).

After some regrouping on the part of city officials, New York not only reimposed the curfew that winter at all parks, but also issued a set of draconian ordinances that would eliminate the homeless from many public areas of the city. Announced by Parks and Recreation commissioner Henry J. Stern (quoted in Dunlap, 1989b, p. B1), the ordinances included:

- No individual person shall lie upon or spread possessions upon a bench so as to interfere with its use by other persons.
- No person shall reside in a park or sleep overnight or make preparation to sleep overnight, including laying down of bedding, or creating or building a shelter or other structure for the purpose of comfort or protection during sleep.
- No person shall possess, store, accumulate, stockpile or warehouse personal belongings within or adjacent to any park which cause or create the appearance that such person actually lives or intends to live or sleep overnight in the park.
- No person shall leave personal belongings unattended within or adjacent to any park for more than two consecutive hours.
- No person shall use any water fountain, drinking fountain, pool, sprinklers, reservoir, lake or any other water contained in the park for the purpose of washing or cleaning himself or herself, his or her clothing or other personal belongings.
- No person shall appear in any park under the influence of alcohol, or other drug to the degree that he may endanger himself, other persons or property, or unreasonably annoy persons in his vicinity.
- No person shall engage in any commercial activity or commercial speech in any park, except in connection with public entertainment pursuant to a permit.
- No begging and panhandling in all parks and streets adjacent to or abutting a park (including sidewalks of such abutting streets).

Predictably, advocates denounced the imposition of curfews and ordinances. Robert Hayes characterized the imposition of a curfew as "so much nonsense and pretense" as to be essentially a "meaningless gesture" (quoted in Levine, 1989a, p. B1). The Reverend James Parks Morton, dean of the Cathedral of St. John the Divine, wrote to Commissioner Stern, saying: "I fear in all this the appearance of a 'sweep mentality' as a response to homelessness. For this city to keep its integrity—even its soul—homelessness has to be regarded primarily as a human emergency, not a public nuisance." And George Horton, director of the Office for the Homeless and Hungry at Catholic Charities, said: "This kind of rule-making is one more assault on people who are assaulted every day. As long as we're not doing justice to them, we ought to be careful when we start to take away people's ability to survive" (quoted in Dunlap, 1989a, p. A31).

These statements appear to have had little effect, and on July 6, 1989, about 200 police officers and a dozen Parks Department workers tore down the homeless shantytown at Tompkins Square Park, where, according to the *New York Times,* about 100 people were living. Seventeen people were arrested for disorderly conduct and eight people, including six police officers, were injured. The next night about 200 people protested, chanting: "Out of the park and into the street, no police state." Protesters also burned an American flag, while many in the crowd said they were enraged by the police action. Several threw glass bottles at the police (*New York Times,* "Razing of Shanties Starts Confrontation in Tompkins Square," July 6, 1989, p. B4). The issue of the parks encampments in general, and Tompkins Square in particular, just would not go away. From 1989 to 1991, a guerrilla war was waged around Tompkins Square, with homeless people and squatters and their supporters erecting tents and flags, only to have police remove them. Every so often the small confrontations grew larger; in December 1989, for example, police and officials equipped with fire engines and Parks Department trucks again dismantled the shantytown, with protesters chanting: "Sieg heil," "No housing, no peace," and "New York City, you can't hide; we charge you with genocide" (Kifner, 1989, p. B1; see also Tom Brokaw, cited in Vanderbilt Television News Archive, December 15, 1989, NBC). Again, on June 3, 1991, for example, hundreds of police officers drove about 200 homeless people from Tompkins Square Park (Kifner, 1991, p. A1).

Though Tompkins Square was the most visible site of the battles between police and the homeless, New York City officials also drove out encampments of homeless people at Riverside Park on the Upper West Side, and in front of the New York Coliseum in Columbus Circle in Midtown. Moreover, police and others engaged in a cat-and-mouse battle with squatters in the East Village and elsewhere. For example, in 1989, hundreds of police were used to clear a former school building of squatters in the Lower East Side, leading to thirty-eight arrests (McKinley, 1989b, p. 1). In the Bronx in 1990, 200 police officers and fire marshals evicted homeless families from an apartment (Nieves, 1990, p. B2).

In some ways, New York City exemplified the most intense "class struggle" aspects of the conflict over homelessness as well as gentrification, drawing in tenants and at least some radicals and citizens who were angry about housing. As an out-of-work carpenter predicted after a Tompkins Square Park raid: "Within five years, the [Lower] East Side will be just as preppie as the West Side. You've got people paying $2,000 a month in rent, and they don't want this eyesore [the park]" (quoted in McKinley, 1989a, p. B1). Yet in all likelihood, for each person showing support, there were many who saw the issue only in "quality of life" terms. A mother with a young daughter in a stroller was quoted in the *New York Times* as saying: "I want to have this park back. It's impossible to enjoy the park when people are living here" ("I Want This Park Back," July 8, 1989, p. 1). In a *New York Times* editorial, a mother complained of heroin and crack addicts among the park dwellers and of finding hypodermic needles:

> My grandmother came to the Lower East Side from a Communist country and my mother still lives here. I have lived here all 33 years of my life and presently work in a local day care center, where one of our students was pricked with a used hypodermic needle found while playing in the park. I am raising my children here, as difficult as Tompkins Square Park's present status makes that task. We are hardly the "yuppie scum" so frequently depicted in the press accounts regarding the park. My family and I would like to be able to use the park and be able to invite people. (Acevedo, 1990, p. 1)

In California, while events lacked the violence of the Tompkins Square Park altercations, tempers flared and, in some cases, virulent anti-homeless rhetoric marked the scene. In the seaside community of Santa Cruz in 1990, for example, more than 500 protesters staged a Fourth of July "Take Back the Town" demonstration against "bums" and "squatters." The anti-homeless protesters "collected more than 2,000 signatures to extend countywide an ordinance that prohibited camping in Santa Cruz city parks" (Casuso, 1990, p. 1). When a pro-homeless rally was held, it sparked an angry counter-demonstration, with participants shouting, "Homeless, go to hell!" (Agnos, 1990, p. 7).

California's cities seemed to compete that summer over which could be the toughest on the homeless. In scenic Santa Barbara, the city council voted for what would later be described as the most stringent anti-homeless law in the country, one that banned the homeless from all public streets, beaches, sidewalks, and parking lots (*Los Angeles Times,* "Homeless Action Causes Shame, Dismay," June 30, 1991, p. 4; Wilkerson, "Plight of Homeless Losing U.S. Attention," 1991, p. 3). Advocates for the homeless felt so strongly opposed to the law that many came to Santa Barbara from Los Angeles by bus to join a protest. Many of the protesters slept on Santa Barbara's streets, baiting police to arrest them (Corwin, 1990, p. 35).

In 1990, Orange County city Santa Ana rounded up homeless people who lived downtown and confined them. As would later be recounted in a court case, police officers stationed atop buildings spotted homeless individuals with binoculars and radioed their location to officers patrolling the streets. Officers on the ground arrested the homeless individuals, handcuffed them, and drove them to Eddie West Field for booking and fingerprinting. At the stadium, police officers chained the homeless to benches for up to six hours without food or water. City officials also confiscated and destroyed the possessions of the homeless. Santa Ana subsequently paid $50,000 to settle lawsuits brought by homeless persons whose property had been destroyed by city employees. A year later, the city paid $400,000 to settle lawsuits brought by homeless persons arrested during the course of this sweep (*Los Angeles Times,* "Bureaucracy Watch: Homeless Go-Round," August 29, 1990, p. 6; Rivera and Eng, 1991, p. 1; Martinez, 1992, p. 4). Astoundingly, in light of the court's "stinging rebuke" of the city and the monetary settlements, Santa Ana as well as the nearby cities of Fullerton and Orange moved in 1992 to again ban homeless people (Simon, 1992, p. 9).

Most of the nationally covered backlashes against the homeless seemed to take place in San Francisco and Santa Monica, perhaps because of their reputations as liberal cities and also because the issue of homeless had become so politicized there. Few cities had as liberal a reputation as Santa Monica, the trendy Los Angeles suburb that was even dubbed "Soviet Monica" by opponents. Known as a "haven for the homeless," a considerable backlash arose there in 1990, triggered in part by the killing of an eighty-nine-year-old woman by a vagrant wielding scissors. Leslie Dutton led an anti-homeless group that called for ending a "no questions asked" food program, a ban on homeless panhandling, and later an ordinance, as in other California cities, to ban the homeless from living on the streets. As reported nationally:

> Santa Monica has been a haven for the homeless, feeding 350 people
> a day on the City Hall lawn, providing shelter and medical care, and
> generally assisting alcoholics, former mental patients and others with
> nowhere to live and no one who cares. But now thousands of residents
> in the affluent Los Angeles suburb are saying enough is enough. They
> want the homeless jailed for drinking or sleeping in public, handouts
> withheld from the able-bodied and the city attorney thrown out for
> allegedly coddling the ne'er-do-wells. (Tye, 1990, p. 1)

The anti-homeless campaign centered on Robert Myers, the liberal city
attorney, who refused to endorse anti-homeless legislation. Dutton and
his group, Santa Monicans for the Citizens Protection Act, secured a
ballot question known as "Proposition Z" to change the city attorney's
position from an appointed one to an elected one. However, the
proposition failed on the November 1990 ballot.

The group continued its agitation, however, even making T-shirts
saying "Greetings from Santa Monica, Skid Row by the Sea" (Hill-
Holtzman, 1991, p. 1). Pressure by citizens and by a commission
appointed to develop a new policy on homelessness eventually forced
Myers to write an anti-encampment law. After a few attempts at
compromise, Myers eventually "refused to write an 'oppressive' law
aimed at preventing people from living in the city's parks" (*Los Angeles
Times,* "Official Refuses to Draft Law to Oust Homeless," January 23,
1992, p. 2). In June 1992, Santa Monica ended its food program, and in
September the city council fired Myers (Hill-Holtzman, 1992b, p. 9; Hill-
Holtzman, 1992a, p. 1).

Interestingly, actor and homeless activist Martin Sheen would join
Myers in leading a "feed in" to protest the new law (*Los Angeles Times,*
"Santa Monica: 'Feed-In' Protests Law to Curb Homeless Gatherings,"
March 13, 1993, p. 2). More important, as in Miami, Santa Ana, and
elsewhere, the courts eventually ruled the anti-homeless legislation
passed by Santa Monica unconstitutional, given their determination that
the banning of large groups acted as a "prior restraint" on free speech
(Hill-Holtzman, 1993, p. 1).

San Francisco, like Santa Monica, had a reputation for being among
the more liberal cities of the United States and also, under Mayor Art
Agnos, a former social worker, a "good" city for the homeless. However,
by this period (1989–1990), Agnos began to use force to keep homeless
people out of certain areas. In 1989, Agnos confronted activists and
homeless people in front of city hall and ordered them out of the plaza;
also that year the city began gating its subway entrances at night to keep

the homeless out (Basheda, 1989, p. 31; Rimer, 1989, p. 1). By 1990, Agnos was backing wide police sweeps aimed at removing the homeless from parks and plazas, saying they were better off in the city's shelters (Peter Jennings, cited in Vanderbilt Television News Archive, July 6, 1990, ABC; *Los Angeles Times,* "Homeless Rousted from S.F. Civic Center," July 7, 1990, p. 30).

Yet Agnos seems to have lost his reelection campaign greatly due to his perceived early liberalism on the homeless issue and the perceived deterioration of the city. In a lead-up article to the late 1991 campaign, the *Chicago Tribune* noted: "now the focus is on the underside of life, the panhandling, litter and graffiti that seem to have multiplied in recent years. Residents are tired of facing the homeless in the streets, according to polls, and suburbanites are staying home rather than venture into a city they view as inhospitable" (Adams, 1991, p. 22).

Conservative former police officer Frank Jordan, in his bid for mayor against Agnos, used the homeless issue in his campaign ads, which included images of a homeless man pushing a shopping cart. Jordan called on the city to get tough on the homeless and accused Agnos of making San Francisco a "magnet for the homeless." Although other issues were of course raised in the campaign, Jordan's victory in December 1991 was read clearly as a backlash against the homeless (Adams, 1991, p. 22; Reuters, 1991, p. 16; Warren and Paddock, 1991, p. 3).

Although not every city cracked down on the homeless, the many articles on "backlash" and "compassion fatigue" in the early 1990s also noted actions in Atlanta, Georgia (police sweeps to rid city streets of the homeless in preparation for the Olympic Games); Portland, Oregon; Chicago, Illinois (police sweeps to evict homeless encampments from O'Hare Airport); Phoenix, Arizona; Philadelphia, Pennsylvania; Washington, D.C.; Berkeley and San Jose, California; Richmond, Virginia; and even Martinsburg, West Virginia. And the political tide was turning, as was clearly evident in Washington, D.C.'s 1990 vote rescinding an earlier vote to provide shelter to all homeless people. Although mayoralty and gubernatorial elections are always subject to multiple issues, several elections, such as the defeat in Massachusetts of Democrat Michael Dukakis to Republican William Weld in 1990 and certainly the later victory of Rudolph Giuliani in New York City in 1994, can be attributed to the packaging of "homelessness" alongside crime, drugs, and other disorders that were claimed to be imperiling urban life.

It should be noted that to many citizens and self-described moderate politicians (even liberal ones like Agnos), the fact that shelters had been built and other services provided served as a basis for a new consensus in the 1990s (see Chapter 7) that those remaining on the streets had only themselves to blame, because they were somehow recalcitrant. As a result of this consensus for a new criminology, many efforts to "clear the streets" of the homeless would no longer make headline news in later years. It is important to keep this in mind, as many politicians insisted that they were not "anti-homeless," but only against disorder and crime.

Cutting Services and Benefits to the Homeless

The many articles noting the changing mood toward homelessness also revealed significant cutbacks in a variety of states and municipalities in this period, in some cases erasing gains made only recently for the poor and the homeless. These cutbacks were widespread by the early 1990s, with the situations in Philadelphia, Pennsylvania; Massachusetts; and Illinois being prime examples.

Between 1989 and 1992, Mayor Wilson Goode's administration in Philadelphia made dramatic cuts in the city's homeless services. Despite strong protests (see, for example, *Los Angeles Times,* "Hearing on Aid Cuts Disrupted in Philadelphia," April 22, 1989, p. 20), the city halved the number of its shelter beds and the number of homeless people served (Tye, 1990, p. 1). The city also instituted a mandatory fee for homeless people—a practice that was adopted by other cities—who now had to pay for their shelter, as well as income restrictions in order for homeless people to qualify for shelter (Dugger, 1992, p. A31). The city also banned drug abusers from the shelters, and began a program of random drug testing. In addition to these measures, Philadelphia joined the long list of cities that were banning homeless people from sleeping on the streets, and began using street sweepers to remove their belongings (a practice later ruled unconstitutional). Business leaders applauded, having earlier charged that "it is nearly impossible for . . . patrons to walk without being importuned by beggars or having to sidestep inert bodies." The Center City Proprietors Association added that crack addicts and homeless people had laid "siege" to downtown Philadelphia, driving customers to suburban malls (Hinds, 1990, p. A14). Opponents like Sister Mary Scullion, a Roman Catholic nun who directed Women of Hope, remarked of the street sweeps: "Doesn't it remind you of South Africa, which used to ban certain people from certain places?" (quoted in Hinds, 1990, p. A14). City officials echoed what would become the new buzzword of the

1990s (at least toward poor people): "personal responsibility." The free open shelters "allowed folk who were on drugs to relieve themselves of personal responsibility," said Barbara J. McLean, acting director of Philadelphia's Office of Services to the Homeless and Adults. "They knew they would be housed and get food at no charge" (quoted in Dugger, 1992, p. A31).

Ironically, in Massachusetts, always considered a liberal state, and certainly a leader on the issue of homelessness, it was soon after the defeat of Dukakis for president that a series of major cuts went into effect. In December 1988, a homeless prevention effort to subsidize at-risk families that had been "announced with great fanfare" a year before was cut. Sue Marsh of the Massachusetts Coalition for the Homeless blasted the governor and declared: "It's dead. That program has been totally gutted" (quoted in Mohl and Loth, 1988, p. 1). The cuts were actually far worse a year later, when the administration cut welfare benefits to 4,000 people and, to the distress of Mayor Raymond Flynn and others, made major cuts in mental health services (Negri, 1990, p. 56). The combination of the continued recession and the election of the more libertarian governor William Weld, however, resulted in even more severe cuts in the years that followed. Presaging what would become a nationwide move, Massachusetts proposed the gutting of its general assistance welfare. This welfare is the only form of assistance that many poor people are eligible for if they do not have children (in some states, general assistance was supplemented by other benefits, though often minimally). General assistance both helped prevent homelessness and was often the only income to provide potential rent money to get people off the street. Despite widespread protests by poor people and their advocates, labor unions, and liberals like Boston mayor Raymond Flynn, Weld succeeded in 1991 in changing "general relief" to a program called Emergency Assistance to the Elderly, Disabled, and Children, cutting 14,000 poor but unemployed people off the rolls (*Boston Globe,* "Weld's Slap at the Disabled," February 12, 1992, p. 14). Despite the victory of removing the nondisabled from Massachusetts's welfare rolls, 1992 saw proposals to cut still another 10,000 people (Hanafin and Locy, 1992, p. 1; Locy, 1992, p. 37). In another move, aimed directly at homeless families, the Boston Housing Authority dropped its preference for them on waiting lists, deciding instead to limit their presence in public housing (Canellos, 1992, p. 31).

Massachusetts was hardly unique, and in fact some states moved more quickly to eliminate benefits in the absence of liberal advocacy groups and other opponents. In Illinois, for example, Governor Jim Edgar moved relatively quickly in 1991 to dismantle Illinois's general assistance program. The program there allocated a mere $165 a month for each recipient, far lower than in states like California, New York, and Massachusetts, and could barely provide funding for anyone to find housing. Despite protests at the state House of Representatives and in Chicago, and efforts by advocates to present the cuts as "penny wise and pound foolish" because they would drive so many onto the streets (Stein, 1991, p. 3; Fountain, 1991, p. 1; Lorentzen, 1991, p. 18), the legislature cut general assistance broadly and made it a temporary program. The state also terminated all medical aid to general assistance recipients, cut its low-income energy assistance program, and cut its special needs payments to AFDC families (*Chicago Tribune*, "States Cutting Programs for Poor, Study Says," December 19, 1991, p. 8). A study conducted in 1993 showed that Illinois had eliminated "all but a small fraction of people who were receiving general assistance . . . [with] 66,000 individuals . . . cut off the Illinois rolls. . . . [The cuts are] believed to have swelled the ranks of Chicago area homeless to 60,000 or more" (Lyon, 1993, pp. 10–11).

Massachusetts and Illinois were joined by California, Michigan, New Jersey, Ohio, and Washington, D.C., in either eliminating general assistance altogether or cutting it broadly in 1991–1992, and other states soon followed. So, ironically, only about five years after "Hands Across America" and other symbolic events to address homelessness, this changed environment produced more homeless, as those teetering on the brink were denied access to income that might have helped them pay rent or deposits for apartments. Of course, this also occurred in an atmosphere in which both Democrats and Republicans were now moving toward a position of "ending welfare as we know it," which might provide one hint as to why things were changing.

The Contemporary Commentary on the Backlash

Since the mass media often lack introspection and analysis, it is somewhat surprising that a variety of articles, some quite sophisticated, appeared particularly in 1990–1992 citing a variety of reasons for "compassion fatigue" or a "backlash" against the homeless. Advocates themselves often provided thoughtful insights about these changes. Still, several issues, particularly involving contradictions in how the advocates had themselves constructed the problem of homelessness, were not addressed by the media.

Two proximate issues that were named by many observers as early as 1989 as causing backlash against homeless people were the increasing crime rate and the perceived "assertiveness" of homeless people. By 1990, the downturn in the economy was also being cited by many commentators. In early 1989, it was an advocate, George McDonald, founder of the Doe Fund, who brought up the impact of the crack cocaine epidemic, to which he believed that most of the drop in public sympathy for the homeless could be attributed. Peter Smith, of the Partnership for the Homeless, estimated that of the 35,000 single homeless adults in New York City, almost 40 percent were addicted to crack. "There's no doubt that fear is now playing a part," he said about the public's changing perception (quoted in Levine, 1989b, p. B1). Since the issue was rarely returned to and it is not possible to validate the numbers given by Smith or where they came from, it is hard to know more about the prevalence of crack. Surprisingly, the issue of crack as well as the general increase in crime rates in some big cities was not significantly addressed by journalists in relation to homelessness. No doubt, though, whether or not a majority or even a large minority of homeless people ever used crack, they often were found in neighborhoods where the crack epidemic was most apparent.

A significant reason for the lack of sympathy for the homeless was that crimes were blamed on homeless people themselves, as in an August 1989 article by *New York Times* reporter Jeffrey Schmalz. Reporting on a backlash in Hollywood, Florida, he said:

> The difference between 10 days ago and now is the story of murder— a bus driver and a passenger shot to death here on July 23 by, the police say, a homeless man. The man then wounded a passing motorist and stole his car for the getaway, the police say. A 44-year-old suspect was arrested three days later in Nebraska.
>
> The difference is also the story of what a tenuous line the homeless walk and of how compassion for them, or at least tolerance and indifference, can turn overnight into fear and anger.
>
> The shootings here are the latest in a handful of murders around the country involving homeless suspects, murders that have turned some towns or neighborhoods against street people. In Melbourne, Fla., in November, business owners called for the closing of a soup kitchen after a drifter was arrested on a charge of murdering an interior designer. Just last weekend a stabbing death on the Upper West Side of Manhattan raised suspicions that it had been committed by a homeless man. Residents complained of being watched, followed and harassed by panhandlers. (Schmalz, 1989, p. A14)

While Schmalz was of course correct—each incident of reported violence by a homeless person (true or not) set off a noisy backlash—it is unlikely that many among the public (at least those who were not poverty-stricken and did not live in ghettos) distinguished clearly between homeless and poor people on the streets of the inner cities of the United States. Reactions to the poor generally were changing, and the crack epidemic and increased scares about violent crime affected many issues at the time.

Most commentators also noted an increasingly "assertive" character of homeless people. Usually the charge was made around the issue of panhandling and other day-to-day street confrontations, with reports of some homeless people yelling at those who did not give money, and even spitting or cursing at them (for example, see Tye, 1990, p. 1). It is interesting in terms of this assertiveness that no commentator seems to have identified this period, the late 1980s to early 1990s, as being the peak period of homeless activism by protesters as well (see Cress and Snow, 1996). Although there seem to be no data to causally relate assertiveness and activism, it may be that what the public is willing to tolerate from the poor relates greatly to the age-old deference expected of the poor, if they are to remain "deserving." It makes sense that assertive poor and homeless people would seem less deserving to many who were once charitably inclined. An intriguing aspect of the issue is the degree to which sympathy for homeless people rests on their very inertness and lack of resistance.

Finally, rather than bringing people together, the arrival of a severe recession by 1990 was seen by many as hurting the homeless cause. Not only were contributions down, but as Sue Marsh of the Massachusetts Coalition for the Homeless put it, "[the recession] has not made people more compassionate. Rather, it has made people look inward more and say, 'I don't have the ability to worry about anyone else'" (quoted in Tye, 1990, p. 1).

Taking into account the roles of crack, crime, aggressive panhandling, and the recession, however, many observers did see the nature of Americans' short issue attention span, and their naivete about what was needed, as a clear brake on the early enthusiasm. As early as November 1989, advocate Kim Hopper saw the public as experiencing a growing sense of helplessness: "They're thinking," Hopper said. "It's still going on after all these years and after all this money has been poured into it, maybe it's time to get tough. The public is being misled into thinking that these folks have had their chance" (quoted in Rimer, 1989, p. 1). When Mitch Snyder killed himself in July 1990, a *Chicago Tribune* reporter put it succinctly:

While he understood much about his country, both Snyder and his movement fell victim to the foreshortened national attention span. America grew weary of the homeless who wouldn't go away, who bumped up against them at subway stops and waved paper cups in their faces and who didn't look or sound like Tom Joad in "The Grapes of Wrath." In time, opinion changed and hearts were turned against Snyder and the homeless. (Daley, 1990, p. 4)

Two weeks later, Douglas Lasdon, executive director for the Legal Action Center for the Homeless in New York, said: "There is less sympathy for the homeless. We've had 10 years of modern homelessness, and people have been walking past it for so long they're getting frustrated" (quoted in Casuso, 1990. p. 1).

As Larry Tye, in his well-reasoned article "Seeking Shelter, the Street People Are Finding Scorn" in the *Boston Globe,* suggested:

In another sense, the rising resentment has less to do with what is happening on the street and more with public frustration at the persistence of the problem. Set up a shelter and give people food, many thought, and the problem will vanish. The reality is that with so little low-income housing, and with rents soaring, more people are being forced into homelessness. Americans are tired of seeing the homeless, of being confronted by them. They aren't used to insoluble problems, and they say, "If you can't solve the problem at least get it out of sight," said Scott Shafer, press secretary to Mayor Art Agnos of San Francisco, who opened shelters and counseling programs to handle the homeless removed from the streets. "People are suffering from compassion fatigue." (Tye, 1990, p. 1)

Ellen Uzelac (1990, p. 1A), in a well-referenced article in the *Baltimore Sun* titled "Persistent Poverty Produces 'Compassion Fatigue',", quoted a fifty-year-old hairdresser from northern California who said: "You drive downtown, and all you see is bums. I'm sick of it." "Compassion?" she exclaimed when asked. "Don't talk to me about compassion." Uzelac noted how "the plight of the homeless—something of a cause celebre the past few years—is losing support even as the problem worsens." "People are tired of not seeing any progress," said Thomas L. Kenyon, president of the National Alliance to End Homelessness. Uzelac also cited George Wilkinson, a futurist with United Way of America. Commenting on American impatience and pragmatism, he noted: "People are angry and frustrated. They want to see something work. If I buy a product, I want it to work. If it doesn't work, I'm angry. Damn it, you expect things to work."

Charles Kieffer, a crisis center director who had created a course on homelessness, noted that the proposed solutions to homelessness were insufficient: "If people feel like they've already done their bit and they don't see their acts of charity have consequence, then they start turning the other way. The needs associated with real solutions to the real problems are not addressed by immediate acts of caring and kindness. If we begin to see the homeless more as a symptom than as a problem, maybe we will begin to get some perspective."

Further analytic articles also brought forth the idea that the nation had been naive in its expectations for ending homelessness. Said Mary Brosnahan, executive director of the National Coalition for the Homeless, in 1991:

> People are a bit weary. They have heard all the solutions for the last 10 years, but it doesn't seem to make a dent in the problem. In the early, naive days of the homeless crisis, people pinned their hopes on the legions of soup kitchens and armories-turned-shelters to reduce the number of people sleeping in doorways and soliciting money on street corners. But the numbers only grew. (Quoted in Wilkerson, 1991, p. 3)

Similarly in a December 1991 piece, Marsha Mercer analyzed the more than decade-old crisis this way:

> When the homeless and hungry first appeared here in the early 1980s, people were shocked. How can this be? we asked ourselves, reaching into our pockets and purses for spare change. Some blamed Reagan, who insisted that the homeless wanted to live that way. Presidential insensitivity aside, though, we assumed that the hardship was temporary, a blip on the screen, an aberration that would disappear as quickly as it came. We were too optimistic, if not naive. Reagan long ago returned to the ranch, but the ranks of the homeless and hungry have continued to grow. (Quoted in *Chicago Tribune,* "A Compassion Fatigued Nation Hardens Its Heart to the Homeless," December 26, 1991, p. 27)

Although many polls at the time showed people abstractly supporting aid to the homeless, a joint *New York Times* and *CBS News* poll conducted in January 1992 showed that younger people tended to feel less upset than older people when seeing a homeless person (see Table 6.1). Clearly the public was split on whether they found the sight of homeless people upsetting, with women affected more negatively than men, and those older than forty-four reacting more negatively than those younger than thirty. The survey also found that more Americans were now seeing homeless people in person, a factor that might have led to increased anger rather than compassion (see Table 6.2). While the survey did not make a definitive link between more contact with homeless people and less compassion, a prominent advocate for the homeless, Episcopal bishop Paul Moore of New York, commented that "the persistence of homelessness and poverty on the streets is having a very insidious effect" (quoted in Steinfels, 1992, p. A1).

Many polls still showed sympathy for homeless people, however, and even a willingness to spend taxpayer money to assist them (see, for example, Barbanel, 1989, p. A1; Goldberg, 1991, p. 18). The National Coalition for the Homeless in these years frequently countered the "compassion fatigue" argument by citing these polls (*Newsletters of the National Coalition for the Homeless,* 1988–1993). Nevertheless, there are many ambiguities to these numbers. First, were the majorities who supported the homeless coming from areas where the vast number of homeless people lived, or from suburban, rural, and small city areas that had been more buffeted by the

Table 6.1 Public Attitudes on Seeing a Homeless Person (percentage)

	"Feel Upset"	"Do Not Feel Upset"
All Adults	42	44
Ages 18–29	35	55
Ages 30–44	44	45
Ages 45–64	45	41
Ages 65 and older	45	30
Men	37	50
Women	47	39

Source: Joint *New York Times* and *CBS News* poll, January 20, 1992.

Table 6.2 "Have You Seen a Homeless Person?" (percentage)

	Personally	Only on Television (or Read About)
January 1992	58	39
December 1990	54	45
January 1989	51	48
January 1986	36	59

Source: Polls by the *New York Times.*

crisis? It is difficult to believe that the politicians who rousted the homeless and cut assistance in states like Illinois, California, New York, Florida, and Philadelphia were acting against the will of the public. It could be true that the more removed people were from large concentrations of homeless people, the more they sympathized. Second, the polls did not make clear how money should be spent on the homeless: for shelters, for housing, for increased police security to protect citizens? Given the absence of these specifics, it is very possible that while many people were still sympathetic to the homeless, they were now more puzzled as to what should be done about the problem.

Politics and the Contradictions of the Advocates' Strategy

Most overlooked by the media, however, was a set of other reasons why homelessness as a social problem worth trying to solve was fading from people's minds. First, the political environment had changed radically since the early to middle 1980s. Second, because of the way the issue of homelessness had been constructed by advocates and others, there had always been the possibility of a backlash, given the contradictions inherent in this construction.

Politically, although the issue of homelessness on its own probably never helped win an election, the environment of the Democratic Party under Ronald Reagan was amenable to the presence of many activists interested in homelessness (of course, not all activists were interested in electoral politics). As noted earlier, liberals and activists felt that the terrible suffering that homelessness represented was a vivid symbolic reminder of what they considered the harshness of the budget cuts of the Reagan period and the economic recession. Fighting a popular president, the Democrats welcomed all issues, and mounted campaigns that sought to attract a range of activists, such as those in support of peace and disarmament, those against intervention in Central America, women's rights groups, gay rights groups, AIDS activists, as well as anti-homeless and anti-poverty activists. However, the Democrats had lost by a large margin in the 1984 presidential race, and already some party leaders felt the time had come to move to the center. A lively primary season for the 1988 election began with the more centrist "new Democrat" Gary Hart in the lead prior to the exposure of his relationship with Donna Rice. With his departure, the race came down to Michael Dukakis of

Massachusetts, the Reverend Jesse Jackson, and Tennessee senator Albert Gore. Homeless advocacy groups such as the National Coalition for the Homeless put major energy into both registering homeless people to vote and supporting candidates, with Jackson clearly the sentimental favorite. Though many liberals were unimpressed with Dukakis as a candidate, the 1988 election campaign saw a major strategy by George H. W. Bush and his adviser Lee Atwater to paint Dukakis as a liberal, most famously in charging that he was a card-carrying member of the American Civil Liberties Union (in connection with the flag-burning amendment), and that as governor he had released African American prisoner Willie Horton, who on furlough proceeded to kill another victim. Whether Dukakis lost solely because of these issues or, as others opined, because of his rather wooden, lackluster appearance became irrelevant, for the campaigns after this were marked by a gradual victory of centrist Democrats.

Best represented by the Democratic Leadership Council (DLC), founded in 1985, but now joined by Bill Clinton, Al Gore, Patrick Moynihan, Sam Nunn, Chuck Robb, Bruce Babbitt, Lawton Chiles, and Dick Gephardt, the strategy of the Democrats was to distance themselves from traditional liberalism and populism. Most important, the Democrats also sought the center by emphasizing issues of perceived middle-class concern rather than powerful fractions of the old New Deal coalition such as labor unions, anti-poverty groups, and African American groups. The front-runners in the 1992 primary were in fact two centrists, Bill Clinton of Arkansas and Paul Tsongas of Massachusetts, both of whom distanced themselves from many of the old maxims of liberal Democratic elections. Gone were any associations of issues related to poverty, for in fact the DLC had already concluded that the party had to support some form of welfare reform to remove the albatross of assisting the "undeserving" poor. Also out were appeals to poverty issues, the stance against capital punishment, broad antiwar appeals, and other issues thought to have lost the Democrats three straight presidential elections and five of the preceding six.

As the 1991–1992 election season got under way, there was some notice of the absence of talk about homelessness (and about poverty in general). In a late 1991 news article, Steven Holmes talked of the issue of homelessness as "having been put to sleep" and repeated criticisms by Jesse Jackson and Ray Flynn that both Democratic and Republican candidates had nothing to say on the issue:

Whether sleeping on grates or in temporary shelters, or panhandling from shoppers, the homeless seem to be everywhere this holiday season, everywhere but in the campaign for the Presidency, where they are referred to only obliquely, if at all. The virtual disappearance of homelessness from the political debate is a study of how changes in the economy, perceived shifts in public opinion and a new mix of candidates can drive into the shadows what had been a major issue. And the issue of homelessness is receding even as the problem appears to be getting worse. (Holmes, 1991, p. 1)

Some months later, the *Los Angeles Times* also reported that little or no attention was being given to "urban issues," including homelessness but also AIDS, street crime, and deteriorating schools. New York City mayor David Dinkins had finally summoned the remaining candidates to "an urban summit at City Hall. With the campaign almost over, the men have finally agreed to a series of debates" (Jehl, 1992, p. 8). In 1992, as the Democrats held their convention in New York City, a dispirited crowd of protesters expressed their anger: "As the Democrats were gaveled to order on the convention floor Monday afternoon, angry protesters on the street outside waved signs asking the party: 'Do You Care?' 'Why are you sweeping and excluding the homeless from your convention?' and 'Why have you betrayed the homeless?'" Advocates certainly no longer regarded the current Democratic nominees as allies:

"First of all, we'd just like to hear Bill Clinton say the word 'homeless.' We haven't heard him say it yet," said Dave Giffen, program director for the Coalition for the Homeless. "Affordable housing has to be made a part of the platform. Reagan slashed the budget for affordable, low-income housing from $35 billion to $7 billion. We want to see that money fully restored." Father Greenlaw of Holy Apostles Soup Kitchen isn't counting on the Democrats to thin the ragged line that daily winds for blocks around his church's iron fence. "No. Categorically no," he said, wearily. "It seems the Clinton-Gore team has premised its appeal to middle-class voters, reaching out to a younger generation, but not really looking to redirect our national priorities from the devastation of the Reagan-Bush years." (Anderson, 1992, p. 1)

This, of course, was not a temporary situation, but represented what would become conventional wisdom for Democratic presidential candidates in 1996, 2000, 2004, and 2008: avoiding issues of concern to the poor. For that matter, most candidates for other offices adopted this strategy as well. The poor, never popular with voters in the United States, had had their turn in symbolic fashion, and now it was time to turn away from the hardships of street people, ghettos, welfare mothers, and other thorny and depressing issues.

Advocates and allies had clearly centered the responsibility for homelessness on Reagan and Reaganomics, and already under the George H. W. Bush administration, this strategy was failing. But that homelessness would continue as a major problem through Democratic as well as Republican administrations was not anticipated, and provoked a crisis for advocates in the 1990s. A similar situation occurred with other social problems, such as AIDS, for which activism relied on Reagan as the enemy.

Another contradiction that came to haunt advocates was their portrayal of the homeless problem as being "new," as well as their support for shelters and other ameliorative services rather than structural change. The portrayal of a new homeless problem that was different from the old skid row days was well intentioned. However, as more and more Americans *saw* the homeless (as indicated by surveys), these people did not look all that "new." Even if more women and children were now homeless, it was not women and children who tended to be seen on subways or on the streets panhandling or waiting in shelter lines.[1] Primarily, the homeless people who were seen were men. And while the point that more of the homeless were now minorities was remarked on early by observers, advocates rarely commented on this fact. The effort to conjure up the image of a "deserving" white mother, in fact, did not square with the visible presence of thousands of black men (and women). One sympathetic observer, the Reverend Spencer C. Gibbs, the newly appointed general presbyter for the Presbyterian Church in New York City, said that in walking about a mile and a half in Manhattan, "I counted upwards of 33–34 black men on one side of the street begging for loose change. As a black man, it makes me depressed." He asked: "What effect does this have on the young black children, especially males, who repeatedly see black men on the streets shabbily dressed and apparently unable to provide for themselves?" (quoted in Steinfels, 1992, p. A1). More systematically in 1993, the US Mayors Conference found that 56 percent of the homeless populations counted were African American, an overrepresentation of about 400 percent (cited in Marek, 1993, p. 3). These estimates were fairly consistent over the years, and meant that, if Latinos and Native Americans were also counted, about 70 percent of homeless people were people of color.

This is not a small point. The history of homelessness clearly has always been bound with social class, but in the post-1979 period it became an issue deeply embedded in race. This was a sober realization that the public well realized, as did Jesse Jackson, Al Sharpton, and most African American mayors and activists. It was never discussed by homeless activists, however, who might have assumed, given the racist history of the United States, that recognition of this fact would only make matters worse. Still, this discontinuity of avoiding the generally male, and particularly minority male, aspect of homelessness perhaps ended up hurting the activist cause.

Finally, as examined in Chapters 4 and 5, there were ambiguities in the demands of politicians, advocates, and activists for immediate aid like shelters as opposed to longer-term solutions such as housing. The failure of temporary solutions was well evident by the late 1980s and early 1990s. For many people, the desire for shelters and services was not simply altruistic, but also, as has been true historically in the United States, an effort to put poor people and other "problem" populations out of sight. But paradoxically, the shelters and soup kitchen services did no such thing, not only because many homeless people rejected the shelters because of the poor conditions and social control imposed there, but also because shelters, unlike institutions such as asylums or prisons, do not provide continuous supervision. Open usually only from early evening to early morning, shelters pushed people out onto the streets during the day, where they were again visible to the public, as were long lines for beds and food. The construction of the homelessness issue of the early 1980s had reached its limit, and the sober realization stage had set in by the early 1990s.

Race and Homelessness

A key factor in the treatment of homelessness may have been a growing awareness of race among the public. This is speculative, though, because surprisingly there is almost no literature on the relationship between race and homelessness. But we do know that almost every survey of street people has found a preponderance of African Americans, ranging from 40 percent to a high of 56 percent.[2] Such figures are dramatic, not only due to their overrepresentation of blacks in the homeless population compared to the general population of the United States (about 12 percent), but also in terms of the highly elevated poverty rate for blacks (about 25 percent). No other group except Native Americans is so overrepresented in the homeless population in the United States. While none of the counts of homeless people are without problems, the consistency of the findings means either that the figures are accurate or that the visible homeless population comprised more African Americans.[3] The reasons why African Americans exceeded white, Latino, Asian, and other racial or ethnic groups in the homeless population are probably already apparent. For one thing, the presence of large numbers of African Americans in the inner cities by the 1960s and 1970s meant that the full brunt of both deindustrialization and gentrification hit them harder than it did other minority groups who were much less predominant in the cities (there are, of course, exceptions, such as the Puerto Ricans in New York City). The work of William Julius Wilson and his colleagues has been critical in documenting the impact of deindustrialization on the ghettos (Wilson, 1996; Smelser, Wilson, and Mitchell, 2001; Wilson, 2004; Wilson and Taub, 2006; Wilson, 2009). Second, no group has suffered as harshly from the war on drugs and its increased incarceration as African Americans, particularly black men. And third, the impact of welfare reform may have disproportionately affected African American women because of the overrepresentation of blacks on AFDC rolls and because African Americans are more likely to be "sanctioned" (punished or cut off the rolls) than other groups (Cheng, 2009).

Why would race be so significant in the changing reaction to homelessness in the United States in the late 1980s and 1990s? One suggestive study of racial associations with homelessness, by Arthur Whaley and Bruce Link (1998), may provide an answer. It was found that among the whites surveyed, the more they associated the majority of the homeless with African Americans, the more dangerous they saw the population as being (Whaley and Link, 1998). We must keep in mind, whatever may have changed since then in the United States, that the era of the mid-1980s through the 1990s was filled with harsh debates about crack and the war on drugs, crime (and the visualization of Willie Horton and other criminals), and welfare reform, also often considered as a racial as well as class and gender issue. This is by no means to argue that the outcome of homeless policy would have been entirely different absent the large number of African Americans. As we have seen historically, treatment of the homeless in the nineteenth century and in the 1930s, when vast majorities were white, was often harsh. Nevertheless, the visible presence of a large number of people of color on the streets could not have helped the rhetoric of advocates that homelessness crosses all lines and can happen to anyone.[4]

Notes

1. No doubt there were sections of cities that had large numbers of homeless families. However, the quicker disposition of their cases, resulting in the families being moved into public housing or welfare hotels, meant that they were less visible on the streets. Men were also more likely to avoid shelters, panhandle, and otherwise congregate in public view.

2. Sources include the Department of Housing and Urban Development, annual assessment data, 2006–2010; the US Mayors Conference, 1991, 1993, 1998, 2006, 2009; the US Census, 2000; and the National Law Center on Poverty, 2004.

3. Difficulties with all homeless counts include their urban bias as well as their relative concentration on shelter users and visible homeless people. It could be argued (although I have seen no such argument) that a more complete census of the homeless that counts rural and suburban people and the many nonvisible homeless people might be different, for example showing more Caucasian people.

4. Although "people of color" includes Asians and Latinos/Hispanics as well as African Americans and Native Americans, Asians are underrepresented in the visible homeless (a range of 1 to 3 percent) and Latinos/Hispanics are not counted significantly higher in the homeless population (12 to 15 percent) than in the general population. It is important to note, again, that homeless counts are not without problems, and also that the United States is a large nation with considerable demographic variability; in many areas, the majority of the homeless are white or Latino/Hispanic. Nevertheless, these figures fit with some other data on extreme poverty, that is, that African Americans are vastly overrepresented.

7

From Social Problem to Bureaucratic Problem, 1994–Present

The forces that made homelessness a major political and social issue of the 1980s were well on their way to declining by the early 1990s. In the 1989–1992 period, the very discussion of "compassion fatigue," together with the newly hostile reaction to the homeless, was news itself, but by the time of the Bill Clinton administration, media were showing a strong decline in coverage of homelessness that would last through the first decade of the twenty-first century.

One reason for the decline in coverage may well have been the uptick in the economy in much of the 1990s. While this uptick never extended to the poor or to many working-class people (this economic recovery was better characterized as a "jobless recovery" or probably even more accurately as a "wageless recovery"), it did provide for a more optimistic period for the middle class. As Barbara Ehrenreich (1989) so well put it, in the United States the middle class is the "universal class"—it sees itself as being "everyone." The middle class is the most dominant class in politics and the mass media. A changed climate for them may well have changed their view of the homeless and poor. If homelessness as a crisis was to some extent a crisis of fear caused by the downturns of the early 1980s, it would stand to reason that as anxiety fell, news that homelessness continued to exist became less compelling to opinion-shapers.

Particularly important as a marker of loss of interest in the poor generally was the passage of welfare reform legislation in 1996. Homelessness, like many other once-politicized issues, came to be institutionalized as a primarily social service and advocacy issue in the 1990s and 2000s along with issues like domestic violence, AIDS, drugs, and veterans' services. Social services offer a solution of sorts, a network of providers, be they social workers, doctors, counselors, educators, or administrators, to address the problem. Generally, as social problems come to be seen as social service issues, they become depoliticized and bureaucratized, and kept away from public view. Of course, at various times in various localities, and more rarely at a national level, the issue of homelessness became more politicized as a result of protest or a particular news angle.

Loss of Interest Among the Media

There is little doubt that coverage of homelessness declined in the major newspapers and broadcast networks beginning in the early 1990s and continuing (with some ebb and flow) to the present. Numerical counts are always subject to limitations. It is difficult (due to the large number of articles in the *Los Angeles* and *New York Times*) to separate stories about homeless people by topic or eliminate repetitive stories. Another weakness in the data is that there is a huge difference between front-page news stories and those tucked away in the middle of a paper (see Goldberg, 2002, for some data on the decline of front-page stories about the homeless in the *New York Times*). Still, for the years in which references to "homeless*ness*" are documented, the high points of coverage are so similar and the steep nature of the decline is so parallel that idiosyncratic developments in one particular source are likely minimized.

Coverage of homelessness in both the *Los Angeles Times* (1,059 citations) and the network news (53 citations) peaked in 1990, while in the *New York Times* (829 citations) coverage peaked in 1989 (possibly because the coverage in New York City started earlier). By the mid-1990s, the citations had dropped markedly in all three sources. Coverage in the *Los Angeles Times,* which experienced the most consistent downward cycle of the three sources, dropped to 521 citations in 1995 (49 percent of its 1990 high point) and to 335 in 1996 (32 percent of its high point). Coverage in the *New York Times* dropped to 583 citations in 1995 (70 percent of its 1989 high point) and to only 205 citations in 1996 (25 percent of its high point), an even more dramatic decrease compared to the *Los Angeles Times*. The Vanderbilt Television News Archive documents a similar drop, from 53 television shows mentioning "homeless" in 1990 to only 12 in 1995 (23 percent of its 1990 high point).

The trend continued in the next decade. In 2000, the *Los Angeles Times* had 358 citations (34 percent of its high point); the *New York Times* had 235 citations (28 percent of its high point); and the Vanderbilt Television News Archive had 21 citations (40 percent of its high point). By 2008, the *Los Angeles Times* had only 171 citations (16 percent of its high point), the *New York Times* had only 125 citation (15 percent of its high point), and the Vanderbilt Television News Archive had only 19 citations (36 percent of its high point).

These are hardly small declines. They indicate that the story of homelessness, which had been a major event in the 1980s, had become quite minor by the 1990s and continuing into the 2000s. Additionally, while "homelessness" had sometimes been considered the most pressing issue in the 1980s in news polls, it ceased to be after that (for example, by 2008, "poverty, hunger, and homelessness" rated a mere 2 percent as a major concern among the public in the United States; Gallup Poll, 2008, p. 66).[1] Finally, the election cycle had little or no effect on the prevalence of stories about homelessness, as the presidential election years were devoid of discussion of the topic.

Clinton, the "Contract with America," and Welfare Reform

It did not escape notice that attention to homelessness was falling and that some of this decline coincided with the election of Bill Clinton. In an article on "media bias," journalist Bernard Goldberg (2002) devoted a chapter of a book to "How Bill Clinton Cured Homelessness." Noting how the surge of news coverage of homelessness occurred under Ronald Reagan, Goldberg claimed that the media "made it look as if the Reagan administration had practically invented homelessness" (p. 69). "Then in the early 1990s a miracle descended upon the land. Homelessness disappeared. It was over. It no longer existed in the entire United States of America! It was a fantastic story. A too-good-to-be-true story!" (p. 71). While Goldberg's article is satiric and itself biased, it cannot be dismissed; the coalition that emerged to construct homelessness as a social and political problem was part of the anti-Reagan movement and supported by a range of interest groups loyal to the Democratic Party or to its left. It was clear as soon as George H. W. Bush departed that even critical advocacy groups were muting their tone (as they usually do) for a Democratic president, even one who did not arouse huge enthusiasm on their part (see *Newslet-*

ters of the National Coalition for the Homeless, 1992–1993, for their attempts at optimism about Clinton after less-than-enthusiastic election coverage); the *New York Times* itself noted Clinton's distance from advocates while they cautiously praised him (DeParle, 1993, p. A13). Still, the decline in coverage was, as of 1993, not a complete free fall. It would actually be the 1994–1996 period of welfare reform, the balanced budget amendment, and the move to the right by the Democrats and the Republicans that would effectively move homelessness even further out of the news.

Clinton (even absent Republican pressures) was clearly not a warrior for assistance to the poor. Running in 1992 to "end welfare as we know it," he was not inclined to raise social benefits for the homeless or any other segment of poor people while cutting the most controversial public assistance program in the United States. He did say a few sympathetic things about homeless people, of course, but major changes were not contemplated. Whatever Clinton's personal views may have been, he saw the issue of welfare as an albatross around the neck of the Democratic Party; he was more liberal on what social service experts call the "in kind" or noncash programs such as medical aid and childcare. While of course there are differences between the population that received Aid to Families with Dependent Children in the early 1990s (mostly women with children) and the homeless, poor people have always existed on a continuum in which welfare recipients, given their low benefits and difficulties in employment, housing, and other issues, often fall into homelessness, just as welfare recipients and even homeless people do find their way off assistance and off the streets when economic conditions and personal problems improve. At a time when "welfare" of almost all types was being highly stigmatized, it would become clear to even the strongest advocate that the major issue of the 1990s was how deep the cuts would be, not any expansion of benefits. The National Coalition for the Homeless and other advocacy groups, for example, started a "Welfare Reform with a Heart" campaign in the debate, in an "if you can't beat them, join them" effort to minimize the damage (*Newsletters of the National Coalition for the Homeless* 14, no. 1 [1995]).

Any hopes that advocates, liberals, or leftists might have had, evaporated with the Republican "Contract with America" in 1994, which called for a strong move to the right, emphasized by a proposed law to balance the federal budget and draconian cuts in welfare and other social service programs. The congressional victory of the Republicans in 1994 put Newt Gingrich into the leadership, and certainly made it appear that the public supported such measures (indeed, regarding welfare, polls overwhelmingly favored a reduction or elimination). The major difference between the parties came with the Democrats' advocacy of more noncash supports such as childcare and medical aid as opposed to the Republicans' deeper cuts.

What ensued in 1995–1996 was dramatic, in that cuts in several programs appeared simultaneously with passage of the Personal Responsibility and Work Opportunity Reconciliation Act, the formal name for the welfare reform, which ended the AFDC program. The National Coalition for the Homeless charged that the 104th Congress was "wag[ing] war on poor and homeless," and that, "if the policy changes currently debated in Washington become the law of the land, we will see homelessness as we have never seen it before" (*Newsletters of the National Coalition for the Homeless* 14, no. 4 [July–August 1995]). Nor, of course, was the National Coalition for the Homeless alone; a report in Massachusetts quoted in the *Boston Globe* spoke of "an unprecedented assault" on the poor, driven by the "systematic destruction" of the social safety net (quoted in Greenwald, 1997, p. B4). An advocate in Illinois suggested that what was happening was "horrifying at the least" (Lovett, 1998, p. 14).

In addition to cuts in eligibility for public housing, Section 8 housing assistance, Food Stamps, and Medicaid, the two major legislative changes that would swell the numbers of homeless people, though not further any concern for them, were the passage of the aforementioned Personal Responsibility Act (welfare reform) and the cuts to Supplemental Security Income (SSI) and Social Security Disability Insurance (SSDI) programs for those who were substance users.

The Personal Responsibility Act ended the entitlement to public assistance of poor people with children (meaning there was no statutory right to benefits; they were subject to state rules and finances, the latter of which were hitched to 1996 spending). For the first time, limits were placed on how long recipients could be on the rolls both on a lifetime basis (five years) and on a consecutive basis (two years in many states). Control was set at the state level and savings from cutting the welfare rolls (which were considerable) could simply accrue to state coffers (though some states committed the money to poverty programs). "Welfare" was now a job program in which, except for disabled people or women with young infants (usually six months old at most), work, training, or workfare (forced work) was required to remain on assistance. Even college education was not a suitable alternative except in two states. Teenage parents were banned from welfare unless they agreed to live with their families or to marry and go to school. Recipients who failed to name the fathers of their children (even rape victims) would not receive welfare. Many recipients would be thrown off the rolls of states by the use of "sanctions," which were imposed for a long list of infractions, ranging from failing to show up for an appointment, to failing to attend a seminar or training, to not notifying the welfare office of a change of address. Books by Sharon Hays (2003) and Gwendolyn Mink (1998) note how the punitive welfare reform combined a bias against women as well as a class and racial agenda that had been growing in the culture since the 1960s, when the specter of "welfare queens" was first raised in response to the large growth in the rolls of AFDC recipients, particularly single women of color. A twenty-five-year campaign by those on the right (but increasingly supported by the public and centrist politicians) had succeeded. Within a five-year period, from 1996 to 2001, welfare rolls dropped from 12.2 million to 5.3 million recipients (Hays, 2003, p. 8).

While the Personal Responsibility Act was complicated by a wide range of state policy differences, the ejection of those with substance abuse problems from the disability rolls was simple and quick. The issue of those on SSI or SSDI who drank or used drugs was brought to the public eye by an investigation in 1994 led by Senator William Cohen of Maine (Sennett and Murphy, 1994, p. 19). While no one disputed at the time the eligibility of these recipients, the investigators charged that the "system was out of control" and sensationalized the fact that some recipients were using their aid money to buy more alcohol and drugs. Congress easily passed a statute that denied both SSI and SSDI assistance to those substance users who were not enrolled in a bona fide alcohol or drug treatment program. Ironically, Congress did not recognize the need for treatment centers, much less increase their numbers, which generally speaking were unaffordable for the very poor. It was a true dilemma for those poor who were caught in the system. The National Coalition for the Homeless estimated that the change immediately resulted in the rejection of 40,000 people from the disability rolls, and would lead to a further rejection of at least 50,000 people a year (*Newsletters of the National Coalition for the Homeless* 15, no. 2 [May–June 1995]).

A variety of studies on welfare reform were conducted, and many of them found that increased homelessness was the result of the dramatic shrinking of welfare rolls across the nation (for example, on Wisconsin, see Healy, 1997, p. 10; on New York State, see Hernandez, 1998, p. 1; on Chicago, see Dworkin, 2000; on Connecticut, see Bok and Simmons, 2002). It is true that because of the strong economy of the late 1990s and early 2000s (which ended with the terrorist attacks of September 11, 2001), many former welfare recipients took low-paying jobs at a far higher rate than expected. Still, even if welfare reform did not enormously increase homelessness, as some predicted, it at least countermanded the economic growth that would otherwise have been expected to lead to less homelessness. Instead, all reports indicated that homelessness rose in sampled cities.[2] Welfare cuts joined the ongoing environment of deindustrialization and gentrification as well as punitive policies such as the drug war to counteract whatever help the better economy might have created for homeless people.

Because of the consensus on welfare reform (in contrast to critics' predictions), there was lack of major unrest about the cuts. There were, of course, some protests among social workers, liberal advocates, and poor people. However, generally these were small and peaceful and became less and less newsworthy. News about poverty and homelessness, much less new prescriptions to end them, came to a virtual halt outside of marginal publications. As was part of the intent of centrist Democrats, the "war on poverty" had now been put into the dustbin of history, and the poorest in society—their support perhaps taken for granted—had been eliminated as a key constituent in the Democratic Party coalition. Both Clinton and the Republicans had gambled successfully not only that the nation's values of work and marriage would lead to support for welfare reform, but also that reaction from poor communities would be muted. Certainly the unpopularity of AFDC among the poor also helped make changes perhaps seem less dramatic to some recipients than to other observers. Even critical observers like Sharon Hays (2003) noted that many poor people and some social workers were at least willing to give Temporary Assistance for Needy Families (TANF), the replacement program for AFDC, "a try" at first.

The "Broken Windows" Theory and the Bush Administration's "Chronic Homelessness" Initiative

Two other important developments of the 1990s and 2000s were the widespread use of criminological theory to add a communitarian veneer to increasingly hostile attacks on homeless people led by figures such as Mayor Rudolph Giuliani of New York City, and the George W. Bush administration's somewhat idiosyncratic approach to homelessness.

As we have seen, the rousting of the homeless has a long history. Though its justification was usually not very sophisticated, it took as obvious the need to protect the public from crime, "aggressive" panhandling, loitering, and other disturbances. Beginning with the popular "broken windows" theory, which emerged in the 1980s through the work of James Q. Wilson and George Kelling (1982), however, a more sophisticated raison d'être was developed. According to this popular theory, neighborhoods in decline are affected not just by major crime, but also by deterioration in lifestyle. The disrepair of broken windows was given as an example; a small thing like this leads to more crime and vandalism, and in turn to declining morale, which eventually causes people to move and property values to decline further. An array of "small offenses" frequently ignored by police and city planners like graffiti, homeless loitering, "squeegee men," untowed cars, prostitution, and public drinking were now added to the list of tasks that police needed to undertake to "save" the cities (leading to a new thrust in community policing). Perhaps no leader came to be more associated with this theory than Giuliani (and also his police chief, William Bratton, who later used Giuliani's approach in Boston and Los Angeles as well). Giuliani's well-publicized efforts to "clean up" the tourist zones of New York City, such as Times Square, made much of Midtown a virtual "Disney zone," cleared not only of disorder and homeless people, but also of low-income people and people of color altogether. Massive police dragnets went after the famous "squeegee men," and then after homeless people loitering in the wrong areas. The importance of this new justification was its popularity, not only in New York City, but also in other parts of the nation where citizens had clearly tired of seeing disorder and visual blight. The lack of concern for what happened to homeless people (and many poor and working-class people, particularly people of color) conveniently made these cleanup ventures easier. Civil libertarians often stood alone in protest. The vilification of homeless people was now complete; as some politicians and officials said, homeless people should use the services available to them, and not be on the streets.

The election of George W. Bush was not a major event in the history of homelessness, nor did it compare with either the Reagan or Clinton presidency in terms of cuts to social benefits. Despite his conservative reputation, Bush generally did little to improve or worsen the conditions of the growing number of homeless people. His major initiative was a somewhat misleading effort (because of its smart rhetoric) centered on ending "chronic homelessness" and creating a "continuum of care." The initiative clearly had a medicalized vocabulary, portraying homelessness as a mental or other health condition that was "chronic" and therefore needing a wide network of available residences that could serve the homeless population, just as hospitals, clinics, hospices, and other such institutions serve the ill.[3]

The initiative was clever in that by distilling all homelessness down to its "chronic" form (estimated to comprise about 20 percent of the overall homeless population), it seemed more realistic, and localities were actually asked to prepare plans to end homelessness within ten years. By focusing on those who used shelters the most and presumably had the most problems, the largest cost savings, and perhaps societal savings in terms of unrest, would accrue. The *New York Times* found this approach highly laudable and even cited it as a new consensus on the old disputes between right and left ("Ending Chronic Homelessness," 2002, p. A24; Bernstein, 2002, p. B6).

Typical of the institutionalization of homelessness, local providers and advocates now spent countless hours in meetings where they developed all sorts of fanciful paper plans to end homelessness (at least "chronic" homelessness). But there was a major problem, throughout the Bush administration, in that no new resources were added to make this venture work, and in some cases, such as housing funding, resources continued to be cut. Moreover, differentiating a "chronic" from an "acute" homeless person or family, except perhaps in a small town, is almost impossible and subject to abuse and misrepresentation. In my experience, those on the streets the longest are most likely to move in and out of different cities and towns and to disappear from the radar altogether. It can be quite easy to see "reductions" in the chronically homeless by simply looking around each year to find those you knew last year and seeing fewer of them. Predictably, the National Coalition for the Homeless rejected the approach, even calling the term "chronic homeless" offensive (*Newsletters of the National Coalition for the Homeless* 23, no. 4 [Winter 2004]). Despite this, the specter of a conservative administration calling for an "end to homelessness" while movements and protests for the homeless had nearly vanished again suggests the changed context of the twenty-first century and the cleverness of the approach.

Of course, among several recessions, the Hurricane Katrina disaster, and a continuation in policies from welfare reform to the drug war, homelessness increased throughout the George W. Bush administration, and there is currently little sign of new initiatives from the Barack Obama administration.[4] In fact, the deep recession of the twenty-first century has brought more attention to homelessness as fears of the middle class rise.

Ritual and Institutionalization

The last step in the rise and fall of social problems is the institutionalization of an issue within the public and nonprofit sectors of the welfare state. On one level, institutionalization consists of grassroots service workers taking positions in shelters, mental health and substance abuse clinics, transitional residences, counseling agencies, and other such services that were created during the earlier stages of a social problem. Many activists become, as Michael Lipsky (1980) describes, "street-level bureaucrats" who are now charged with administration of the problem clientele. Ironically, it is often the former activists or at least those who believed they were the forces for change who come to enforce the new laws and rules of this administration. These street-level bureaucrats become service providers, negotiating with federal bureaucrats and state and local officials on a regular basis to obtain money and then run their own agencies. They become enmeshed in a ritualized game of funding—for example, annual competition for McKinney Act funding—that places them in competition with their peers for money. In terms of homelessness and poverty, in most parts of the United States large players such as the Salvation Army, the Volunteers of America, and Catholic Charities dominate the hierarchy at local levels, splitting the money provided. Another smaller group of institutionalized actors are those who remain as advocates on a state or national basis, usually with far less of a presence than in earlier days. Their actions are now more moderate and legislative in nature.

As I noted in an earlier book (Wagner 2000, chap. 6), and as well described also by Stanley Aronowitz (1996), social services become a sort of graveyard for social movements. As they provide jobs, they also restrict political activity by law, and provide an illusion that day-to-day service is a somewhat political task rather than what it is—a service function of the state or a contracted nonprofit organization. One might say for issues like homelessness, as well as for others like domestic violence, AIDS, and rape, that institutionalized service becomes a politics of nostalgia. Often former activists in movements such as the gay and lesbian, women's, and now the homeless movement are absorbed within the service system. Many activists in fact do leave or "burn out" from these organizations, because the original nature of battered women's shelters or AIDS assistance, for example, was movement-oriented and based on the work of nonprofessionals. These organizations, once funding becomes more widespread, follow the practices of professionalism in service, such as fundraising, grant-writing, and lobbying, leaving behind the days of protest.

A glance at the newspaper of the National Coalition for the Homeless, the *Safety Network,* now more than twenty-five years old, provides some examples of the decline of a movement and the rise of institutional concerns. Though the newspaper never presented a completely unified view, in the 1980s soaring rhetoric about the injustice of homelessness was common, along with righteous indignation over the politics of the Reagan-Bush era. Protests and rallies were covered, as well as litigation strategies and policy analyses of both causes and remedies for homelessness. It is true that even in the 1980s, the coalition's newspaper acted as a sort of clearinghouse on homelessness, and included reports on new books written, occasional job ads, and information on training institutes, workshops, and conferences. By the mid-1990s, the latter notices became more prominent and more professional. In addition to breaks in publication and less soaring rhetoric, many of the concerns of the *Safety Network* shifted to funding battles for McKinney monies; ritualized marches (such as the annual Homeless Memorial Day in honor of those homeless people who have died on the streets); civil rights issues, particularly hate crime legislation, which became a major concern; voting rights measures for the homeless, and so on. Some reports spoke of the ongoing institutionalization of homelessness; the gaining of voice mail for the homeless; the issue of tobacco use among the homeless; a website created for homeless people to reunite with their families; an essay contest among the homeless on the importance of voting; declarations of homeless months; and even reference books available on homelessness, including a new encyclopedia on the topic (*Newsletters of the National Coalition for the Homeless,* 1995–2009).

It is not of course a matter of whether the concerns of the 1990s and 2000s were valid, but rather that the emphasis in the *Safety Network,* and in other parts of the previously homeless social movement, moved from concerns about ending homelessness, or at least significantly decreasing it, to living with homelessness and managing homelessness. Supporting symbolic events and countering negative events (for example, a focus on outlawing "bum videos") became a more routinized focus, common to the institutionalization period. Homeless people became a sort of "class," like women, people of color, or the disabled, with long-term interests and rights. In this sense, the treatment of homelessness since the mid-1990s has echoed the ambiguities about homelessness as an issue in the post-1960s era.

From Economics to Identity Politics

Historically, homelessness in the nineteenth and most of the twentieth century was seen as an economic issue whose origins paralleled the conditions of working-class and other poor people. Hence, despite the huge stigma of being homeless, there was widespread sympathy for the homeless in both the nineteenth and most of the twentieth century among some elements of the working population, at least in labor unions and left-wing parties. To the sympathetic, the "homeless" were members of the working population who had fallen on difficult times, particularly during the depressions so common in the United States prior to World War II.

When homelessness became an issue again in the late 1970s and 1980s, the economic aspect was still present, given the severe recession of the time, and accounts by advocates of the combined effect of economics, the housing crisis, Reagan-era cutbacks, and the like were emphasized. Many activists and advocates analyzed the issue in terms of left-wing politics, from populist to Marxist.

Still, the events of these decades took place in a markedly different environment than that of homelessness in the 1930s, for example. Not only was popular opinion deeply divided about any social class basis of homelessness, with many blaming mental illness, alcoholism, and deinstitutionalization as causes, but the left itself was far different than in previous eras. The left generally was quite weak and composed of a variety of small identity elements, many a function of the civil rights and post–civil rights eras, such as the women's, gay and lesbian, and racial-minority movements. For activists of these periods, a politics of identity—"we're here and we're going to stay here"—was always familiar and powerful. To a great extent, not only homelessness but also the poverty movements became more centered in identity politics.

Identity politics can be seen as the opposite of the universal appeal of previous social movements. That is, trade unionism or socialism, for example, spoke of a general betterment of society that would come about if their movements were successful. A similar claim was made for the movements of the 1960s. Even though civil rights or the women's movement would seem not to apply to everyone, gains to all people were seen in a society that remedied racism and sexism. As the unrest of the 1960s faded, much narrower views were privileged. Stemming initially from the "black pride" and "black power" movements, each activist group in society praised its own differences in identity ("we're here and we're queer," for example), and at least parts of each movement demurred at a universal appeal. What Americans who were outside these movements ultimately absorbed was the idea that people should accept and be kind to the affected groups, rather than the initial appeals to pursue a just society. Hence, "identity politics" stands very close to what came to be called "political correctness," as its acceptance was often one of style rather than real social and political change.

One example of this change is the widespread priority in the 1990s and 2000s of homelessness-related hate crime legislative efforts (only a few of which have been successful so far) among advocates and providers. Certainly the large numbers of awful attacks on defenseless homeless people were a cruel and bitter series of episodes in US history (though hardly new; they were once advocated by major newspapers in the nineteenth century). The downside of this legislative effort, particularly as it requires more time and effort, is that it makes homelessness into a permanent condition and obscures its economic and social class nature. For women or people of color, there is no choice of status, and hate crime legislation for these groups was part of a civil rights goal to protect them from violence. But homelessness is not a condition people are born into and stay in; it is not an identity in the same way. The major issue is how to get them into homes. Moreover, if hate crimes against the homeless should be illegal, why should it not be against the law to attack poor people generally? Many people who attack low-income people are not aware of the housing status of their victims. Some poor people who are housed look homeless, and many homeless people do not look homeless. A further question is whether, if hate crimes are determined on a social class basis, the many thousands of robberies and other criminal acts committed by poor people against the wealthier classes should also then be considered hate crimes. There are certainly criminals who await affluent victims in suits, who might provide a better "take" than robbing a working person would. The implication is that the identity politics of the post-1960s obscures a primarily economic issue. Homeless people are seen as a rather permanent class of victims with a set of new rules that parallel those for other victim groups, as the idea of ending homelessness fades.

The annual Homeless Memorial Day rallies, usually involving candlelight vigils and posters with the names of homeless people who have died, constitute another example of ritualized identity politics. While an emotionally moving experience (at least the first time one attends), the effort makes no demands and offers no solutions. The effect on the audience (primarily the media) is presumably sympathy. But how this sympathy is to be shown, perhaps through charitable contributions, is unclear.

This tendency can be seen in much of the politics of poverty of recent years. In the days when more powerful social movements existed—the 1930s and 1960s—groups formed and mobilized with the intent to accomplish a clear goal, a specific policy or benefit. My own experience with elements of the Poor People's Economic and Human Rights Campaign[5] shows that the emphasis of groups of poor people around the country, while often militantly worded, has moved away from policy goals to more of a "we're here" emphasis with rallies and marches against the prevalence of poverty and homelessness in what is otherwise portrayed as an affluent country. The idea is that somehow the majority of Americans will be moved by sympathy to *do something* (though, again, it is not always clear what they should do). In 2010, for example, the PPEHRC sponsored a long march of poor people from New Orleans to Detroit for the World Social Forum. The march did not seem to have any clear policy intent, but like many political actions (typified by the "Million Man March" in the 1990s) it again tended to signal the "we're here" identity politics.

Identity politics in my view is too weak a basis on which to establish a movement, particularly a movement that by definition includes only a minority of Americans (even taking the highest estimates of the poverty rate), and one that does not always arouse sympathy. Activists tend to repeatedly copy the civil rights movement, which was successful at a particular point in time with a particular issue (equal rights for African Americans), but which is not necessarily appropriate for the current time period or current issues. For civil rights, the great brutality of southern officials against peaceful protesters awakened a large enough percentage of white Americans to injustice toward African Americans that (some) success was achieved. Even here, the failure of the civil rights movement to lift many African Americans and Latinos out of poverty suggests the weakness of identity politics as an organizing tool.

The possibility of de-stigmatizing the poor and the homeless is far different than for larger groups (such as women and African Americans) and for groups that are not dramatically large but are diffused throughout the population (such as the lesbian, gay, bisexual, and transgender movement). The fact is that few middle- and upper-class Americans know any homeless people or, often, any poor people. This makes sympathy far more difficult to achieve. Can people whose lives are removed from poverty support major efforts to end it based only on sympathetic conscience?

Notes

1. The poll was conducted prior to the beginning of the Great Recession in late 2008.

2. Each year after the welfare reform, the US Mayors Conference reported more homelessness and hunger (see *Newsletters of the National Coalition for the Homeless*).

3. The specific points of ending chronic homelessness were in themselves unobjectionable. The administration demanded more planning by institutions, from prisons to hospitals to foster care, to make sure their clients were not discharged into homelessness. It also advocated a variety of types of "supportive" or "transitional" housing, long a goal of advocates, for those who needed help adjusting to society because of mental illness, addiction, or simply length of time on the streets. Whether such efforts, even if successful, could reduce homelessness significantly is debatable.

4. Obama never mentioned poverty, homelessness, welfare, or similar concerns in his campaign. He also stated that he had been wrong to oppose welfare reform. See, for example, *ABC News,* "Obama Shifts on Welfare Reform," July 1, 2008.

5. See www.economichumanrights.org. Jennifer Gilman and I were active in this effort on and off during the 2000s. Early on, a perceptive student of mine who joined a local group, the Portland Organization to Win Economic Rights (POWER), a constituent group of the PPEHRC, asked me a provocative question: "How does this differ from identity politics?" Indeed, it seems that much of this effort certainly was linked to identity politics.

8

Conclusion

Can any of the various efforts to reduce (or end) homelessness in the period since 1979 be regarded as successful? It turns out that this is not an easy question to answer. Not only does it rest on differing goals and assumptions held by different actors, but the empirical evidence needed to answer it is lacking.

One issue that has been minimized in this book is the fact that homelessness is not a permanent status but consists of different individuals day to day. It cannot be measured in the same way that the conditions of women or African Americans or the disabled (such "ascribed status," as sociologists call it, does not apply to homeless people). In each period of history when there has been homelessness, there have been many successful exits from homelessness, assisted at times by economic opportunities, by social service workers, or by positive changes in the conditions of life. There is no doubt that no matter how many millions of people became homeless at some point in the past three decades, many of them became housed (even if they more rarely moved out of poverty status).[1] Others, of course, died on the streets or spent considerable years there. We do not have good data on exits from the streets, so in many ways we do not know for sure whether various social policies or social services have "worked." Nor do we have much data on the earlier periods of history discussed in Chapter 3.

It is far easier, then, to look at the structural issues that cause homelessness—the conditions that allow people to continue to fall in and out of homelessness. Although here too there are arguments about numbers and other evidence, we have some points of consensus.

For example, the end of the deep depression of 1873–1877 helped reduce homelessness and other forms of extreme poverty to an extent that was noticeable at the time. My work (Wagner 2008b) following a cohort of almshouse residents uses census and other historical data to show that many "inmates" (as they were called) appear in the 1880 census as housed working people. Some other longitudinal studies, beginning with the classic work of Stephen Thernstrom (1973), show similar mobility in good economic times. In the 1930s, despite the reforms of the New Deal, however, it does not appear that extreme poverty and homelessness (always linked, of course) declined to a great degree until the economic climate changed with the war production boom of 1940. No doubt many programs, from the Federal Emergency Relief Administration and the Transient Bureau to public works projects, helped bring many thousands of individuals out of homelessness, but ultimately, as far as can be determined, those who left the streets were continually replaced by newly or returning homeless people.

The "new homeless" who appeared in the late 1970s and early 1980s emerged in a country that was very different from the United States of earlier periods of high homelessness. Whether it was 1873 or 1933, the national media, newspapers and then radio, was nowhere near as dominant in people's construction of social issues. Nor were advocacy or professional groups dominant in the naming and defining of social problems. As a simplification, issues such as homelessness and poverty were greatly confined to the local political system because of the organization of the Poor Law system, which until the Social Security Act of 1935 was completely local. Such problems were dealt with at a city or town level. People of course knew about homelessness and often had strong opinions about homeless people, but these opinions were often based on their own social class rather than on news accounts or expert views (as discussed in Chapter 3). Moreover, to the extent that homeless and other poor people caused social unrest, their concerns were often addressed locally. For example, in the depression of the 1890s, many cities in the Northeast began public works projects in response to protest. In the 1930s, political protest in a number of large cities also provoked many of the reforms of that era (see Piven and Cloward, 1993 [1971], 1977).

The world of contemporary affairs is quite different. Social problems seem ever present and growing, and even compete with each other.

Many of these problems are not necessarily known to the public through personal experience. Be it crime, homelessness, AIDS, climate change, sexual abuse, or drugs, the public often believes that any given problem, by the very nature of its portrayal as a "problem," is necessarily a growing problem, even in the absence of personal experience. Of course, some problems, such as economic downturns and war, have always been public problems, and presumably have more personal impact (though still not for everyone). Another difference today is the ability of advocates—people acting on behalf of others—to define issues rather than those actually affected. We are so accustomed to claims about problems that we do not expect testimony from the affected populations (in other than an anecdotal way), but instead rely on authority figures such as charity officials, advocacy groups, public officials, clergy, and mental health professionals to advise us.

In this newer market of "social problems," the original advocates for the homeless deserve generally high praise. A group who had always (at least in modern society) suffered stigma was fairly quickly converted into a "new homeless" group who, it was argued, were not at fault for their poverty and dislocation. Though it took many years for this view to win a large number of adherents, the construction of the issue was obviously intended to answer in advance the refusal of many people to care about those who were down on their luck, whose tattered clothes, smelly bodies, and unhappy visages did not make them likely candidates for sympathy. The coincidence of the deep recession of the early 1980s helped this construction, as many Americans were shocked not only to see homeless people, but also by the other economic failures they witnessed around them. Although in some ways the issue came full-circle when the Democrats won the White House, the victory of Ronald Reagan, despite its large majority, left enough people unhappy that many were willing to join hands on homelessness and dissent on other issues that were also seen as caused by Reaganomics.

The long-run results of the social construction of homelessness in the 1980s were less positive. But this construction of homelessness was also never thought of as a long-term strategy. Of course, we need to remind ourselves that in the early 1980s, people did not think homelessness would last. Most advocates, experts, allies, and others never anticipated the continuation of homelessness for decades to come. Ending homelessness was to be a quick, makeshift operation. Hence part of the new social construction of homelessness was the hope that a different national administration would solve the problem. With the benefit of hindsight, we see that what happened was not a result of one recession or one president, much less of only deinstitutionalization or housing policies. In fact, a major economic change has occurred in the United States, deeply undercutting standards of living for most working people and ending the country's dominance of the world economy. Wages have remained at best constant with inflation (meaning no real growth), unemployment has remained high even in recovery periods, and the poverty rate has not significantly decreased even in nonrecession years. A new and larger class of low-wage workers has been created in the United States, from which a smaller subclass has been cast out—people who have no jobs, homes, or social support. Such a prediction in 1980 would have seemed absurd (when the term "underclass" was coined in the 1980s, it was a response to these developments, but generally in a negative way that blamed the poor themselves for these conditions; see, for example, Auletta, 1982; Katz, 1993).

The major economic changes were paralleled by a rather surprising lack of political resistance by the population to changes in the workplace (the decline of unions and wages, for example) and to the role of the welfare state (the constant cuts in social benefits). Because of these two facts—economic decline and political quiescence—a whole series of movements and causes have declined. Radicalism, socialism, and even liberalism have become weaker forces in the United States as the old New Deal politics has faded.

In this sense the failure of the broader structural efforts on the part of some of the advocates and many of the homeless protesters themselves can be seen as unsurprising. How would the United States embrace redistributive programs to assist the poorest members of society with housing or jobs or income or other benefits when in fact these remedies were generally being rejected? The advocates and homeless protesters were marching against a continuing trend in which the government role in assisting its population has become stigmatized. The relative failure of the Obama administration to reverse this trend shows how dominant the environment is. This neoliberal environment has become globalized, with Latin America the only exception.

This is not to diminish specific criticisms of the homeless movement made in this book: the targeting of the Reagan administration as the sole culprit in the crisis, the overselling of the "new homeless" despite the prevalence of minority men, and the ambiguity between immediate demands for shelter and other services and the more structural long-term needs for housing and income. Still, it is difficult to know whether different appeals would have resulted in a different outcome. A more militant effort may have galvanized more poor people on the edge of homelessness to join protests, and may have had more influence, but we need to weigh this possibility against the possibility that a militant movement might have caused even more anger and backlash among the general public. During the 1980s and 1990s, with few exceptions, such as the Los Angeles riots of 1992, there were not many major disorders in the cities, and even riots were based (at least ostensibly) on racial rather than class issues.

In view of the limits of the reforms of the 1980s as well as the lack of any order, it is not surprising that the two best-known advocates, Mitch Snyder and Robert Hayes, left the homeless movement in 1990. Snyder's suicide, of course, may have been based on personal issues as well as his pessimism about the homeless campaign. Hayes gave up his leadership around the same time. Though other concerned and conscientious leaders emerged in the 1990s and 2000s, they were not well-known or covered by the media. A number of indigenous advocates either left or reappeared in other broader movements.

Still, even in the absence of structural reforms to eliminate homelessness, some gains for the homeless campaign can be claimed. A large number of ameliorative programs exist that have helped some homeless people, particularly where the economy and the housing market are not as bleak. Homeless people have gained civil rights protections, and thus have joined the class of people who are (sometimes) protected by law. Even though media coverage is now far less, homeless people are treated with respect most of the time when they are portrayed. Meanwhile, a network of institutions manages these people, and the favored ones may do well, though the more recalcitrant ones do not. There are certainly formerly homeless people who are very grateful for the aid they received from social workers and other human service workers and from specific social agencies or charities. Whether these increased service ventures will remain in these days of new cutbacks, and whether these services can be considered "new" considering cutbacks that have been made in other programs, are complexities that few probably consider. Oddly, these gains are the ones that most mimic the older methods of the nineteenth century—the flophouses and municipal lodging houses, and the small amounts of aid under the Poor Laws—rather than being truly modern innovations.

In these ways, the social construction of homelessness as a problem by advocates, activists, the media, and experts has been most effective at a symbolic level (transforming the homeless from a despised class into victims of society) and in terms of civil rights (the right to vote and the right to receive social benefits, with many court cases won on behalf of the homeless). The construction of the issue has been far less successful in changing, much less ending, the economic and social conditions that produce homelessness, and would continue after the issue left the front pages.

The Difficulties of Social-Problem Activism

As discussed briefly in Chapter 7, "identity politics" has failed to arouse a universal (or even majority) basis for political and social action. A broader connected issue has been the adaptation of the social-problem approach by activists in an attempt to win public support.

Historically, homelessness, if it was judged a problem at all, was connected to the fate of the "common man," particularly the working class and others not far removed from the poorhouses and poor relief. Like unionism or socialism, the issue of tramps and bums was an issue of working people, at least rhetorically.

While there has long been an academic field of social problems, there has been significant growth in media, political, and specialist attention to them since the early 1980s—the creation of what Joseph Gusfield (1989) has called a "social problems industry." There are many reasons for this trend, but more important here is its impact on the movements of the left, particularly the movements of poor people.

Social problems that affect a relatively small number of people are generally too weak for constructing social movements, much less electoral campaigns. Whether it is homeless people, sex workers, deaf people, transgendered people, or one of the many other special populations or issues in the limelight, the relatively small number of people affected limits their potential for a large base of support. The repeated strategy of these movements and of the left has been to appeal to others based on sympathy or a concern for human rights generally.

While it is true that sometimes moral issues need to be pursued no matter the cost, it is also true that a seemingly large collection of issues and populations now exist on the menu of progressive groups. It is possible that the scattered nature of the objectives of social movements makes it difficult to identify with or see one's own interests as being linked to them.

In other words, most people do not actually expect to become homeless. This number includes many who legitimately have little to fear, but no doubt also includes some people who might actually face this prospect in the future. The campaigns and advocacy around homelessness have generally relied either on abstract sympathy and generosity or on the broad statement that "it can happen to anyone." Simply repeating the latter statement again and again clearly does not change people's minds when they do not have friends or neighbors in this position.

Given the relatively small numbers of homeless people in the United States, homelessness is unlikely to be a "winning issue" in the political system. Somewhere within the issue of homelessness, there may be a set of economic concerns—for paying the rent, for keeping one's home, for meeting daily needs—that develops a majority sentiment in the United States. This is no easy task, and oddly it has not seemed particularly easier in the current recession. One reason, and perhaps hardly even the chief reason, is the competition and proliferation of social problems, which has in many ways exhausted the average citizen. Does he or she become concerned about climate change, or the possibility of poverty and homelessness through the recession, or the battle over gay marriage, or the issue of the federal debt? With so much information and so many issues, how are people to prioritize their concerns and efforts, and how are they to make sense of the world? And if people lack the ability to think coherently about ideology and theory, as may be the case among many Americans, how can they choose which issues to engage?

Admittedly this is hardly the only reason for the lack of any oppositional culture in the United States. But a key part of developing such a culture would be to rethink how problems are presented and organized. The cultural gulf between the small number of activists and the larger public is deep and difficult to bridge.

Finally, an understated issue in homelessness (but arguably with any cause) is the role of the two-party system in alternately soliciting issues, absorbing them, and abandoning them. Movements or advocacy causes do not exist in isolation. They must stir some interest among the powerful, at least at a local level, but preferably at a higher level. In the opposition, a party may look for issues that symbolically support its views. Such was the case with the Democratic Party and homelessness. However, once in power, the elected party often chooses to pay only symbolic attention to an issue, and sometimes none at all. Just as some socially conservative issues failed to make the political agenda under

President Reagan, many issues that were of interest to Democratic Party lawmakers at some point did not make it onto the agendas of the Clinton and Obama administrations. Political governing brings forward a different calculus than being in the opposition; votes must always be counted (at least in the form of polls) to judge whether or not a partisan issue will sway the public. Issues involving great financial expense (such as redistribution of resources) or high political costs will often be avoided. These electoral and governing issues are perhaps the greatest stumbling block for social-problem advocates.

Thoughts About Social Constructionism

Since most social constructionism (like this book) is of a case-study nature, it is important to bring out some theoretical points that may be useful to others. In addition, it appears that relatively few case studies have been grounded in the broad economic issues of American society. Thus, while there are many articles on the construction of new social problems, from missing children to mental disorders to hate crimes, there are far fewer studies of "older" problems or those that have broader political and economic implications.

As noted in Chapter 2, social constructionist perspectives are basically compatible with social conflict perspectives. This is not to say that these are the only useful perspectives in the social sciences, of course, but joining them together can help better explain social problems than can either set of perspectives alone.

Historical Background

Many social constructionist studies do not provide much of a historical background to the social problems studied. This is of course more appropriate for the newer social problems, such as stalking, hate crimes, cyber crimes, identity theft, and sexual abuse among the clergy. However, for older social problems (whether of the same name or not), historical background seems needed. For homelessness, it is important to know there was a time when it was not a social problem. And it is equally important to know how stigmatized the condition became in Western society and throughout Western history. The political and social efforts to aid the homeless in earlier times were greatly limited, just as efforts since 1979 have been. Whether the issue is unemployment, drugs, disease, foreign conflict, poverty, or smoking, to name just a few topics, it is still generally true that social problems that failed to gain majority support in the past are unlikely to have a great deal of support. It is also generally true that deeply stigmatized issues, such as drugs (and smoking tobacco as well), are deeply embedded in race and class in the United States. History is still our best predictor of what will happen to a social issue.

The Primacy of Politics and Economics

In many case studies (as in this book), social constructionists accent the role of various claims-makers, including advocacy or reform groups, as well as media coverage of the issue at hand. But for issues deeply embedded in the economic and political system, such as homelessness, the key variables of success are not just the claims-makers and the media, but also the political and economic resistance that stands in the way of change. Those issues that are central to either distribution of resources (government policy on business and labor, and taxation, for example) or redistribution (such as the welfare state) bring forth an array of forces that oppose change, and these forces are often supported by government officials and bureaucrats. Many people believe that mere advocacy or explanation of the unfairness of certain aspects of the social system should be enough to effect change, but this unfortunately has not often been the case historically.

In the case of homelessness, little or no consideration was ever given by political (or corporate) elites to major changes in distribution or redistribution to assist the homeless (and others at risk of homelessness) in the areas they most needed it, such as housing and income. The implications of spending significant money on the very poor would have had sharp political and economic ramifications. But it also would have been an almost unique interference in the private housing market. Just as we have recently seen considerable battle over attempts to change a private system of healthcare, the government, except for a few means-tested programs like public housing, has stayed out of the real estate industry for a reason. This is not to say that all opposition to change within these systems is elitist or self-serving. It is also true that fashioning an equitable policy to assist the poorest people (the homeless) would be challenging in terms of how to handle those near the border of homelessness or even near the border of poverty. But these many technical aspects were generally not addressed by those officials and elites who had the capability to do so.

Minimalist Politics: Easy Solutions to Deeper Problems

The political solution to competing political positions is often the one that is the most minimal and symbolic. In other words, a social system that is not prepared to change its policies of distribution and redistribution confronts social problems primarily through symbolism (witness "Hands Across America") or through relatively small ameliorative programs (like shelters, soup kitchens, case management, and transitional housing) that provide some aid but do nothing to seriously affect the powerful stakeholders in the economy, thereby avoiding the possibility of structural change. The failure of major political, corporate, or other leaders to even consider serious changes in power leads to what we have discussed as the "sober realization" stage, in which proposed solutions to social problems suddenly appear rather disappointing to the public as well as advocates.

Much of recent politics in the United States supports such a view. When Americans become aroused enough, there is fear that political change will occur at the polls, and so political parties, along with advocates and others, jockey for change. Yet except at very exceptional times in US history, this change has been relatively small. The battle over healthcare illustrates this well. A growing dissatisfaction with the state of private health insurance has surfaced on and off for at least two decades as more and more Americans either lose their coverage or are forced to pay more for their healthcare. Still, neither of the two presidents who took on healthcare—Clinton and Obama—proposed significant changes to the private healthcare industry in the United States, despite exaggerated claims to the contrary. The very complexity of their plans was the result of devising a set of small changes to soothe the partisans while avoiding significant changes that would provoke a major revolt from the powerful stakeholders. Hence the paradox of the Obama administration in adding 31 million customers to private, for-profit insurance, many of whom will have to pay the majority of their healthcare costs.

No doubt some readers will disagree with this analysis. However, the extent to which the US political and economic system usually succeeds in deferring or ignoring appeals of advocates and other claims-makers (and even the media) when the political and economic expense would be too great should at least be explored by social constructionists. Conversely, even when vast numbers of citizens oppose something (witness the big-business bailouts of 2008), the economic and political elites move ahead despite the opposition. In others words, we should no longer assume that the United States functions as a true democracy.

Group Size Matters

Most people approach social problems as if they were of one cloth. But a problem strongly felt by most women, for example, is a far more potent issue than one felt by most Native Americans. Illustrating the concept of "innumeracy" (Best, 2001), many people often wildly overestimate the sizes of minority population groups in the United States, such as Native Americans and African Americans. But it is important to know their true size in order to understand their relative power. The elderly are a growing population group, and a group that votes. Generally, they have more power than younger people. An issue of interest to both African Americans and Latinos is far more powerful than an issue of interest to only one of these groups, and in fact there is much disagreement between these two groups, which prevents broader action.

With the issue of homelessness, the relatively small percentage of the population affected at any given moment needs to be taken into account. It is true that, over many years, many millions will become homeless at least temporarily. But this is a misleading statement. Most people who become temporarily homeless do not identify as homeless; in fact, even some people who are long-term homeless do not identify as homeless.[2] This, along with the low likelihood that the homeless and formerly homeless will vote, makes it relatively easy for politicians to ignore the issue.

Of course, some groups are strategically located in the US political system. Cuban Americans, while of far lower numbers than other Latinos such as Chicanos, are disproportionately powerful because of their location in the swing state of Florida and their history of strong lobbying and high voter turnout. Numbers do not tell the whole story, of course. But some sense of power needs to be brought into the study of social problems, which sometimes treats differently powerful groups as equals. Homeless people, mentally ill people, small minority groups, and groups with low voter turnout (such as the poor) must be analyzed differently than groups who have much more power.

Can an Issue Be De-stigmatized?

Many of the issues that sociologists deal with, including homelessness, are considerably stigmatized. This is the reason why, in the early 1980s, some advocates portrayed homelessness as "new," to avoid the "skid row bum" stigma given the fact of increasing numbers of women and children among the homeless. While this claim was not completely ineffective, eventually the large proportions (at least on the streets) of adult males, particularly nonwhites, became visible to the public. Nor is it clear that women who looked ragged or mentally "off" or had a bottle in their hand fared perceptually well either. Stigma runs deep, and seeing one person who fits the negative stereotype may have more influence (confirmation bias) than seeing twenty who do not.

We have seen very successful efforts at de-stigmatization in the early twenty-first century, the issue of gay and lesbian rights being a good example. Despite continued opposition, in 1960 or even 1970 it would have seemed almost impossible to believe that gays and lesbians would gain the kind of social acceptance they have in parts of the United States today, that they would gain positive media coverage, and that they would begin to succeed in gaining legal protection. Unlike the homeless or Native Americans, to take another example, gay and lesbian people, while a minority of the population, are situated throughout society. Statements like "they are your brothers, sisters, parents, and children" have resonated because so many people have discovered that they are true. This is not the case (despite the claim of some advocates to the contrary) with homelessness. Most people do not know anyone who is homeless, and many middle- and upper-class people do not know anyone who is poor. Similarly, except in a few specific areas of the nation, it is very possible not to know any Native Americans, particularly those who have tribally recognized blood quotients (usually at least 25 percent). Because the homeless are not only numerically small but also highly stigmatized, the rhetoric of "they are your sisters and brothers" does not ring true for most of the public.

Conclusion

This book shows that the struggle against homelessness in the past three decades has shown a lack of real progress in addressing the basic social and structural causes of deep poverty that are embedded in the problem of homelessness. More recently, the "Occupy Wall Street" movement has stirred hope that some of the key underlying issues at stake (capitalism and income inequality) might actually be confronted. Whether these broad slogans can be translated into clear political objectives and policies remains unclear. Given the grip of the two-party system on the political arena of the United States, as well as the complex rules of divided government, it is difficult to imagine immediate changes.

Notes

1. Unfortunately, the research on this has been limited. I have addressed academic audiences about my own personal experiences in the nearly two decades since I studied the homeless of Portland, Maine (Wagner, 1993). Regardless of anecdotes about homeless people who have done well, it should be noted that those who stay in an area are more likely to become housed than those who leave. Also, of course, some people die while homeless.

2. David Snow and Leon Anderson (1993), and I as well (Wagner, 1993), have noted the tendency of many homeless people to embrace "role-distancing" strategies to dissociate themselves from the label "homeless."

Bibliography

Abramovitz, M. 1988. *Regulating the Lives of Women.* Boston: South End.

Acevedo, E. 1990. Letter to editor. *New York Times,* October 13, pp. 1, 24.

Adams, J. A. 1991. "Campaign Throwing Mud at San Francisco." *Chicago Tribune,* October 13, p. 22.

Agnos, A. 1990. "Perspective on the Homeless: Off the Streets, into the Safety Net." *Los Angeles Times,* July 20, p. 7.

Albert, E. 1989. "AIDS and the Press: The Creation and Transformation of a Social Problem." In Best, J., ed., *Images of Issues: Typifying Contemporary Social Problems.* New York: Aldine de Gruyter.

Alters, D. 1986. "Roots of Homelessness Debated at Conference." *Boston Globe,* March 28, p. 16.

Anderson, L. 1992. "Homeless Bid for Heart of the Party." *Chicago Tribune,* July 14, p. 1.

Andrews, A. 1984. "100 Camp at Common's Tent City." *Boston Globe,* June 5, p. 1.

Applegate, D. 2006. *The Most Famous Man in America: The Biography of Henry Ward Beecher.* New York: Doubleday.

Arce, A., Tadlock, M., Vergare, M., and Shapiro, S. 1983. "A Psychiatric Profile of Street People Admitted to an Emergency Shelter." *Hospital and Community Psychiatry* 34: 812–817.

Aronowitz, S. 1996. *The Death and Rebirth of American Radicalism.* New York: Routledge.

Associated Press. 1984. "Statehouse Roundup; Dukakis Budget Praised by Poor." *Boston Globe,* February 18, p. 1.

———. 1985. "'Walk for Hunger' to Be Held Today." *Boston Globe,* May 5, p. 35.

Auletta, K. 1982. *The Underclass.* New York: Random.

Austin, C. 1983a. "Churches Increasing Services to Needy in Time of Hardship." *New York Times,* April 17, p. A47.

———. 1983b. "Manhattan Church a Leader in Shelter of Homeless." *New York Times,* February 27, p. A42.

Awalt, C. 1991. "Brother, Don't Spare a Dime." *Newsweek,* September 30, p. 13.

Barbanel, J. 1989. "Poll Shows New Yorkers Fault City Efforts for the Homeless." *New York Times,* June 29, p. A1.

Barnicle, M. 1985. "No Room at the Inn." *Boston Globe,* December 9, p. 21.

———. 1988. "What's Going on Here?" *Boston Globe,* January 12, p. 17.

Barron, J. 1987. "Thousands March Against Homelessness." *New York Times,* December 21, p. B3.

Basheda, V. 1989. "Police Turn Back Homeless Marchers at S.F. City Hall." *Los Angeles Times,* July 15, p. 31.

Baum, A., and Burnes, D. 1993. *A Nation in Denial: The Truth About Homelessness.* Boulder: Westview.

Baxter, E., and Hopper, K. 1981. *Private Lives/Public Spaces: Homeless Adults on the Streets of New York City.* New York: Community Service Society.

Beck, J. 1986. "Joining Hands Against Hunger." *Chicago Tribune,* May 26, p. 8.

Becker, H. 1973. *The Outsiders: Studies in the Sociology of Deviance.* 2nd ed. New York: Free Press.

Beckett, K. 1994. "Setting the Public Agenda: 'Street Crime' and Drug Abuse in American Politics." *Social Problems* 41(3): 425–447.

Belcher, J., and Toomey, B. G. 1988. "Relationship Between the Deinstitutionalization Model, Psychiatric Disability, and Homelessness." *Health and Social Work* 13(2) (Spring): 143–145.

Belcher, J., Toomey, B. G., and Ephross, P. H. 1989. "Toward an Effective Practice Model for the Homeless Mentally Ill." *Social Casework* 70(7): 421–427.

Berger, P., and Luckmann, T. 1966. *The Social Construction of Reality.* Garden City, NY: Doubleday.

Bernstein, N. 2002. "A Plan to End City Homelessness in 10 Years." *New York Times,* June 13, p. B6.

Best, J. 1989. "Dark Claims and Child Victims: Statistical Claims About Missing Children." In Best, J., ed., *Images of Issues: Typifying Contemporary Social Problems.* New York: Aldine de Gruyter.

———. 2001. *Damned Lies and Statistics: Untangling Numbers from the Media, Politicians, and Activists.* Berkeley: University of California Press.

Bird, D. 1980. "Maze of Tunnels Remain Refuge of the Homeless." *New York Times,* March 17, p. B1.

Black, C. 1988. "Dukakis' Economic Views Capture Voter Support, Poll Indicates." *Boston Globe,* May 25, p. 16.

Blau J. 1992. *The Visible Poor: Homelessness in the United States.* New York: Oxford University Press.

Blumer, H. 1971. "Social Problems as Collective Behavior." *Social Problems* (Winter): 298–306.

Bogard, C. 2003. *Seasons Such as These: How Homelessness Took Shape in America.* New York: Aldine de Gruyter.

Bok, M., and Simmons, L. 2002. "Post-Welfare Reform, Low-Income Families, and the Dissolution of the Safety Net." *Journal of Family and Economic Issues* 23(3) (September): 217–238.

Boston Globe. 1980a. "Joan Ford and Her Six Children." July 26, p. 1.

———. 1980b. "After the Lights Are Packed Away." December 25, p. 1.

———. 1980c. "Some Offers of Help Extended." September 18, p. 1.

———. 1982a. "Group Seeks More Shelters for Homeless." December 17, p. 1.

———. 1982b. "37 Who Died on the Streets." February 19, p. 1.

———. 1985a. "Dukakis Budget Hit on Help for Poor." March 30, p. 28.

———. 1985b. "A Policy for the Homeless." January 10, p. 16.

———. 1985c. "Short Circuits." June 2, p. 25.

———. 1986a. "A Constitution, Not a Catalog." July 31, p. 18.

———. 1986b. "Pine Street Inn Under Fire." July 24, p. 14.

———. 1992. "Weld's Slap at the Disabled." February 12, p. 14.

Brace, C. L. 1967 [1872]. *The Dangerous Classes of New York.* Montclair, NJ: P. Smith.

Bradlee, B., Jr. 1986. "Human Chain of Charity Is Set for Tomorrow." *Boston Globe,* May 24, p. 1.

Broder, S. 2002. *Tramps, Unfit Mothers, and Neglected Children: Negotiating the Family in Nineteenth Century Philadelphia.* Philadelphia: University of Pennsylvania Press.

Brown, J. 1981. "Thousands Forced to Live on Street." *Chicago Tribune,* December 17, p. N1.

———. 1982. "Chicago Streets Are Their Home." *Chicago Tribune,* June 13, p. 5.

Bruce, R. V. 1959. *1877: Year of Violence.* Indianapolis: Bobbs-Merrill.

Bunting, K. 1979. "Nomads on the Road to Nowhere." *Los Angeles Times* (Orange County Edition), August 4, p. 8.

———. 1980. "Mission Hunts for Home." *Los Angeles Times,* November 7, p. A1.

Burbank, J. 1985. "Santa Monica Chamber Urges Citizen's Arrests to Curb Panhandling." *Los Angeles Times,* November 24, p. 1.

Burt, M. 1993. *Over the Edge: The Growth of Homelessness in the 1980s.* New York: Sage.

Campbell, C. 1981. "City Agrees to Detail Its Gateway Plan for Housing Derelicts." *New York Times,* August 15, p. 2.

Canellos, P. S. 1992. "HA Seeks OK to Limit Priority for Homeless." *Boston Globe,* September 11, p. 31.

Carmody, D. 1981. "New York Is Facing 'Crisis' on Vagrants." *New York Times,* June 28, p. A1.

———. 1984. "City Sees No Solution for Homeless." *New York Times,* October 10, p. B4.

Casuso, J. 1990. "Compassion for Homeless Turns to Fear." *Chicago Tribune,* July 22, p. 1.

Chambliss, W. 1994. "Policing the Ghetto Underclass: The Politics of Law and Law Enforcement." *Social Problems* 41(2): 177–194.

Chapman, S. 1987. "Finding the Real Causes and Cures of Homelessness." *Chicago Tribune,* November 29, p. 3.

Cheng, T. 2009. "Racial Inequality in Receiving Transitional Support Services and Being Sanctioned Among TANF Recipients: A Group Threat Hypothesis." *Journal of Social Service Research* 35(2): 115–123.

Chicago Tribune. 1981. "The Street Walkers: Why?" June 28, p. 1.

———. 1982a. "Chicago's Homeless Thousands." December 14, p. 18.

———. 1982b. "Mayors Ask Aid for Needy This Winter." November 23, p. 7.

———. 1983. "Four Nuns Coming Soon to Aid the Poorest of Poor." January 24, p. 1.

———. 1989. "More People See Homeless in Their Towns, Poll Reports." January 23, p. 4.

———. 1991. "States Cutting Programs for Poor, Study Says." December 19, p. 8.

Clayton, J. 1985a. "City Studies Conditions at Shelter Site for Homeless." *Los Angeles Times,* May 7, p. 1.

———. 1985b. "Police Shut Down Makeshift Home for Skid Row Residents." *Los Angeles Times,* May 11, p. 1.

Coakley, M. 1982. ". . . and the Depth of Human Despair Is Growing." *Chicago Tribune,* June 13, p. 5.

Coffey, R. 1987. "The Chic Play a One-Night Stand as Mother Teresa." *Chicago Tribune,* March 6, p. 21.

Cohen, S. 1972. *Folk Devils and Moral Panics: The Creation of the Mods and Rockers.* Oxford: Blackwell.

Corwin, M. 1990. "Santa Barbara Police Avoid Protest Arrests." *Los Angeles Times,* October 27, p. 35.

Cox, P. 1986. "South End, Pine Street Inn Scene of Protest by Union." *Boston Globe,* July 23, p. 18.

Cress, D., and Snow, D. 1996. "Mobilization at the Margins: Resources, Benefactors, and the Viability of Homeless Social Movement Organizations." *American Sociological Review* 61(6) (December): 1089–1109.

———. 2000. "The Outcomes of Homeless Mobilization: The Influence of Organization, Disruption, Political Mediation, and Framing." *American Journal of Sociology* 105: 1063–1104.

Cresswell, T. 2001. *The Tramp in America.* London: Reaktion.

Croteau, D. 1995. *Politics and the Class Divide.* Philadelphia: Temple University Press.

Crouse, J. 1986. *The Homeless Transient in the Great Depression in New York, 1929–1941.* Albany: State University of New York Press.

Curry, G. 1987. "House Oks More Homeless Aid." *Chicago Tribune,* March 6, p. 6.

———. 1989. "Homeless Are Sent Packing from Subways." *Chicago Tribune,* October 25, p. 6.

Dabili, A. 1984. "Still They Come: State Tries Hard, but Problem of Homeless Far from Solved." *Boston Globe,* November 26, p. 1.

Daley, B. 1988. "Homeless Woman Hits NYC Policy, Says Housing, Not Forced Hospitalization Is Answer to Problem." *Boston Globe,* February 19, p. 86.

Daley, S. 1986. "Is 'Hands' the Latest Benefit Boffo?" *Chicago Tribune,* May 23, p. 1.

———. 1990. "Man Who Wanted to House a Nation Departed with Empty Feeling." *Chicago Tribune,* July 8, p. 4.

Daniels, L. 1979a. "Murdered 'Shopping-Bag Lady' Cremated, a Mystery to the End." *New York Times,* April 20, p. B4.

———. 1979b. "Vagrant Found Raped and Slain off E. 42nd Street." *New York Times,* February 13, p. B3.

Davis, L. R. 1983. Letter to editor. *Los Angeles Times,* December 10.

De Atley, R. 1986. "Helping 'Hands' Yields Just $16 M, and Funds Still Sit." *Boston Globe,* August 24, p. 20.

deCourcy Hinds, M. 1990. "Philadelphia Journal: Reclaiming the Streets Yet Tearing at the Soul." *New York Times,* February 16, p. A14.

DeParle, J. 1993. "Advocates for Homeless Meet with Clinton." *New York Times,* December 23, p. A13.

Derbyshire, J. 2003. "Throw the Bums Out: But Do So with Compassion—Coolidge Style Compassion." *National Review* 55(12) (June): 25–26.

Deutsch, A. 1949. *The Mentally Ill in America.* New York: Columbia University Press.

Dickson, P., and Allen, T. 2006. *The Bonus Army: An American Epic.* New York: Walker & Company.

Dietz, J. 1980a. "Boston State, a Roof for Homeless." *Boston Globe,* November 20, p. 1.

———. 1980b. "Homeless and Sick, Now They Are Cold Too." *Boston Globe,* November 4, p. 1.

———. 1980c. "Homeless Families Say Welfare Aid Withheld." *Boston Globe,* August 1, p. 1.

———. 1980d. "Homeless Get Home." *Boston Globe,* December 6, p. 1.

———. 1980e. "Mahoney Leads Tour of Shelter for Homeless." *Boston Globe,* December 12, p. 1.

———. 1980f. "Whither the Mental Patient Who Is Poor?" *Boston Globe,* August 26, p. 1.

———. 1981. "May 1st to Send 65 to the Streets." *Boston Globe,* April 14, p. 1.

———. 1984. "Centerpiece; Homeless Mentally Ill Neglected, Study Says." *Boston Globe,* September 13, p. 1.

Dordick, G. 1997. *Something Left to Lose.* Philadelphia: Temple University Press.

Downs, A. 1972. "Up and Down with Ecology: The Issue Attention Cycle." *Public Interest* 32 (Summer): 38–50.

Dugger, C. W. 1992. "New York and Other Cities Diverge over How to Help the Homeless." *New York Times,* March 1, p. A31.

Dunlap, D. 1989a. "Park Rules to Limit Homeless Anger Many." *New York Times,* April 16, p. A31.

———. 1989b. "Stern Seeks Expanded Rules to Curb Abuse of Parks in New York." *New York Times,* March 15, p. B1.

Dworkin, J. 2000. "Families Hardest Hit: Effects of Welfare Reform on Homeless Families." Chicago: National Welfare Monitoring and Advocacy Partnership.

Dwyer, T. 1981. "Boston's Streets Are Their Home." *Boston Globe,* July 20, p. 1.

Economic Report of the President. 2011. Washington, DC: US Government Printing Office. www.gpoaccess.gov/epo.

Ehrenreich, B. 1989. *Fear of Falling: The Inner Life of the Middle Class.* New York: Pantheon.

Fink, L. 2001. *Major Problems in the Gilded Age and the Progressive Era.* 2nd ed. Boston: Houghton Mifflin.

Fitzgerald, M. 1979. "Rental Shortage." *Los Angeles Times,* January 5, p. C6.

Fleming, K. 1987. "The Case for Hospitalizing the Mentally Ill." *Los Angeles Times,* November 15, p. 3.

Fonseca, I. 1996. *Bury Me Standing: The Gypsies and Their Journey.* New York: Vintage.

Foucault, M. 1977. *Discipline and Punish: The Birth of the Prison.* New York: Pantheon, 1977.

———. 1980. *Power/Knowledge.* New York: Pantheon, 1980.

Fountain, J. W. 1991. "Homeless Head to Capital Group Touring State to Protest Budget Cuts." *Chicago Tribune,* May 13, p. 1.

Frantz, D. 1982. "Uptown Storefront Draws Fire." *Chicago Tribune,* January 28, p. N1.

Fuentes, G. 1985. "21st Ward Raps Shelter Plans." *Chicago Tribune,* July 24, p. 3.

Funiciello, T. 1993. *The Tyranny of Kindness: Dismantling the Welfare System to End Poverty in America.* New York: Atlantic Monthly.

Gallup Poll. 1979–. Wilmington, DE: Scholarly Resources.

Gans, H. 1994. "The Positive Functions of the Undeserving Poor." *Politics and Society* 22(3) (September): 269–283.

Geertz, C. 1973. *The Interpretation of Cultures: Selected Essays.* New York: Basic.

———. 1983. *Local Knowledge: Further Essays in Interpretive Anthropology.* New York: Basic.

Geist, W. 1985. "About New York: The Homeless Find 11th St., and a Block Is Upset." *New York Times,* January 26, pp. 1, 25.

George, J. 1988. "Ward Is Critical of Police in Clash." *New York Times,* August 11, p. A1.

Geremek, B. 1994. *Poverty: A History.* Oxford: Blackwell.

Glave, J. 1986. "Man with Sword Kills 2, Wounds 9 in Rampage on Staten Island Ferry." *Boston Globe,* July 8, p. 3.

Goffman, E. 1974. *Frame Analysis: An Essay on the Organization of Experience.* New York: Harper and Row.

Goldberg, B. 2002. "How Bill Clinton Cured Homelessness." In B. Goldberg, *Bias: A CBS Insider Exposes How the Media Distorts the News.* Washington, DC: Regnery.

Goldberg, H. 1991. "Poll Supports More Spending on Homeless." *Los Angeles Times,* January 13, p. 18.

Golden, S. 1992. *The Women Outside: Meanings and Myths of Homelessness.* Berkeley: University of California Press.

Goodwin, M. 1983. "Costs to Shelter Homeless in City Climbing Sharply." *New York Times,* October 2, p. A1.

Greeley, T. 1984. "A Glimmer of Hope for San Diego's Homeless." *Los Angeles Times,* January 3, p. 1.

Greenwald, M. 1997. "Study Sees Assault on Federal, State Aid for Poor." *Boston Globe,* January 22, p. B4.

Gregory, K. 1981. "Empathetic Journal of 'Invisible' Women." *Los Angeles Times,* May 24, p. K5.

Gusfield, J. 1989. "Constructing the Ownership of Social Problems: Fun and Profit in the Welfare State." *Social Problems* 36(5) (December): 431–441.

Haberman, C. 1980. "Mental Patients 'Dumped' Koch Says." *New York Times,* July 29, p. B3.

Hall, S., McMullan, J., and Ratner, R. 1978. *Policing the Crisis: Mugging, the State, and Law and Order.* New York: Holmes and Meier.

Hanafin, T., and Locy, T. 1992. "Much Pain, No Gain for Poor Portraits of State's Wounded Show Where Budget Ax Falls." *Boston Globe,* April 9, p. 1.

Harrington, M. 1962. *The Other America: Poverty in the United States.* New York: Macmillan.

Hays, S. 2003. *Flat Broke with Children: Women in the Age of Welfare Reform.* Oxford: Oxford University Press.

Healy, M. 1997. "Shelters Bulge at Welfare Vanguard; Social Services: Wisconsin, Which Is Leading Nation in Reforms, Sees Surge in Homelessness; Officials Vigorously Deny New Programs Are to Blame." *Los Angeles Times,* March 1, p. 10.

Heiner, R. 2001. *Social Problems: An Introduction to Critical Constructionism.* New York: Oxford University Press.

Herman, R. 1980. "Carey Says City Worsens Plight of the Homeless." *New York Times,* December 29, p. B1.

Hernandez, R. 1998. "Homeless Shelters Suffer as Welfare Rolls Decline." *New York Times,* June 14, pp. 1, 38.

Higgins, R. 1982. "More Wait in Line for Their Daily Bread." *Boston Globe,* January 14, p. 1.

Hill-Holtzman, N. 1991. "A Lightning Rod for Anger over Homeless." *Los Angeles Times,* November 10, p. 1.

———. 1992a. "Santa Monica Council Fires City Attorney Government: Robert Myers Had Resisted Orders to Crack Down on the Homeless; His Ouster Comes at an Explosive Meeting as His Supporters Hiss and Scream." *Los Angeles Times,* September 10, p. 1.

———. 1992b. "Santa Monica Enforces a New Policy Toward Homeless People Government: The City Ends Its Meals Program at City Hall and Issues the First Citations for Living in a Public Place; The Emphasis Is on Social Services; Legal Challenges Are Expected." *Los Angeles Times* (Valley Edition), June 19, p. 9.

———. 1993. "Law Limiting Use of Parks by Homeless Overturned Courts: Santa Monica Ordinance Aimed at Keeping Large-Scale Feeding Programs out of Public Areas Is Unconstitutional, Judge Rules; Concerns over Freedom of Speech Are Cited." *Los Angeles Times,* April 27, p. 1.

Hinds, M. D. 1990. "Philadelphia Journal: Reclaiming the Streets Yet Tearing at the Soul." *New York Times,* February 16, p. A14.

Hoch, C., and Slayton, R. 1987. *New Homeless and Old.* Philadelphia: Temple University Press.

Hochman, S. 1985. "Stewart to Sing for the Homeless." *Los Angeles Times,* September 21, p. 7.

Holmes, S. 1991. "Homelessness Rises, but Not as Issue." *New York Times,* December 25, pp. 1, 9.

Hombs, M. E., and Snyder, M. 1983. *Homelessness in America: The Forced March to Nowhere.* Washington, DC: Community for Creative Non-Violence.

Hope, M., and Young, J. 1986. *The Faces of Homelessness.* Lexington, MA: Heath.

Hopper, K. 2003. *Reckoning with Homelessness.* Ithaca: Cornell University Press.

Horowitz, A. 2002. *Creating Mental Illness.* Chicago: University of Chicago Press.

Houston, J. 1982. "Protest for Poor Marches to State Building, City Hall." *Chicago Tribune,* December 24, p. 11.

Jackson, M. 1995. *At Home in the World.* Durham: Duke University Press.

Jansson, B. 2004. *The Reluctant Welfare State: A History of American Social Welfare Policies.* 7th ed. Pacific Grove, CA: Brooks/Cole.

Jasper, J. 2000. *Restless Nation: Starting Over in America.* Chicago: University of Chicago Press.

Jehl, D. 1992. "Clinton and Brown Appeal to Voter Dissatisfaction in New York Debates Campaign: Both Seek the Role of Outsider; Arkansas Governor Tries to Shed Front-Runner Status He Says Has Hurt Him." *Los Angeles Times,* April 1, p. 8.

Jencks, C. 1994. *The Homeless.* Cambridge: Harvard University Press.

Jenkins, P. 1992. *Intimate Matters: Moral Panics in Contemporary Great Britain.* New York: Aldine de Gruyter.

Johnson, A. B. 1990. "Is Mental Illness a Cause or Effect?" *Portland Press Herald,* July 29, p. 11.

Kaiser, C. 1979. "A State Justice Orders Creation of 750 Beds for Bowery Homeless." *New York Times,* December 9, p. 81.

Katz, M. 1986. *In the Shadow of the Poorhouse.* New York: Basic.

———. 1989. *The Undeserving Poor: From the War on Poverty to the War on Welfare.* New York: Pantheon.

———, ed. 1993. *The "Underclass" Debate: Views from History.* Princeton: Princeton University Press.

Kay, L., and Conklin, M. 1989. "Odds and INS." *Chicago Tribune,* January 2, p. 2.

Kelley, J. 1984. "Names and Faces." *Boston Globe,* February 15, p. 1.

Kennedy, J. 1986. "Judge Orders Plan to Increase Welfare." *Boston Globe,* June 27, p. 15.

Kennedy, S. 1983. "Contributors to Neediest Cite Homeless." *New York Times,* February 20, p. A56.

Kenney, C. 1986. "Home Is Where the Heart Breaks; for the Most Innocent of Society's Victims, an Emergency Shelter; or Run-Down Hotel Room Is a Place Called Home." *Boston Globe,* November 23, p. 15.

Kerr, P. 1986. "Millions Join Hands Across U.S. to Aid the Homeless and Hungry." *New York Times,* May 26, p. 1.

Keyssar, A. 1986. *Out of Work: The First Century of Unemployment in Massachusetts.* Cambridge: Cambridge University Press.

Kifner, J. 1989. "Tent City in Tompkins Square Park Is Dismantled by Police." *New York Times,* December 15, p. B1.

————. 1991. "New York Closes Park to Homeless." *New York Times,* June 4, p. A1.

Kozol, J. 1988. *Rachel and Her Children.* New York: Fawcett.

Kunzl, T. 1984. "'Hunter' Reaps Harvest for State's Needy." *Los Angeles Times,* July 15, p. 10.

Kusmer, K. 2002. *Down and Out, on the Road: The Homeless in American History.* Oxford: Oxford University Press.

Lambert, B. 1987. "Koch and Public Opinion: Getting the Homeless off the Streets." *New York Times,* September 8, p. B3.

Lauter, D. 1987. "Senate Passes $423-Million Measure to Aid Homeless." *Los Angeles Times,* April 10, p. 1.

Lee, B. A., Jones, S. H., and Lewis, D. W. 1990. "Public Beliefs About the Causes of Homelessness." *Social Forces* 69(1): 253–265.

Levine, R. 1989a. "Curfew Back at the Parks in New York." *New York Times,* January 10, p. B1.

————. 1989b. "Metro Matters; The Homeless: A Problem Koch Wants to Lose." *New York Times,* January 30, p. B1.

Levitan, S., Mangum, G., and Mangum, S. L. 1998. *Programs in Aid of the Poor.* Baltimore: Johns Hopkins University Press.

Levy, R. 1985. "Ruling the Roost." *Boston Globe,* April 25, p. 77.

Lewis, D. 1982. "Rally for Boston Housing, Jobs." *Boston Globe,* May 9, p. 1.

Liebow, E. 1993. *Tell Them Who I Am.* New York: Free Press.

Limbaugh, R. 1991. "The Rush Hours." *New York Times Magazine,* January 13, p. 8.

Linder, L. 1981. "Homeless Moving into Abandoned Dwellings in a Philadelphia Slum." *Los Angeles Times,* October 4, p. 2.

Link, B., Schwartz, S., Moore, R., and Phelan, J. 1995. "Public Knowledge, Attitudes, and Beliefs About Homeless People: Evidence for Compassion Fatigue?" *American Journal of Community Psychology* 23(4): 533–555.

Link, B., and Toro, P. 1991. "Images of the Homeless: Public Views and Media Messages." *Housing Policy Debate* 2(3): 21–36.

Lipsky, M. 1980. *Street-Level Bureaucracy.* New York: Sage.

Lipsky, M., and Smith, S. 1989. "When Social Problems Are Treated as Emergencies." *Social Service Review* 53: 5–25.

Lipton, F., Sabatini, A., and Katz, S. 1983. "Down and Out in the City: The Homeless Mentally Ill." *Hospital and Community Psychiatry* 34: 817–821.

Locy, T. 1992. "Group Sues State over Cuts in Welfare." *Boston Globe,* April 24, p. 37.

Lorentzen, M. 1991. "Street Nightmares." *Chicago Tribune,* May 18, p. 18.

Los Angeles Times. 1978. "Indigents Ousted at Visitors' Center." December 10, p. C6.

———. 1981. "'Reaganville' Protest Ends with 6 Arrests." November 27, p. A2.

———. 1982a. "Mayors Seek Winter Help for Homeless." November 22, p. A2.

———. 1982b. "Tent-City Protests Decry Economic Policy." October 26, p. F4.

———. 1987. "House Concerned About Cost, Senate Votes $923 Million for Homeless." June 28, p. 4.

———. 1989. "Hearing on Aid Cuts Disrupted in Philadelphia." April 22, p. 20.

———. 1990a. "Bureaucracy Watch: Homeless Go-Round." August 29, p. 6.

———. 1990b. "Homeless Rousted from S.F. Civic Center." July 7, p. 30.

———. 1991. "Homeless Action Causes Shame, Dismay." June 30, p. 4.

———. 1992a. "Judge Orders Miami 'Safe Zones' Where Homeless Won't Be Rousted." November 17, p. 17.

———. 1992b. "Official Refuses to Draft Law to Oust Homeless." January 23, p. 2.

———. 1993. "Santa Monica: 'Feed-In' Protests Law to Curb Homeless Gatherings." March 13, p. 2.

Lovett, D. 1998. "Reform Hasn't Stopped Homelessness." *Chicago Tribune,* July 8, p. 14.

Lyon, J. 1993. "Social Change: Negotiating the Mine Field (and Mind Field) of Urban Want." *Chicago Tribune,* May 30, pp. 10, 11.

Magnet, M. 1987. "America's Underclass: What to Do?" *Fortune,* May 11, p. 130.

Marcuse, P. 1988. "Neutralizing Homelessness." *Socialist Review* 18: 69–96.

Marek, L. 1993. "Study Says City Homeless Largely Black." *Chicago Tribune,* December 22, p. 3.

Martinez, G. 1992. "Memos Tell Plan to Roust Homeless Courts: Transient's Lawsuit Cites Santa Ana Documents Telling of Strategy to Remove People's Belongings from Civic Center." *Los Angeles Times* (Orange County Edition), March 18, p. 4.

Marvasti, A. 2003. *Being Homeless: Textual and Narrative Construction*. Lanham: Lexington Books.

Marx, K. 1977 [1872]. *Capital: A Critique of Political Economy.* New York: Vintage.

Marx, K., and Engels, F. 1985 [1848]. *The Communist Manifesto.* Harmondsworth: Penguin.

McCarthy, C. 1981. "A National Call for Mercy." *Boston Globe,* January 31, p. 1.

McFadden, R. 1985. "Coalition Asserts City Is Unprepared for Surge in Homeless This Winter." *New York Times,* October 6, p. A42.

———. 1988. "Park Curfew Protest Erupts into a Battle and 38 Are Injured." *New York Times,* August 8, p. A1.

McGarry, T. W. 1983. "Your Honors: Lend Hand to Help Homeless." *Los Angeles Times,* July 21, p. V1.

McKee, W. 1983. Letter to editor. *Los Angeles Times,* November 6.

McKinley, J. C., Jr. 1989a. "City Moves to Clean Up Tompkins Square After Raid." *New York Times,* July 7, p. B1.

———. 1989b. "Police Seal Building After a Protest by Squatters." *New York Times,* October 28, pp. 1, 29.

McLellan, D. 1982. "Homeless Women in Suburbia." *Los Angeles Times,* August 2, p. F1.

Mead, L. 1986. *Beyond Entitlement: The Social Obligation of Citizenship.* New York: Free Press.

Mehegan, D. 1986. "Demonstrators for Homeless Evicted, South End House Is Ruled Unsafe." *Boston Globe,* November 30, p. 38.

Mercer, M. 1991. "A Compassion Fatigued Nation Hardens Its Heart to the Homeless." *Chicago Tribune,* December 26, p. 27.

Michaelson, J., and Sahagan, L. 1982. "New Wave of the Homeless." *Los Angeles Times,* June 11, p. A3.

Miller, H. 1991. *On the Fringe: The Dispossessed in America.* Lexington, MA: Heath.

Mink, G. 1998. *Welfare's End.* Ithaca: Cornell University Press.

Mohl, B., and Loth, R. 1998. "Dukakis Expected to Cut Spending $250 M." *Boston Globe,* December 7, p. 1.

Monkkonen, E., ed. 1984. *Walking to Work: Tramps in America, 1790–1935.* Lincoln: University of Nebraska Press.

Montgomery, D. 1993. *Citizen Worker: The Experience of Workers in the United States with Democracy and the Free Market During the Nineteenth Century.* New York: Cambridge University Press.

Montgomery, P. 1981. "House Homeless in Armory, Judge Orders City and State." *New York Times,* October 21, p. B1.

Moore, P., Jr. 1982. "Koch, Reagan, and the Poor." *New York Times,* January 31, p. 21.

Morone, J. 1990. *The Democratic Wish: Popular Participation and the Limits of American Government.* New York: Basic.

Murray, C. 1984. *Losing Ground: American Social Policy, 1950–1980.* New York: Basic.

Muth, M., and Morehouse, W. 1981. "Shelters Provide Last Chance for 'Street People' Passed Over by Rest of Society." *Los Angeles Times* (reprinted from *Christian Science Monitor*), December 25, p. N6.

National Coalition for the Homeless. 2009. Fact sheet, July. www .nationalhomeless.org/factsheets/why.html.

Negri, G. 1986. "Backers of Homeless Continue to Occupy South End Building." *Boston Globe,* November 29, p. 13.

———. 1990. "10 Are Arrested at State House While Protesting Welfare Cuts." *Boston Globe,* November 9, p. 56.

Nelson, B. 1984. *Making an Issue of Child Abuse: Political Agenda Setting for Social Problems.* Chicago: University of Chicago Press.

Newsletters of the National Coalition for the Homeless. various years. www.nationalhomeless.org/factsheets/why.html.

New York Times. 1979a. "Careless of the Mentally Ill." October 24, p. A30.

———. 1979b. "The Danger of Dumping the Mentally Ill." December 26, p. A26.

———. 1980. "Patients Left Out in the Cold." December 20, p. 24.

———. 1981. "The City: Koch Revises Plan on Aiding Homeless." March 28, p. 2.

———. 1982a. "National Group Formed to Help the Homeless." May 9, p. A14.

———. 1982b. "Noho Residents' Opposition Kills Plan for Homeless Shelter." December 26, p. A46.

———. 1983. "The City: Homeless Picket Legal Aid Society." April 8, p. B3.

———. 1986a. "Koch Gives Response to Reagan on Hotels." November 21, p. B3.

———. 1986b. "Why Was Mary Ventura Released?" June 21, p. 1.

———. 1989a. "I Want This Park Back." July 8, pp. 1, 22.

———. 1989b. "Razing of Shanties Starts Confrontation in Tompkins Square." July 6, p. B4.

———. 2002. "Ending Chronic Homelessness." March 13, p. A24.

Nieves, E. 1990. "Squatters Face Giving Up a Building to the Homeless." *New York Times,* December 4, p. B2.

Noy, D. 2009. "When Framing Fails: Ideas, Influence, and Resources in San Francisco's Homeless Policy Field." *Social Problems* 56(2) (May): 223–242.

O'Brien, R., ed. 2004. *Voices from the Edge: Narratives About the Americans with Disabilities Act.* New York: Oxford University Press.

O'Connor, A. 2001. *Poverty Knowledge: Social Science, Social Policy, and the Poor in Twentieth-Century U.S. History.* Princeton: Princeton University Press.

Overend, W. 1983a. "Homelessness Seen as a Political Issue." *Los Angeles Times,* October 27, p. D7.

———. 1983b. "Shelter Offers New Hope for the Homeless." *Los Angeles Times,* July 8, p. F1.

———. 1983c. "A Time of Crisis for Our Brothers' Keepers." *Los Angeles Times,* May 1, p. 1.

Paddio, M. 1982. Letter to editor. *Los Angeles Times,* October 2.

Pear, R. 1987. "President Signs $1 Million Bill to Aid Homeless." *New York Times,* July 24, p. A1.

Peirce, N. 1982. "Hope for the Homeless." *Los Angeles Times,* September 24, p. 11.

Pertman, A. 1985. "An Appeal for the Needy." *Boston Globe,* July 24, p. 3.

Peszke, M. 1985. "Connecticut Opinion: Why Are We Turning Our Streets into Asylums?" *New York Times,* January 27, p. 22.

Peterson, I. 1983. "Warm Season Masks but Doesn't End Problem of the Homeless." *New York Times,* June 3, p. A16.

Phofl, S. 1977. "The 'Discovery' of Child Abuse." *Social Problems* 24(3): 310–323.

Piven, F. F., and Cloward, R. 1977. *Poor People's Movements.* New York: Pantheon.

———. 1993 [1971]. *Regulating the Poor: The Functions of Public Welfare.* New York: Vintage.

Polanyi, K. 1957. *The Great Transformation.* Boston: Beacon.

Quigley, J., Raphael, S., and Smolensky, E. 2001. *Homelessness in California.* Sacramento: Public Policy Institute.

Quill, E. 1980. "A Man in Search of a Roof." *Boston Globe,* November 8, p. 1.

Quindlen, A. 1979. "Facilities for 'Shopping Bag Ladies' and Battered Women Are Planned." *New York Times,* May 26, p. 23.

Reinarman, C., and Levine, H., eds. 1997. *Crack in America: Demon Drugs and Social Justice.* Berkeley: University of California Press.

Reuters. 1991. "Bitter Mayoral Race Splits San Francisco." *Chicago Tribune,* December 8, p. 16.

Rimer, S. 1989. "Doors Closing as Mood on the Homeless Sours." *New York Times,* November 18, p. 1.

Rivera, C., and Eng, L. 1991. "Judge Hands Protection to Homeless in Sweep Ruling Law: Street People Gained Clout When Crackdown Was Ruled Illegal in Court, but Law Enforcement Lost a Weapon." *Los Angeles Times,* February 10, p. 1.

Roberts, J. J. 2004. *How to Increase Homelessness.* Bend, OR: Loyal Publishing.

Roberts, S. 1988. "Reagan on Homelessness: Many Choose to Live in the Streets." *New York Times,* December 23, p. 26A.

Robinson, J. 1988. "Housing Movement Split over Goals, Tactics." *Boston Globe,* July 18, p. 3.

Ropers, R. 1988. *The Invisible Homeless.* New York: Social Science Press.

Rosen, M. 2003. "Homeless Scare Tactics." *Rocky Mountain News,* November 7, p. 49A.

Rossi, P. 1989. *Down and Out in America: The Origins of Homelessness.* Chicago: University of Chicago Press.

Rousseau, A. M. 1981. *Shopping Bag Ladies.* New York: Pilgrim.

Rubin, E. 1980. "Just the Family Left After Car-Burning." *Boston Globe,* August 10, p. 1.

Rule, S. 1983a. "City Study on Homeless Cites Need for More Aid." *New York Times,* November 11, p. B5.

———. 1983b. "New York Is Facing a Lawsuit on Care of Homeless Families." *New York Times,* March 31, p. A1.

Sanborn, F. 1878. "Social Science in Theory and Practice." *Journal of Social Science* 9 (September): 8.

Schmalz, J. 1988. "Miami Police Want to Control Homeless by Arresting Them." *New York Times,* November 4, p. A1.

———. 1989. "Hollywood Journal—New Message to Homeless: Get Out." *New York Times,* August 3, p. A14.

Schneider, J. 1985. "Social Problems Theory: The Constructionist View." *Annual Review of Sociology* 11: 209–229.

Schwartz, T. 1979a. "50 SRO Tenants Charge Harassment." *New York Times,* December 28, p. B3.

————. 1979b. "Homeless Given Help on the Streets." *New York Times,* September 1, p. 21.

Secter, B. 1981. "Flood of Young Strains Skid Row Mission." *Los Angeles Times,* February 5, p. A3.

Seigenthaler, K., Papajohn, D., Siegel, A., Greenbaum, K., and Reckterrwald, W. 1986. "Millions Line Up to Join Hands and Hearts; State Does Its Part for the Hungry." *Chicago Tribune,* May 26, p. 1.

Sennett, C., and Murphy, S. 1994. "SSI Checks Often Used for Drink, Drugs." *Boston Globe,* February 26, p. 19.

Shields, T. 2001. "Network News Construction of Homelessness, 1980–1993." *Communication Review* 4(2): 193–218.

Shipp, E. R. 1982. "Lawsuit That Sought Homes for Homeless Dismissed by a Judge." *New York Times,* October 5, p. B8.

————. 1986. "Do More for Homeless, Say Half of Those Polled." *New York Times,* February 3, p. B3.

Simon, H. 1992. "Punishing Homeless for Living: Still Cruel, but Not Unusual." *Los Angeles Times* (Orange County Edition), June 14, p. 9.

Sims, C. 1990. "Some Police Skeptical of Any Plans to Roust Beggars." *New York Times,* May 12, pp. 1, 25.

Skocpol, T. 1996. *Boomerang: Clinton's Health Security Effort and the Turn Against Government in U.S. Politics.* New York: Norton.

Smelser, N., Wilson, W. J., and Mitchell, F., eds. 2001. *America Becoming: Racial Trends and Their Consequences.* Commission on Behavioral and Social Sciences and Education, National Research Council. Washington, DC: National Academies Press.

Snow, D., and Anderson, L. 1993. *Down on Their Luck: A Study of Homeless Street People.* Berkeley: University of California Press.

Snow, D., Anderson, L., Baker, S., and Martin, M. 1986. "The Myth of Pervasive Mental Illness Among the Homeless." *Social Problems* 33(5) (June): 407–423.

Snow, D., Anderson, L., and Benford, R. D. 1992. "Master Frames and Cycles of Protest." In Morris, A. D., and Mueller, C. M., eds., *Frontiers in Social Movement Theory.* New Haven: Yale University Press.

Snow, D., Anderson, L., Soule, S. A., and Cress, D. M. 2005. "Identifying the Precipitants of Homeless Protest Across 17 U.S. Cities, 1980–1990." *Social Forces* 83(3): 1183–1210.

Sommer, S. 1987. "When Will 'Hands Across America' Touch the Poor?" *Los Angeles Times,* February 11, p. 5.

Stanley, A. D. 1992. "Beggars Can't Be Choosers: Compulsion and Contract in Postbellum America." *Journal of American History* 78 (March): 1265–1293.

State of Maine. 1833. *The Powers and Duties of Town Officers.* Hallowell, ME: Glazier, Masters.

Stein, S. 1991. "200 Welfare Recipients, Advocates Petition Edgar Not to Cut Funds." *Chicago Tribune,* February 13, p. 3.

Steinfels, P. 1992. "Apathy Is Seen Greeting Agony of the Homeless." *New York Times,* January 20, p. A1.

Stricker, F. 2007. *Why America Lost the War on Poverty—and How to Win It.* Chapel Hill: University of North Carolina Press.

Taylor, B. 1984. "Some Choose to Be Homeless, President Says." *Boston Globe,* February 1, p. 1.

Thernstrom, S. 1973. *The Other Bostonians: Poverty and Progress in the American Metropolis, 1880–1970.* Cambridge: Harvard University Press.

Timmer, D., Eitzen, S., and Talley, K. 1994. *Paths to Homelessness.* Boulder: Westview.

Toro, P. A., and McDonnell, D. M. 1992. "Beliefs, Attitudes, and Knowledge About Homelessness: A Survey of the General Public." *American Journal of Community Psychology* 20(1) (February): 53–80.

Torrey, E. Fuller. 1988. *Nowhere to Go: The Tragic Odyssey of the Homeless Mentally Ill.* New York: Harper and Row.

———. 1991. "Who Goes Homeless?" *National Review* 43(15) (August): 34–36.

———. 2008. *The Insanity Offense: How America's Failure to Treat the Seriously Mentally Ill Endangers Its Citizens.* New York: Norton.

Trachtenberg, A. 1982. *The Incorporation of America: Culture and Society in the Gilded Age.* New York: Hill and Wang.

Trattner, W. 1984. *From Poor Law to Welfare State.* London: Free Press.

Tye, L. 1990. "Seeking Shelter, the Street People Are Finding Scorn." *Boston Globe,* August 27, p. 1.

United Press International. 1981. "The Street Walkers: Why?" *Chicago Tribune,* June 28, p. 1.

Uzelac, E. 1990. "Persistent Poverty Produces 'Compassion Fatigue'; Advocates for Poor Fear Impact on Giving." *Baltimore Sun,* December 2, p. 1A.

Vanderbilt Television News Archive. Vanderbilt University, Nashville, TN. http://tvnews.vanderbilt.org.

Waddington, P. A. J. 1986. "Mugging as a Moral Panic: A Question of Proportion." *British Journal of Sociology* 37(2): 245–265.

Waggoner, W. 1983a. "Concern for Homeless Stirs Gifts to Neediest." *New York Times,* January 11, p. B7.

————. 1983b. "Plight of Poor Inspires Verse of Neediest Cases Contributor." *New York Times,* January 3, p. B2.

Wagner, D. 1993. *Checkerboard Square: Culture and Resistance in a Homeless Community.* Boulder: Westview.

————. 1997. *The New Temperance: The American Obsession with Sin and Vice.* Boulder: Westview/HarperCollins.

————. 2000. *What's Love Got to Do with It: A Critical Look at American Charity.* New York: New Press.

————. 2005. *The Poorhouse: America's Forgotten Institution.* Lanham, MD: Rowman and Littlefield.

————. 2008a. "Homelessness." In Hutchison, R., *Encyclopedia of Urban Studies.* Thousand Oaks, CA: Sage.

————. 2008b. *Ordinary People: In and Out of Poverty in the Gilded Age.* Boulder: Paradigm.

Wagner, D., and Cohen, M. 1991. "The Power of the People: Homeless Protesters in the Aftermath of Social Movement Participation." *Social Problems* 38(4): 543–561.

Walker, T. 1983. "'Hobo' Rides Rails for the Homeless." *Los Angeles Times,* July 29, p. C1.

Warren, J., and Paddock, R. 1991. "Jordan Defeats Agnos in S.F. Mayor's Race Election: Former Police Chief Capitalizes on Pledge to Clear City of Homeless and Litter in Ousting Incumbent." *Los Angeles Times,* December 11, p. 3.

Weber, M. 1978. *Economy and Society.* Berkeley: University of California Press.

Weinraub, B. 1980. "Visiting Reporters at Convention Saw New York as a Bleak Town." *New York Times,* August 16, p. 9.

————. 1986. "Reagan Decides to Join 'Hands Across America.'" *New York Times,* May 24, p. 1.

Whaley, A., and Link, B. 1998. "Racial Categorization and Stereotype-Based Judgments About Homeless People." *Journal of Applied Psychology* 28(3): 189–205.

Wilkerson, I. 1991. "Plight of Homeless Losing U.S. Attention." New York Times News Service. *Chicago Tribune,* September 2, p. 3.

Williams, J. C. 2005. "The Politics of Homelessness: Shelter Now and Political Protest." *Political Research Quarterly* 58(3): 497–509.

Wilson, D. 1986. "Living in a Never-Never Land and Where the Government Foots the Bill." *Boston Globe,* December 16, p. 15.

Wilson, J. Q., and Kelling, G. L. 1982. "Broken Windows." *Atlantic* 249(3) (March): 29–38.

Wilson, W. J. 2004. *Race, Class, and the Postindustrial City: William Julius Wilson and the Promise of Sociology.* Albany: State University of New York Press.

———. 2009. *More Than Just Race: Being Black and Poor in the Inner City.* New York: Norton.

Wilson, W. J., and Taub, R. 1996. *When Work Disappears: The World of the New Urban Poor.* New York: Knopf.

———. 2006. *There Goes the Neighborhood: Racial, Ethnic, and Class Tensions in Four Chicago Neighborhoods and Their Meaning for America.* New York: Knopf.

Witcher, G. 1987. "Activists Hit Governor on Causes of Poverty." *Boston Globe,* January 18, p. 32.

Witcher, G., and Mohl, B. 1987. "State Court Orders Rise in Welfare." *Boston Globe,* January 6, p. 1.

Woolch, J., and Dear, R. 1993. *Malign Neglect: Homelessness in an American City.* San Francisco: Jossey-Bass.

Woolgar, S., and Pawluch, D. 1985. "Ontological Gerrymandering: The Anatomy of Social Problems Explanations." *Social Problems* 32(3): 214–227.

Wright, T. 1997. *Out of Place: Homeless Mobilizations, Subcities, and Contested Landscapes.* Albany: State University of New York Press.

Index

About the Book

Whose fault is homelessness? Thirty years ago the problem exploded as a national crisis, drawing the attention of activists, the media, and policymakers at all levels—yet the homeless population endures to this day, and arguably has grown. David Wagner offers a major reconsideration of homelessness in the United States, casting a critical eye on how we as a society respond to crises of inequality and stratification.

Incorporating local studies into a national narrative, Wagner probes how homelessness shifted from being the subject of a politically charged controversy over poverty and social class to posing a functional question of social service delivery. At the heart of his analysis is a provocative insight into why we accept highly symbolic policies that dampen public outrage, but fail to address the fundamental structural problems that would allow real change.

David Wagner is professor of social work and sociology at the University of Southern Maine. **Jennifer Barton Gilman** is an independent scholar.